UNCTAD/DITE/2(Vol. IV)

United Nations Conference on Trade and Development
Division on Investment, Technology and Enterprise Development

International Investment Instruments: A Compendium

Volume IV
Multilateral and Regional Instruments

United Nations
New York and Geneva, 2000

Note

UNCTAD serves as the focal point within the United Nations Secretariat for all matters related to foreign direct investment and transnational corporations. In the past, the Programme on Transnational Corporations was carried out by the United Nations Centre on Transnational Corporations (1975-1992) and the Transnational Corporations and Management Division of the United Nations Department of Economic and Social Development (1992-1993). In 1993, the Programme was transferred to the United Nations Conference on Trade and Development. UNCTAD seeks to further the understanding of the nature of transnational corporations and their contribution to development and to create an enabling environment for international investment and enterprise development. UNCTAD's work is carried on through intergovernmental deliberations, technical assistance activities, seminars, workshops and conferences.

The term "country", as used in the boxes added by the UNCTAD secretariat at the beginning of the instruments reproduced in this volume, also refers, as appropriate, to territories or areas; the designations employed and the presentation of the material do not imply the expression of any opinion whatsoever on the part of the Secretariat of the United Nations concerning the legal status of any country, territory, city or area or of its authorities, or concerning the delimitation of its frontiers or boundaries. Moreover, the country or geographical terminology used in the boxes may occasionally depart from standard United Nations practice when this is made necessary by the nomenclature used at the time of negotiation, signature, ratification or accession of a given international instrument.

To preserve the integrity of the texts of the instruments reproduced in this volume, references to the sources of the istruments that are not contained in their original text are identified as "note added by the editor".

The texts of the instruments included in this volume are reproduced as they were written in one of their original languages or as an official translation thereof. When an obvious linguistic mistake has been found, the word "sic" has been added in brackets.

The materials contained in this volume have been reprinted with special permission of the relevant institutions. For those materials under copyright protection, all rights are reserved by the copyright holders.

It should be further noted that this collection of instruments has been prepared for documentation purposes only, and its contents do not engage the responsibility of UNCTAD.

UNCTAD/DITE/2 Vol. IV

UNITED NATIONS PUBLICATION

Sales No. E.00.II.D.13

ISBN 92-1-112484-0

PREFACE

International Investment Instruments: A Compendium contains a collection of international instruments relating to foreign direct investment (FDI) and transnational corporations (TNCs). The collection is presented in five volumes. The first three volumes were published in 1996. *Volumes IV* and *V* are published four years later, in 2000, in order to bring the collection up to date. The last two volumes also expand the collection further by including a number of instruments adopted in earlier years which were not included in the previous volumes.

The collection has been prepared to make the texts of international investment instruments conveniently available to interested policy-makers, scholars and business executives. The need for such a collection has increased in recent years as bilateral, regional and multilateral instruments dealing with various aspects of FDI have proliferated, and as new investment instruments are being negotiated at all levels.

While by necessity selective, the present collection seeks to provide a faithful record of the evolution and present status of intergovernmental cooperation concerning FDI and TNCs. Although the emphasis of the collection is on relatively recent documents (more than half of the instruments reproduced date from after 1990), it was deemed useful to include important older instruments as well, with a view towards providing some indications of the historical development of international concerns over FDI in the decades since the end of the Second World War.

The core of this collection consists of legally binding international instruments, mainly multilateral conventions and regional agreements that have entered into force. In addition, a number of "soft law" documents, such as guidelines, declarations and resolutions adopted by intergovernmental bodies, have been included since these instruments also play a role in the elaboration of an international framework for foreign direct investment. In an effort to enhance the understanding of the efforts behind the elaboration of this framework, certain draft instruments that never entered into force, or texts of instruments on which the negotiations were not concluded, are also included; and, in annexes, several prototypes of bilateral investment treaties are reproduced. Included also are a number of influential documents prepared by business, consumer and labour organizations. It is clear from the foregoing that no implications concerning the legal status or the legal effect of an instrument can be drawn from its inclusion in this collection.

In view of the great diversity of the instruments in this *Compendium* -- in terms of subject matter, approach, legal form and extent of participation of States -- the simplest possible method of presentation was deemed the most appropriate. Thus, the relevant instruments are distributed among the *five volumes of the Compendium* as follows:

- *Volume I* is devoted to multilateral instruments, that is to say, multilateral conventions as well as resolutions and other documents issued by multilateral organizations.

- *Volume II* covers interregional and regional instruments, including agreements, resolutions and other texts from regional organizations with an inclusive geographical context.

- *Volume III* is divided into three annexes covering three types of instruments that differ in their context or their origin from those included in the first two volumes:

   - Annex A reproduces investment-related provisions in free trade and regional integration agreements. The specific function and, therefore, the effect of such provisions is largely determined by the economic integration process which they are intended to promote and in the context of which they operate.

   - Annex B (the only section that departs from the chronological pattern) offers the texts of prototype bilateral treaties for the promotion and protection of foreign investments (BITs) of several developed and developing countries, as well as a list of these treaties concluded up to July 1995. The bilateral character of these treaties differentiates them from the bulk of the instruments included in this *Compendium*. Over 900 such treaties had been adopted by July 1995.

   - Annex C supplies the texts of documents prepared by non-governmental organizations; these give an indication of the broader environment in which the instruments collected here are prepared.

- *Volume IV*, divided into two parts, covers additional multilateral (Part One) and regional instruments (Part Two) not covered in *Volumes I* and *II*, including, but not limited to, those adopted between 1996 and the end of 1999.

- *Volume V* is divided into four parts, as follows:

   - Part One reproduces investment-related provisions in a number of additional free trade and economic integration agreements not covered in *Volume III*.

   - Part Two includes for the first time investment-related provisions in association agreements as well as bilateral and interregional cooperation agreements. These are divided into three annexes. Annex A is devoted to agreements signed between the countries members of the European Free Trade Association (EFTA) and third countries. Annex B covers investment-related provisions in agreements signed between the countries members of the European Community (EC) and third countries as well as other regional groups. Annex C includes types of bilateral agreements related to investment that differ from those covered in other parts.

   - Part Three contains the texts of a number of additional prototype BITs of several developed and developing countries, as well as a list of these treaties concluded between July 1995 and the end of 1998, when the total number of BITs concluded since 1959 reached over 1,730.

   - Part Four reproduces additional texts of recent documents prepared by non-governmental organizations.

Within each of these subdivisions, instruments are reproduced in chronological order, except for the sections dedicated to BIT prototypes.

The multilateral and regional instruments covered are widely differing in scope and coverage. Some are designed to provide an overall, general framework for FDI and cover many, although rarely all, aspects of investment operations. Most instruments deal with particular aspects and issues concerning FDI. A significant number address core FDI issues, such as the promotion and protection of investment, investment liberalization, dispute settlement and insurance and guarantees. Others cover specific issues, of direct but not exclusive relevance to FDI and TNCs, such as transfer of technology, intellectual property, avoidance of double taxation, competition and the protection of consumers and the environment. A relatively small number of instruments of this last category has been reproduced, since each of these specific issues often constitutes an entire system of legal regulation of its own, whose proper coverage would require an extended exposition of many kinds of instruments and arrangements.

The *Compendium* is meant to be a collection of instruments, not an anthology of relevant provisions. Indeed, to understand a particular instrument, it is normally necessary to take its entire text into consideration. An effort has been made, therefore, to reproduce complete instruments, even though, in a number of cases, reasons of space and relevance have dictated the inclusion of excerpts.

The UNCTAD secretariat has deliberately refrained from adding its own commentary to the texts reproduced in the *Compendium*. The only exception to this rule is the boxes added to each instrument. They provide some basic facts, such as its date of adoption, date of entry into force, status as of 1995 and 1999 respectively, and, where appropriate, signatory countries. Also in the case of agreements signed between the EFTA countries or the EC countries with third countries or regional groups -- where only a few samples of the types of agreements with investment-related provisions are included -- a list of similar agreements signed by these two groups of countries has been included to give an indication of the range of countries involved in these types of agreements. Moreover, to facilitate the identification of each instrument in the table of contents, additional information has been added, in brackets, next to each title, on the year of its signature and the name of the relevant institution involved.

Rubens Ricupero
Secretary-General of UNCTAD

Geneva, January 2000

ACKNOWLEDGEMENTS

Volumes IV and *V* of the *Compendium* were prepared by Boubacar Hassane, with major inputs from Abraham Negash, under the guidance of Victoria Aranda and the overall direction of Karl P. Sauvant. Arghyrios A. Fatouros and Peter Muchlinski provided overall advice. Comments on the table of contents were given by Patrick Juillard, Mark Koulen, Maryse Robert, Patrick Robinson and Thomas Waelde. The volumes were typeset by Florence Hudry. The cooperation of the relevant organizations from which the relevant instruments originate is acknowledged with gratitude.

CONTENTS

VOLUME I
MULTILATERAL INSTRUMENTS

VOLUME II
REGIONAL INSTRUMENTS

REGIONAL INSTRUMENTS

VOLUME III

REGIONAL INTEGRATION, BILATERAL AND NON-GOVERNMENTAL INSTRUMENTS

ANNEX C. NON-GOVERNMENTAL INSTRUMENTS

VOLUME IV

MULTILATERAL AND REGIONAL INSTRUMENTS

PART ONE

MULTILATERAL INSTRUMENTS

PART TWO

REGIONAL INSTRUMENTS

VOLUME V

REGIONAL INTEGRATION, BILATERAL AND NON-GOVERNMENTAL INSTRUMENTS

PART ONE

INVESTMENT-RELATED PROVISIONS IN FREE TRADE AND ECONOMIC INTEGRATION AGREEMENTS

PART TWO

INVESTMENT-RELATED PROVISIONS IN ASSOCIATION AGREEMENTS, BILATERAL AND INTERREGIONAL COOPERATION AGREEMENTS

ANNEX A.   INVESTMENT-RELATED PROVISIONS IN FREE TRADE AGREEMENTS SIGNED BETWEEN THE COUNTRIES MEMBERS OF THE EUROPEAN FREE TRADE ASSOCIATION AND THIRD COUNTRIES AND LIST OF AGREEMENTS SIGNED (END-1999)

ANNEX B.   INVESTMENT-RELATED PROVISIONS IN ASSOCIATION, PARTNERSHIP AND COOPERATION AGREEMENTS SIGNED BETWEEN THE COUNTRIES MEMBERS OF THE EUROPEAN COMMUNITY AND THIRD COUNTRIES AND LIST OF AGREEMENTS SIGNED (END-1999)

ANNEX C.   OTHER BILATERAL INVESTMENT-RELATED AGREEMENTS

PART THREE

PROTOTYPE BILATERAL INVESTMENT TREATIES AND LIST OF BILATERAL INVESTMENT TREATIES (MID-1995 — END-1998)

PART FOUR

NON-GOVERNMENTAL INSTRUMENTS

* * *

PART ONE

MULTILATERAL INSTRUMENTS

SINGAPORE MINISTERIAL DECLARATION*
[excerpts]
AND
REPORT (1998) OF THE WORKING GROUP ON THE RELATIONSHIP BETWEEN TRADE AND INVESTMENT TO THE GENERAL COUNCIL
[excerpts]

(WORLD TRADE ORGANIZATION)

The Singapore Ministerial Declaration was adopted by the World Trade Organization's first regular Conference at the Ministerial level in Singapore on 13 December 1996. In the Declaration the ministers agreed to establish a Working Group on the Relationship between Trade and Investment. In accordance with paragraph 20 of the Declaration, in December 1998 the Working Group on the Relationship between Trade and Investment submitted its report to the WTO General Council on the work done in the group in 1997-1998. The General Council adopted the recommendation made by the Working Group at its meetings held on 9-11 and 18 December 1998. At its meeting on 24 September 1999 the Working Group considered and adopted its report for 1999 and submitted it to the General Council. The 1999 report did not contain recommendations.

Investment and Competition

20.   Having regard to the existing WTO provisions on matters related to investment and competition policy and the built-in agenda in these areas, including under the TRIMs Agreement, and on the understanding that the work undertaken shall not prejudge whether negotiations will be initiated in the future, we also agree to:

> *establish a working group to examine the relationship between trade and investment; and

> * establish a working group to study issues raised by Members relating to the interaction between trade and competition policy, including anti-competitive practices, in order to identify any areas that may merit further consideration in the WTO framework.

These groups shall draw upon each other's work if necessary and also draw upon and be without prejudice to the work in UNCTAD and other appropriate intergovernmental fora. As regards UNCTAD, we welcome the work under way as provided for in the Midrand Declaration and the contribution it can make to the understanding of issues. In the conduct of the work of the working groups, we encourage cooperation with the above organizations to make the best use of available resources and to ensure that the development dimension is taken fully into account. The

---

* *Source*: World Trade Organization (1996). "Singapore Ministerial Declaration", WT/MIN(96)DEC; available on Internet (http://www.wto.org/govt/mindec.htm). [Note added by the editor.]

General Council will keep the work of each body under review, and will determine after two years how the work of each body should proceed. It is clearly understood that future negotiations, if any, regarding multilateral disciplines in these areas, will take place only after an explicit consensus decision is taken among WTO Members regarding such negotiations.

*   *   *

REPORT (1998) OF THE WORKING GROUP ON THE RELATIONSHIP BETWEEN TRADE AND INVESTMENT TO THE GENERAL COUNCIL[*]
[excerpts]

D. RECOMMENDATION

Paragraph 20 of the Singapore Ministerial Declaration provides, inter alia, that the General Council will keep under review the work of the Working Group on the Relationship between Trade and Investment established under that provision and will determine, after two years, how the work of the Working Group should proceed.

The Working Group recommends that the General Council decides as follows:

> The Working Group shall continue the educational work that it has been undertaking on the basis of the mandate contained in paragraph 20 of the Singapore Ministerial Declaration. The Work of the Working Group, which shall be reviewed by the General Council, shall continue to be based on issues raised by Members with respect to the subjects identified in the Checklist of Issues Suggested for Study[1]. It is understood that this decision is without prejudice to any future decision that might be taken by the General Council, including in the context of its existing work programme.

ANNEX 1

CHECKLIST OF ISSUES SUGGESTED FOR STUDY

Non-Paper by the Chair

Revision

It was widely recognized that the Working Group's work programme should be open, non-prejudicial and capable of evolution as the work proceeds. It was also emphasized that all elements, not only category I, should be permeated by the development dimension. Particular

---

[*] *Source*: World Trade Organization (1998). "Report (1998) of the Working Group on the Relationship between Trade and Investment to the General Council", WT/WGTI/2, 8 December 1998, (98-4920). [Note added by the editor.]

[1] See Annex 1.

attention should be paid to the situation of least-developed countries. In pursuing the items of its work programme, the Working Group should avoid unnecessary duplication of work done in UNCTAD and other organizations.

_____

I.   Implications of the relationship between trade and investment for development and economic growth, including:

-    economic parameters relating to macroeconomic stability, such as domestic savings, fiscal position and the balance of payments;

-    industrialization, privatization, employment, income and wealth distribution, competitiveness, transfer of technology and managerial skills;

-    domestic conditions of competition and market structures.

In this work, the Working Group should seek to benefit from the experience of Members at different stages of development and take account of recent trends in foreign investment flows and of the relationship between different kinds of foreign investment.

II.   The economic relationship between trade and investment:

-    the degree of correlation between trade and investment flows;

-    the determinants of the relationship between trade and investment;

-    the impact of business strategies, practices and decision-making on trade and investment, including through case studies;
-    the relationship between the mobility of capital and the mobility of labour;

-    the impact of trade policies and measures on investment flows, including the effect of the growing number of bilateral and regional arrangements;

-    the impact of investment policies and measures on trade;

-    country experiences regarding national investment policies, including investment incentives and disincentives;

-    the relationship between foreign investment and competition policy.

III.   Stocktaking and analysis of existing international instruments and activities regarding trade and investment:

-    existing WTO provisions;

-    bilateral, regional, plurilateral and multilateral agreements and initiatives;

    -      implications for trade and investment flows of existing international instruments.

IV.   On the basis of the work above[2]:

    -      identification of common features and differences, including overlaps and possible conflicts, as well as possible gaps in existing international instruments;

    -      advantages and disadvantages of entering into bilateral, regional and multilateral rules on investment, including from a development perspective;

    -      the rights and obligations of home and host countries and of investors and host countries;

    -      the relationship between existing and possible future international cooperation on investment policy and existing and possible future international cooperation on competition policy.

*   *   *

---

[2] The question of the timing of work under section IV was the subject of a decision taken by the Working Group at its meeting of 2-3 June 1997.

UNITED NATIONS GENERAL ASSEMBLY RESOLUTION 51/191
UNITED NATIONS DECLARATION AGAINST CORRUPTION AND BRIBERY IN INTERNATIONAL COMMERCIAL TRANSACTIONS[*]
AND
UNITED NATIONS GENERAL ASSEMBLY RESOLUTION 52/87
ON INTERNATIONAL COOPERATION AGAINST CORRUPTION AND BRIBERY IN COMMERCIAL TRANSACTIONS

United Nations General Assembly resolution 51/191, to which the United Nations Declaration against Corruption and Bribery in International Commercial Transactions is annexed, was adopted by the General Assembly at its fifty-first session on 16 December 1996. United Nations General Assembly resolution 52/87 on International Cooperation against Corruption and Bribery in International Commercial Transactions was adopted by the General Assembly at its fifty-second session on 12 December 1997. These resolutions were preceded by General Assembly resolution 51/59 on Action against Corruption, containing in an annex the International Code of Conduct for Public Officials. The three resolutions complement each other and reflect recent recommendations of the United Nations with respect to corruption and bribery in commercial transactions.

The General Assembly;

Recalling its resolution 3514 (XXX) of 15 December 1975, in which it, inter alia, condemned all corrupt practices, including bribery, in international commercial transactions, reaffirmed the right of any State to adopt legislation and to investigate and take appropriate legal action, in accordance with its national laws and regulations, against such corrupt practices, and called upon all Governments to cooperate to prevent corrupt practices, including bribery,

Recalling also the further work carried out by the General Assembly and the Economic and Social Council on the issue of illicit payments and on elaborating a code of conduct on transnational corporations,[1] consideration of which helped call attention to and raise international awareness of the adverse consequences of bribery in international commercial transactions,

Recalling further its resolution 50/106 of 20 December 1995, in which it recommended that the Economic and Social Council consider the draft international agreement on illicit payments at its substantive session of 1996 and report to the Assembly at its fifty-first session,

---

[*] *Source*: United Nations (1996). "General Assembly Resolution 51/191: United Nations Declaration Against Corruption and Bribery in International Commercial Transactions", *Official Records of the General Assembly: Fifty-first Session*, Supplement No. 49 (A/51/49) (New York: United Nations), pp. 176-178; available also on the Internet (gopher://gopher.un.org/00/ga/recs/51/RES51-EN.191). [Note added by the editor.]

[1] E/1991/31/Add.1.

Welcoming the steps taken at the national, regional and international levels to fight corruption and bribery, as well as recent developments in international forums that have further advanced international understanding and cooperation regarding corruption and bribery in international commercial transactions,

Noting the adoption in March 1996, by States members of the Organization of American States, of the Inter-American Convention against Corruption,[2] which includes an article on transnational bribery,

Noting also significant continuing work relevant to and consistent with the objectives of the present resolution in other regional and international forums, such as the continuing work of the Council of Europe and the European Union to combat international bribery, as well as the commitment by the States members of the Organisation for Economic Cooperation and Development[3] to criminalize bribery of foreign public officials in international commercial transactions in an effective and coordinated manner and further examine the modalities and appropriate international instruments to facilitate criminalization, and to re-examine the tax deductibility of such bribes with the intention of denying such tax deductibility in the member States that do not already do so,

1.   *Adopts* the United Nations Declaration against Corruption and Bribery in International Commercial Transactions, the text of which is annexed to the present resolution;

2.   *Notes* the work being undertaken by the United Nations and in other international and regional forums to address the problem of corruption and bribery in international commercial transactions, and invites all States concerned to pursue the completion of such work;

3.   *Invites* Member States, in accordance with the Declaration, to take appropriate measures and cooperate at all levels to combat corruption and bribery in international commercial transactions;

4.   *Requests* the Economic and Social Council and its subsidiary bodies, in particular the Commission on Crime Prevention and Criminal Justice:

(a)   To examine ways, including through legally binding international instruments, without in any way precluding, impeding or delaying international, regional or national actions, to further the implementation of the present resolution and the annexed Declaration, so as to promote the criminalization of corruption and bribery in international commercial transactions;

(b)   To keep the issue of corruption and bribery in international commercial transactions under regular review;

(c)   To promote the effective implementation of the present resolution;

5.   *Invites* other bodies of the United Nations system, including the United Nations Conference on Trade and Development, whose competence extends to this matter, to take action as appropriate within their mandates to promote the objectives of the present resolution and the

---

[2] See E 1996/99.

[3] See E/1996/106.

Declaration;

6.   *Encourages* private and public corporations, including transnational corporations, and individuals engaged in international commercial transactions to cooperate in the effective implementation of the Declaration;

7.   *Requests* the Secretary-General to inform Member States, the relevant bodies and the specialized agencies of the United Nations system, and international, regional and non-governmental organizations, of the adoption of the present resolution, to encourage action towards making its provisions widely known and to promote its effective implementation;

8.   *Also requests* the Secretary-General to prepare a report, for consideration by the General Assembly at its fifty-third session, on the progress made towards implementation of the present resolution and the steps taken by Member States, international and regional organizations and other relevant institutions to combat corruption and bribery in international commercial transactions; on the results of the work in this regard undertaken by the Commission on Crime Prevention and Criminal Justice and other bodies of the United Nations system; and on measures taken in accordance with the present resolution to promote social responsibility and the elimination of corruption and bribery in international commercial transactions;

9.   *Invites* Member States and competent international, regional and non-governmental organizations to provide relevant information to assist the Secretary-General in preparing the above-mentioned report;

10.   *Decides* to include in the provisional agenda of its fifty-third session, under an item entitled "Business and development", a review of the report of the Secretary-General concerning the implementation of the present resolution.

86th plenary meeting
16 December 1996

Annex

UNITED NATIONS DECLARATION AGAINST CORRUPTION AND BRIBERY IN INTERNATIONAL COMMERCIAL TRANSACTIONS

The General Assembly,

Convinced that a stable and transparent environment for international commercial transactions in all countries is essential for the mobilization of investment, finance, technology, skills and other important resources across national borders, in order, inter alia, to promote economic and social development and environmental protection,

Recognizing the need to promote social responsibility and appropriate standards of ethics on the part of private and public corporations, including transnational corporations, and individuals engaged in international commercial transactions, inter alia, through observance of the laws and regulations of the countries in which they conduct business, and taking into account the impact of their activities on economic and social development and environmental protection,

Recognizing also that effective efforts at all levels to combat and avoid corruption and bribery in all countries are essential elements of an improved international business environment, that they enhance fairness and competitiveness in international commercial transactions and form a critical part of promoting transparent and accountable governance, economic and social development and environmental protection in all countries, and that such efforts are especially pressing in the increasingly competitive globalized international economy,

Solemnly proclaims the United Nations Declaration against Corruption and Bribery in International Commercial Transactions as set out below.

Member States, individually and through international and regional organizations, taking actions subject to each State's own constitution and fundamental legal principles and adopted pursuant to national laws and procedures, commit themselves:

1.   To take effective and concrete action to combat all forms of corruption, bribery and related illicit practices in international commercial transactions, in particular to pursue effective enforcement of existing laws prohibiting bribery in international commercial transactions, to encourage the adoption of laws for those purposes where they do not exist, and to call upon private and public corporations, including transnational corporations, and individuals within their jurisdiction engaged in international commercial transactions to promote the objectives of the present Declaration;

2.   To criminalize such bribery of foreign public officials in an effective and coordinated manner, but without in any way precluding, impeding or delaying international, regional or national actions to further the implementation of the present Declaration;

3.   Bribery may include, *inter alia*, the following elements:

(a)   The offer, promise or giving of any payment, gift or other advantage, directly or indirectly, by any private or public corporation, including a transnational corporation, or individual from a State to any public official or elected representative of another country as undue consideration for performing or refraining from the performance of that official's or representative's duties in connection with an international commercial transaction;

(b)   The soliciting, demanding, accepting or receiving, directly or indirectly, by any public official or elected representative of a State from any private or public corporation, including a transnational corporation, or individual from another country of any payment, gift or other advantage, as undue consideration for performing or refraining from the performance of that official's or representative's duties in connection with an international commercial transaction;

4.   To deny, in countries that do not already do so, the tax deductibility of bribes paid by any private or public corporation or individual of a State to any public official or elected representative of another country and, to that end, to examine their respective modalities for doing so;

5.   To develop or maintain accounting standards and practices that improve the transparency of international commercial transactions, and that encourage private and public

corporations, including transnational corporations, and individuals engaged in international commercial transactions to avoid and combat corruption, bribery and related illicit practices;

6. To develop or to encourage the development, as appropriate, of business codes, standards or best practices that prohibit corruption, bribery and related illicit practices in international commercial transactions;

7. To examine establishing illicit enrichment by public officials or elected representatives as an offence;

8. To cooperate and afford one another the greatest possible assistance in connection with criminal investigations and other legal proceedings brought in respect of corruption and bribery in international commercial transactions. Mutual assistance shall include, as far as permitted under national laws or as provided for in bilateral treaties or other applicable arrangements of the affected countries, and taking into account the need for confidentiality as appropriate:

(a) Production of documents and other information, taking of evidence and service of documents relevant to criminal investigations and other legal proceedings;

(b) Notice of the initiation and outcome of criminal proceedings concerning bribery in international commercial transactions to other States that may have jurisdiction over the same offence;

(c) Extradition proceedings where and as appropriate;

9. To take appropriate action to enhance cooperation to facilitate access to documents and records about transactions and about identities of persons engaged in bribery in international commercial transactions;

10. To ensure that bank secrecy provisions do not impede or hinder criminal investigations or other legal proceedings relating to corruption, bribery or related illicit practices in international commercial transactions, and that full cooperation is extended to Governments that seek information on such transactions;

11. Actions taken in furtherance of the present Declaration shall respect fully the national sovereignty and territorial jurisdiction of Member States, as well as the rights and obligations of Member States under existing treaties and international law, and shall be consistent with human rights and fundamental freedoms;

12. Member States agree that actions taken by them to establish jurisdiction over acts of bribery of foreign public officials in international commercial transactions shall be consistent with the principles of international law regarding the extraterritorial application of a State's laws.

* * *

UNITED NATIONS GENERAL ASSEMBLY RESOLUTION 52/87 ON INTERNATIONAL COOPERATION AGAINST CORRUPTION AND BRIBERY IN COMMERCIAL TRANSACTIONS*

The General Assembly,

Disturbed by the bribery of public officials by individuals and enterprises of other States in relation to international commercial transactions,

Convinced that such practices undermine the integrity of state bureaucracies and weaken social and economic policies by promoting corruption in the public sector, thus diminishing its credibility,

Convinced also that the fight against corruption must be supported by sincere international cooperation efforts,

Recalling its resolution 3514 (XXX) of 15 December 1975, in which it, inter alia, condemned all corrupt practices, including bribery, by transnational corporations and other corporations, their intermediaries and others involved, in violation of the laws and regulations in host countries, reaffirmed the right of any State to adopt legislation and to investigate and take appropriate legal action, in accordance with its national laws and regulations, against such corrupt practices and called upon all Governments to cooperate to prevent corrupt practices, including bribery,

Recalling also Economic and Social Council resolution 1995/14 of 24 July 1995 on action against corruption,

Recalling further its resolution 50/225 of 19 April 1996 on public administration and development,

Recalling in particular its resolution 51/59 of 12 December 1996, in which it adopted the International Code of Conduct for Public Officials, annexed thereto, and recommended it to Member States as a tool to guide their efforts against corruption,

Recalling that by its resolution 51/191 of 16 December 1996 it adopted the United Nations Declaration against Corruption and Bribery in International Commercial Transactions,

Recalling also that in its resolution 51/191 it requested the Economic and Social Council and its subsidiary bodies, in particular the Commission on Crime Prevention and Criminal Justice, to examine ways to further the implementation of that resolution and the United Nations Declaration against Corruption and Bribery in International Commercial Transactions, to keep the issue of corruption and bribery in international commercial transactions under regular review and to promote the effective implementation of that resolution,

---

* *Source*: United Nations (1997). "General Assembly Resolution 52/87 on International Cooperation Against Corruption and Bribery in Commercial Transactions,"*Official Records of the General Assembly: Fifty-second Session*, Supplement No. 49 (A/52/49) (New-York: United Nations), pp. 211-212; also available on the Internet (gopher://gopher.un.org/00/ga/recs/52/RES52-87.EN). [Note added by the editor.]

Taking note of the report of the Secretary-General on action against corruption and bribery[1] and of the report of the Expert Group Meeting on Corruption, held at Buenos Aires from 17 to 21 March 1997,[2]

Welcoming developments that have advanced international understanding and cooperation regarding bribery in transnational business, such as the Inter-American Convention against Corruption adopted by the Organization of American States on 29 March 1996,[3] which includes an article on the prohibition of foreign commercial bribery; the ongoing work of the Council of Europe against corruption, including the elaboration of several international conventions containing provisions on bribery in international commercial transactions; the ongoing work of the World Trade Organization to improve transparency, openness and due process in government procurement procedures; and the ongoing work of the States members of the Organisation for Economic Cooperation and Development, including, as elements, the agreement to prohibit the tax deductibility of bribes paid to foreign public officials in international commercial transactions, and the commitment to criminalize the bribing of foreign public officials in international business transactions,

1.   *Agrees* that all States should take all possible measures to further the implementation of the United Nations Declaration against Corruption and Bribery in International Commercial Transactions[4] and of the International Code of Conduct for Public Officials;[5]

2.   *Urges* Member States that have not yet done so to implement relevant international declarations and to ratify, where appropriate, international instruments against corruption;

3.   *Also urges* Member States to criminalize, in an effective and coordinated manner, the bribery of public office holders of other States in international commercial transactions, and encourages them to engage, as appropriate, in programmatic activities to deter, prevent and combat bribery and corruption, for example, by diminishing institutional barriers through the development of integrated management systems and the promotion of legal reform, in accordance with their fundamental legal principles in both the public and private sectors, by encouraging a greater role for citizens in the development of transparent and accountable government, by supporting the active participation of non-governmental organizations in the identification, planning and implementation of initiatives that raise ethical standards and practices in both government and business transactions and by providing training and technical assistance to other States, as appropriate, and to develop and implement standards of good governance, in particular, accountability and transparency, legitimate commercial and financial conduct and other anti-corruption measures;

4.   *Requests* the Secretary-General to invite each Member State to provide a report on steps taken to implement the provisions of the Declaration, including those dealing with criminalization, effective sanctions, tax deductibility, accounting standards and practices, development of business codes, illicit enrichment, mutual legal assistance and bank secrecy

---

[1] E/CN. 15/1997/3.

[2] E/CN. 15/1997/3/Add.1, annex.

[3] See E/1996/99.

[4] Resolution 51/191, annex.

[5] Resolution 51/59, annex.

provisions, as well as on national anti-corruption strategies and policies, for compilation by the Secretary-General and consideration by the Commission on Crime Prevention and Criminal Justice, with a view to examining further steps to be taken for the full implementation of the Declaration;

5.   *Invites* competent international, regional and non-governmental organizations to provide relevant information to the Commission on Crime Prevention and Criminal Justice on international efforts to combat corruption and bribery;

6.   *Requests* the Secretary-General, subject to the availability of extrabudgetary funds, to intensify technical assistance to combat corruption, providing advisory services to Member States that request such services, and urges Member States to provide the Secretariat with the necessary extrabudgetary funds for such technical assistance;

7.   *Requests* the Commission on Crime Prevention and Criminal Justice to give attention to the question of the bribery of public office holders of other States in international commercial transactions and to include in its agenda for a future session a review of action taken by States to implement the Declaration.

70th plenary meeting
12 December 1997

*   *   *

FOURTH PROTOCOL TO THE GENERAL AGREEMENT ON TRADE IN SERVICES[*]
[excerpts]

(WORLD TRADE ORGANIZATION)

Among the set of ministerial decisions related to services adopted at the Marrakesh Ministerial Meeting in April 1994 which closed the Uruguay Round, was a decision to extend negotiations on trade in basic telecommunications beyond the Uruguay Round. The negotiations began in May 1994 and were concluded by the adoption of the Fourth Protocol to the General Agreement on Trade in Services on 15 February 1997. The WTO members that had accepted the Fourth Protocol as of 28 October 1999 are: Antigua and Barbuda, Argentina, Australia, Bangladesh, Belize, Bolivia, Brunei Darussalam, Bulgaria, Canada, Chile, Colombia, Côte d'Ivoire, Czech Republic, Dominican Republic, Ecuador, El Salvador, European Communities and their member States — Austria, Belgium, Denmark, Finland, France, Germany, Greece, Ireland, Italy, Luxembourg, the Netherlands, Portugal, Spain, Sweden, United Kingdom — Ghana, Grenada, Hong Kong (China), Hungary, Iceland, India, Indonesia, Israel, Jamaica, Japan, the Republic of Korea, Malaysia, Mauritius, Mexico, Morocco, New Zealand, Norway, Pakistan, Peru, Poland, Romania, Senegal, Singapore, Slovak Republic, South Africa, Sri Lanka, Switzerland, Thailand, Trinidad and Tobago, Tunisia, Turkey, United States of America and Venezuela. WTO members that had submitted commitments on basic communications subsequent to the close of negotiations on the Fourth Protocol are: Barbados, Cyprus, Guatemala, Kenya, Kyrgys Republic, Latvia, Suriname and Uganda. The Schedules of Specific Commitments and Lists of Exemptions from Article II of the General Agreement on Trade in Services concerning basic telecommunications that were annexed to this Protocol are not reproduced in this volume.

Members of the World Trade Organization (hereinafter referred to as the "WTO") whose Schedules of Specific Commitments and Lists of Exemptions from Article II of the General Agreement on Trade in Services concerning basic telecommunications are annexed to this Protocol (hereinafter referred to as " Members concerned"),

Having carried out negotiations under the terms of the Ministerial Decision on Negotiations on Basic Telecommunications adopted at Marrakesh on 15 April 1994,

Having regard to the Annex on Negotiations on Basic Telecommunications,

Agree as follows:

Upon the entry into force of this Protocol, a Schedule of Specific Commitments and a List of Exemptions from Article II concerning basic telecommunications annexed to this

---

[*] *Source*: World Trade Organization (1997). "Fourth Protocol to the General Agreement on Trade in Services", S/L/20; available on the Internet (http://wto.org/wto/services/4-prote.htm). [Note added by the editor.]

Protocol relating to a Member shall, in accordance with the terms specified therein, supplement or modify the Schedule of Specific Commitments and the List of Article II Exemptions of that Member.

This Protocol shall be open for acceptance, by signature or otherwise, by the Members concerned until 30 November 1997.

The Protocol shall enter into force on 1 January 1998 provided it has been accepted by all Members concerned. If by 1 December 1997 the Protocol has not been accepted by all Members concerned, those Members which have accepted it by that date may decide, prior to 1 January 1998, on its entry into force.

This Protocol shall be deposited with the Director-General of the WTO. The Director-General of the WTO shall promptly furnish to each Member of the WTO a certified copy of this Protocol and notifications of acceptances thereof.

This Protocol shall be registered in accordance with the provisions of Article 102 of the Charter of the United Nations.

Done at Geneva on 15 April One thousand nine hundred and ninety-seven, in a single copy in the English, French and Spanish languages, each text being authentic, except as otherwise provided for in respect of the Schedules annexed hereto.

*   *   *

FIFTH PROTOCOL TO THE GENERAL AGREEMENT ON TRADE IN SERVICES[*]
[excerpts]

(WORLD TRADE ORGANIZATION)

The World Trade Organization's negotiations on financial services concluded with the adoption of the Fifth Protocol to the General Agreement on Trade in Services on 12 December 1997. The Protocol was opened for acceptance by Governments until 29 January 1999. The WTO members that accepted the Fifth Protocol as of 28 October 1999 are: Australia, Bahrain, Bulgaria, Canada, Chile, Colombia, Costa Rica, Cyprus, Czech Republic, Ecuador, El Salvador, Egypt, European Communities and their member States — Austria, Belgium, Denmark, Finland, France, Germany, Greece, Ireland, Italy, Luxembourg, the Netherlands, Portugal, Spain, Sweden, United Kingdom — Honduras, Hong Kong (China), Hungary, Iceland, India, Indonesia, Israel, Japan, the Republic of Korea, Macau, Kuwait, Malaysia, Malta, Mauritius, Mexico, Nicaragua, New Zealand, Norway, Pakistan, Peru, Romania, Senegal, Singapore, Slovak Republic, Slovenia, South Africa, Sri Lanka, Switzerland, Thailand, Tunisia, Turkey, United States of America and Venezuela. The Schedules of Specific Commitments and Lists of Exemptions from Article II of the General Agreement on Trade in Services concerning financial services which were annexed to this Protocol are not reproduced in this volume.

Members of the World Trade Organization (hereinafter referred to as the "WTO") whose Schedules of Specific Commitments and Lists of Exemptions from Article II of the General Agreement on Trade in Services concerning financial services are annexed to this Protocol (hereinafter referred to as "Members concerned"),

Having carried out negotiations under the terms of the Second Decision on Financial Services adopted by the Council for Trade in Services on 21 July 1995 (S/L/9),

Agree as follows:

[1] A Schedule of Specific Commitments and a List of Exemptions from Article II concerning financial services annexed to this Protocol relating to a Member shall, upon the entry into force of this Protocol for that Member, replace the financial services sections of the Schedule of Specific Commitments and the List of Article II Exemptions of that Member.

[2] This Protocol shall be open for acceptance, by signature or otherwise, by the Members concerned until 29 January 1999.

[3] This Protocol shall enter into force on the 30th day following the date of its acceptance by all Members concerned. If by 30 January 1999 it has not been accepted by all Members concerned,

---

[*] *Source*: World Trade Organization (1998). "Fifth Protocol to the General Agreement on Trade in Services", S/L/45; available on the Internet (http://www.wto.org/services/s145.htm). [Note added by the editor.]

those Members which have accepted it before that date may, within a period of 30 days thereafter, decide on its entry into force.

[4] This Protocol shall be deposited with the Director-General of the WTO. The Director-General of the WTO shall promptly furnish to each Member of the WTO a certified copy of this Protocol and notifications of acceptances thereof pursuant to paragraph 3.

[5] This Protocol shall be registered in accordance with the provisions of Article 102 of the Charter of the United Nations.

Done at Geneva this --- day of [month] one thousand nine hundred and ninety [---], in a single copy in English, French and Spanish languages, each text being authentic, except as otherwise provided for in respect of the Schedules annexed hereto.

*   *   *

PART TWO

REGIONAL INSTRUMENTS

DECISION 285 OF THE COMMISSION OF THE CARTAGENA AGREEMENT: RULES AND REGULATIONS FOR PREVENTING OR CORRECTING DISTORTIONS IN COMPETITION CAUSED BY PRACTICES THAT RESTRICT FREE COMPETITION[*]

(ANDEAN COMMUNITY)

Decision 285 establishing a set of Norms to Prevent or Correct Competitive Distortions Caused by Practices that Restrict Free Competition was adopted by the countries members of the Andean Group, namely, Bolivia, Colombia, Ecuador, Peru and Venezuela, on 21 March 1991. This Decision replaced Decision 230 dealing with the same topic. Decision 285 entered into force on 4 April 1991.

THE COMMISSION OF THE CARTAGENA AGREEMENT,

HAVING SEEN: Chapter VIII of the Cartagena Agreement, Decisions 230, 258, and 281 and Board Proposal 223/Rev. 2;

WHEREAS:

The Commission approved Decision 230, which contains rules and regulations for preventing or correcting practices that could distort competition;

Decision 258 stipulates that the Commission, at the proposal of the Board, shall review the rules and regulations on competition;

Decision 281 stipulates that the Commission, at the proposal of the Board and by March 31, 1991 at the latest, shall review the rules and regulations on competition established in Decision 230;

In order to achieve the objectives of the integration process, it is advisable to perfect Subregional rules and regulations on competition so that they can act as effective mechanisms for preventing or correcting any distortions that could be caused by business behaviors that restrict, hinder or distort that competition;

Due to their origin and scope, it is necessary to distinguish between the practices that are the subject-matter of this Decision, and dumping and subsidy practices and restrictions on exports;

---

[*] *Source*: Andean Group (1991). "Decision 285 of the Commission of the Cartagena Agreement: Rules and Regulations for Preventing or Correcting Distortions in Competition Caused by Practices that Restrict Free Competition", *Gaceta Oficial del Acuerdo de Cartagena*, Year VIII, No. 80, 4 April 1991. [Note added by the editor.]

DECIDES:

I. SCOPE OF APPLICATION

ARTICLE 1

The purpose of the rules and regulations provided for in this Decision is to prevent or correct distortions in competition caused by practices that restrict free competition.

ARTICLE 2

Member Countries or enterprises that have a legitimate interest may ask the Board for authorization or a mandate to take measures to prevent or correct the threat of injury or injury to production or exports, caused by practices that restrict free competition originating in the Subregion or involving an enterprise that carries out its economic activity in a Member Country.

Originating in the Subregion is understood to mean practices carried out by enterprises that pursue their economic activities in one or more Member Countries. The involvement in a Member Country is understood to mean a practice carried out among enterprises whose economic activities are conducted in one or more Member Countries and enterprises located outside the Subregion.

Excluded from this Decision are practices carried out by one or more enterprises located in a single Member Country that do not generate any effects in the Subregion. In those cases the respective national legislation shall be applicable.

For purposes of this Decision, a significant delay in building up national production is considered as a threat of injury.

ARTICLE 3

Practices restricting free competition are understood to mean agreements, parallel behaviors or collusion between enterprises that restrict, impede of distort competition or that could do so.

The agreements referred to in the previous clause may include horizontal or vertical agreements entered into by related parties.

For purposes of this Decision, the abusive exploitation by one or several enterprises of their dominant position in the market, is also considered a practice that restricts free competition.

It is understood that one or several enterprises enjoy a dominant position if they are able to act independently, without considering the competitors, buyers or suppliers, due to factors such as significant participation of the enterprises in the respective markets, the characteristics of supply and demand for the products, the degree of technological development of the products involved, and the access of competitors to financing and sources of supplies, as well as to distribution networks.

ARTICLE 4

The following are considered agreements, parallel behaviors or collusion:

a)   The wrongful of manipulation or direct or indirect setting of prices or other marketing condition, on terms that are discriminatory with relation to what would have prevailed in a normal commercial situations;

b)   The limitation or control of production, distribution, technical development or investments. Also limitations or prohibitions on exporting, importing or competing;

c)   The allocation Distribution of the market or of supply sources, especially maneuvers intended to disrupt the normal supply of raw materials;

d)   Application in trading of unequal conditions to equivalent goods or relationships services, which place some competitors at a disadvantage to others;

e)   Subordination of contract signing to the acceptance of supplementary goods or services that, by nature or according to commercial practice, have nothing to do with the subject-matter of those contracts; and

f)   Other cases with equivalent effects.

ARTICLE 5

The following are considered abuses of a position of dominance in the market:

a)   The wrongful manipulation or direct or indirect setting of prices or other marketing conditions, on terms that are discriminatory with relation to what would have existed in normal commercial situations.

b)   The limitation or control of production, distribution, technical development or investments. Also limitations or prohibitions on exporting, importing or competing;

c)   Unjustified refusal to satisfy demands for purchases of products, among other things, failure to furnish supplies to enterprises with which they are disputing the market for the end product.

d)   Application in trade or service relationships of unequal conditions to equivalent goods or services, which place some competitors at a disadvantage to others;

e)   Subordination of contract signing to the acceptance of supplementary goods or services that, by nature or according to commercial practice, have nothing to do with the subject-matter of those contracts; and

f)   Other cases with equivalent effects.

II. PROCEDURE

ARTICLE 6

The following have the right to submit a written petition:

a)   Member Countries through their respective liaison institutions; and

b)   The enterprise or enterprises that have a legitimate interest, to the extend permitted by national legislation.

The written petition must contain the following information:

- the nature of the restrictive practices and their duration;

- the characteristics of the products or services that are the subject of the practices;

- the characteristics of the products that are affected;

- the enterprises involved;

- the evidence that may make it possible to presume the existence of a threat of injury or injury to production or exports caused by practices that restrict free competition;

- the characteristics of the measures requested.

Upon receipt of the claim, the Board shall proceed to inform the liaison institutions of the Member Countries where the enterprises involved in the investigation carry out their economic activities.

ARTICLE 7

The Board shall not initiate the investigation if the petition is incomplete. In that case, it shall so advise the claimant, indicating in detail what information is missing, within ten working days after presentation of the petition.

If the petition is deemed adequate, within ten working days after its presentation, the Board shall pronounce itself to that effect through a Resolution. Furthermore, that Resolution shall be communicated to the claimant enterprise or enterprises.

ARTICLE 8

During the investigation, the Board may request and collect evidence and information from the liaison institutions and, either through them or directly, from the producers, exporters, importers or consumers with a legitimate interest in the investigation. They may also furnish information or, as the case may be, present pleadings to the Board.

In cases where the Board requests, collects or receives evidence and information directly, it shall report this to the respective liaison institutions.

ARTICLE 9

In exercising its power to request and collect evidence, the Board may decide to treat the information given to it as confidential if the party furnishing that information asks for and justifies such treatment, since as the source of that information, its dissemination may have unfavorable consequences for it.

Moreover, the parts of internal documents prepared by the Board or Member Countries which contain that kind of information may also be of a confidential nature.

When confidential treatment of evidence is sought, the petitioner shall provide a summary of the information that may be disclosed or an explanation of why that information cannot be summarized. In the latter case, the Board does not have to accept that explanation, in which case it may not take that evidence into consideration.

Likewise, even if the petition is justified, the information may not be taken into account if the entity offering it fails to submit a non-confidential summary of its contents, provided that this information is capable of being summarized.

Those interested in the investigation may submit a written request for the information furnished or prepared pursuant to this Decision and this information may be supplied to them if it is not confidential in nature.

This article does not impede the disclosure of general information and, in particular, of the grounds for the Resolutions referred to in this Decision, if required in the course of a judicial proceeding. In making that disclosure, it shall be kept in mind that the trade secrets of those that have a legitimate interest in the investigation must not be revealed.

ARTICLE 10

In the course of the investigation, the Board may, on its own initiative or at the petition of any of the interested parties, call meetings for the purpose of seeking a direct settlement; the commitments made and the results of these meetings shall be recorded in the minutes.

No interested party shall be compelled to attend a meeting and the absence of said party shall not be detrimental to its case.

The Board shall go on record with its opinion through a Resolution that will state what commitments have been assumed and whether the investigation shall be suspended or shall continue at the request of the claimant.

Enterprises or the authorities of the country where the practice is carried out shall furnish the necessary information for verifying compliance with the commitments assumed. If these commitments fail to be fulfilled or the pertinent information is not furnished, the Board shall resume the investigation.

ARTICLE 11

The Board shall have a period of two months as of the date of publication of the Resolution to which Article 7 of this Decision refers, in which to conduct its investigation.

In special cases, the deadline may be extended up to two additional months, in which case the Board must so inform the claimant.

ARTICLE 12

In order to issue its opinion, the Board must consider the existence of positive evidence regarding:

a)   The practices that are restricting free competition;

b)   The threat of injury or injury; and

c)   A cause-and-effect relationship between the practices and the threat of injury or injury.

ARTICLE 13

The determination of the existence of a threat of injury or injury and of the cause-and-effect relationship with the practices restricting free competition may be based, among other things, on the examination of:

a)   The volume of trade in the products that are the subject of those practices, particularly to determine if it has changed significantly, both in absolute terms and in relation to the production and consumption of the Member Country affected;

b)   The prices of the products or services that are the subject of the practices, particularly to determine whether they are considerably different from the prices of similar products or services in the absence of those practices; and

c)   The effects on the production or exports affected by the practices, as deduced from the real or virtual trends in pertinent economic factors, such as: production, domestic sales, exports, distribution, market share, use of installed capacity, employment, stocks, and profits.

ARTICLE 14

At the conclusion of the investigation, and within ten working days after the event provided for in Article 11, the Board shall place issues an opinion through a Resolution, in accordance with its conclusions and based on the available information.

The Resolution shall indicate the characteristics of the measures to be established, the deadlines for their adoption and their duration. Also, when applicable, the conditions that will determine the duration of those measures.

ARTICLE 15

Once the Board has verified, at the request of the liaison institutions or of the interested parties, the change in or elimination of the causes that gave grounds for the Resolution to which the previous article refers, it shall repeal that Resolution partially or totally by amending or derogating it. The Board shall have two months in which to issue its opinion.

The Board may also verify on its own initiative the change in or elimination of the causes that gave grounds for the Resolution in question and amend or repeal it.

III. MEASURES

ARTICLE 16

The Board shall issue its opinion through an injunction if it determines the existence of a practice restricting free competition that threatens to cause or causes injury. It may also decide on the implementation of measures designed to eliminate or lessen the distortions that generated the claim.

Member Countries shall adopt the necessary measures to ensure that the effects of those restrictions cease.

The corrective measures may consist in authorizations to countries where the enterprises that are affected carry out their economic activities, allowing them to apply preferential tariffs, with regard to Subregional tariff commitments, to imports of the products affected by the practice that restricts free competition.

ARTICLE 17

In the event that the threat of injury or injury is evident, the Board may, in the course of its investigation, issue recommendations aimed at bringing the practice to an end.

VI. FINAL PROVISION

ARTICLE 18

This Decision replaces Decision 230 as regards to the rules and regulations for preventing or correcting distortions in competition caused by practices that restrict free competition.

Signed in the city of Lima on the twenty-first of March of nineteen ninety-one.

*   *   *

AGREEMENT BETWEEN THE GOVERNMENT OF THE UNITED STATES OF AMERICA AND THE COMMISSION OF THE EUROPEAN COMMUNITIES REGARDING THE APPLICATION OF THEIR COMPETITION LAWS*
AND
AGREEMENT BETWEEN THE EUROPEAN COMMUNITIES AND THE GOVERNMENT OF THE UNITED STATES OF AMERICA ON THE APPLICATION OF POSITIVE COMITY PRINCIPLES IN THE ENFORCEMENT OF THEIR COMPETITION LAWS

The Agreement between the Government of the United States of America and the Commission of the European Communities regarding the Application of Their Competition Laws was signed in Washington on 23 September 1991. It entered into force on the same date pursuant to article 2 of the Decision of the Council and the Commission of 10 April 1995 Concerning the Conclusion of the Agreement between the European Communities and the Government of the United States of America Regarding the Application of Their Competition Laws, Exchange of Interpretative Letters with the Government of the United States of America, according to which the Agreement shall apply with effect from 23 September 1991 (retroactive effect from 23 September 1991 had been made necessary due to the Decision of the Court of Justice of the European Communities). Subsequently, an Agreement between the European Communities and the United States of America on the Application of Positive Comity Principles in the Enforcement of Their Competition Laws was signed in Brussels and Washington on 4 June 1998. It entered into force on the same date.

THE GOVERNMENT OF THE UNITED STATES OF AMERICA AND THE COMMISSION OF THE EUROPEAN COMMUNITIES,

Recognizing that the world's economies are becoming increasingly interrelated, and in particular that this is true of the economies of the United States of America and the European Communities;

Noting that the Government of the United States of America and the Commission of the European Communities share the view that the sound and effective enforcement of competition law is a matter of importance to the efficient operation of their respective markets and to trade between them;

Noting that the sound and effective enforcement of the Parties' competition laws would be enhanced by cooperation and, in appropriate cases, coordination between them in the application of those laws;

---

* *Source*: European Commission (1995). "Agreement between the Government of the United States of America and the Commission of the European Communities regarding the Application of their Competition Laws", *Official Journal of the European Communities*, L 132, 15 June 1995; available also on the Internet (http://europa.eu.int/comm/dg04/interna/95145b.htm). [Note added by the editor.]

Noting further that from time to time differences may arise between the Parties concerning the application of their competition laws to conduct or transactions that implicate significant interests of both Parties;

Having regard to the Recommendation of the Council of the Organization for Economic Cooperation and Development Concerning Cooperation Between Member Countries on Restrictive Business Practices Affecting International Trade, adopted on June 5, 1986; and Having regard to the Declaration on US6EC Relations adopted on November 23, 1990,

HAVE AGREED AS FOLLOWS:

Article I

Purpose and definitions

1.   The purpose of this Agreement is to promote cooperation and coordination and lessen the possibility or impact of differences between the Parties in the application of their competition laws.

2.   For the purpose of this Agreement, the following terms shall have the following definitions:

A.   'competition law(s)' shall mean (i) for the European Communities, Articles 85, 86, 89 and 90 of the Treaty establishing the European Economic Community, Regulation (EEC) No 4064/89 on the control of concentrations between undertakings, Articles 65 and 66 of the Treaty establishing the European Coal and Steel Community (ECSC), and their implementing Regulations including High Authority Decision No 24654, and (ii) for the United States of America, the Sherman Act (15 USC §§ 167), the Clayton Act (15 USC §§ 12627), the Wilson Tariff Act (15 USC §§ 8611), and the Federal Trade Commission Act (15 USC §§ 41668, except as these sections relate to consumer protection functions), as well as such other laws or regulations as the Parties shall jointly agree in writing to be a 'competition law' for purposes of this Agreement;

B.   'competition authorities' shall mean (i) for the European Communities, the Commission of the European Communities, as to its responsibilities pursuant to the competition laws of the European Communities, and (ii) for the United States, the Antitrust Division of the United Stated Department of Justice and the Federal Trade Commission;

C.   'enforcement activities' shall mean any application of competition law by way of investigation or proceeding conducted by the competition authorities of a Part; and D. 'anticompetitive activities' shall mean any conduct or transaction that is impermissible under the competition laws of a Party.

Article II

Notification

1.   Each Party shall notify the other whenever its competition authorities become aware that their enforcement activities may affect important interests of the other Party.

2.   Enforcement activities as to which notification ordinarily will be appropriate include those that:

(a)   are relevant to enforcement activities of the other Party;

(b)   involve anticompetitive activities (other than a merger or acquisition) carried out in significant part in the other Party's territory;

(c)   involve a merger or acquisition in which one or more of the parties to the transaction, or a company controlling one or more of the parties to the transaction, is a company incorporated or organized under the laws of the other Party or one of its States or Member States;

(d)   involve conduct believed to have been required, encouraged or approved by the other Party; or

(e)   involve remedies that would, in significant respects, require or prohibit conduct in the other Party's territory.

3.   With respect to mergers or acquisitions required by law to be reported to the competition authorities, notification under this Article shall be made:

(a)   in the case of the Government of the United States of America,

(i)   not later than the time its competition authorities request, pursuant to 15 USC § 18 a (e), additional information or documentary material concerning the proposed transaction,

(ii)   when its competition authorities decide to file a complaint challenging the transaction, and

(iii)   where this is possible, far enough in advance of the entry of a consent decree to enable the other Party's views to be taken into account; and

(b)   in the case of the Commission of the European Communities,

(i)   when notice of the transaction is published in the Official Journal, pursuant to Article 4 (3) of Council Regulation No 4064/89, or when notice of the transaction is received under Article 66 of the ECSC Treaty and a prior authorization from the Commission is required under that provision,

(ii)   when its competition authorities decide to initiate proceedings with respect to the proposed transaction, pursuant to Article 6 (1) (c) of Council Regulation (EEC) No 4064/89, and

(iii)   far enough in advance of the adoption of a decision in the case to enable the other Party's views to be taken into account.

4. With respect to other matters, notification shall ordinarily be provided at the stage in an investigation when it becomes evident that notifiable circumstances are present, and in any event far enough in advance of:

   (a)   the issuance of a statement of objections in the case of the Commission of the European Communities, or a complaint or indictment in the case of the Government of the United States of America; and

   (b)   the adoption of a decision or settlement in the case of the Commission of the European Communities, or the entry of a consent decree in the case of the Government of the United States of America; to enable the other Party's views to be taken into account.

5. Each Party shall also notify the other whenever its competition authorities intervene or otherwise participate in a regulatory or judicial proceeding that does not arise from its enforcement activities, if the issues addressed in the intervention or participation may affect the other Party's important interests. Notification under this paragraph shall apply only to:

   (a)   regulatory or judicial proceedings that are public;

   (b)   intervention or participation that is public and pursuant to formal procedures; and

   (c)   in the case of regulatory proceedings in the United States, only proceedings before federal agencies. Notification shall be made at the time of the intervention or participation or as soon thereafter as possible.

6. Notifications under this Article shall include sufficient information to permit an initial evaluation by the recipient Party of any effects on its interests.

Article III

Exchange of information

1. The Parties agree that it is in their common interest to share information that will

   (a)   facilitate effective application of their respective competition laws, or

   (b)   promote better understanding by them of economic conditions and theories relevant to their competition authorities' enforcement activities and interventions or participation of the kind described in Article II (5).

2. In furtherance of this common interest, appropriate officials from the competition authorities of each Party shall meet at least twice each year, unless otherwise agreed, to

   (a)   exchange information on their current enforcement activities and priorities,

   (b)   exchange information on economic sectors of common interest,

   (c)   discuss policy changes which they are considering, and

(d)   discuss other matters of mutual interest relating to the application of competition laws.

3.   Each Party will provide the other Party with any significant information that comes to the attention of its competition authorities about anticompetitive activities that its competition authorities believe is relevant to, or may warrant, enforcement activity by the other Party's competition authorities.

4.   Upon receiving a request from the other Party, and within the limits of Articles VIII and IX, a Party will provide to the requesting Party such information within its possession as the requesting Party may describe that is relevant to an enforcement activity being considered or conducted by the requesting Party's competition authorities.

Article IV

Cooperation and coordination in enforcement activities

1.   The competition authorities of each Party will render assistance to the competition authorities of the other Party in their enforcement activities, to the extent compatible with the assisting Party's laws and important interests, and within its reasonably available resources.

2.   In cases where both Parties have an interest in pursuing enforcement activities with regard to related situations, they may agree that it is in their mutual interest to coordinate their enforcement activities. In considering whether particular enforcement activities should be coordinated, the Parties shall take account of the following factors, among others:

(a)   the opportunity to make more efficient use of their resources devoted to the enforcement activities;

(b)   the relative abilities of the Parties' competition authorities to obtain information necessary to conduct the enforcement activities;

(c)   the effect of such coordination on the ability of both Parties to achieve the objectives of their enforcement activities; and

(d)   the possibility of reducing costs incurred by persons subject to the enforcement activities.

3.   In any coordination arrangement, each Party shall conduct its enforcement activities expeditiously and, insofar as possible, consistently with the enforcement objectives of the other Party.

4.   Subject to appropriate notice to the other Party, the competition authorities of either Party may limit or terminate their participation in a coordination arrangement and pursue their enforcement activities independently.

Article V

Cooperation regarding anticompetitive activities in the territory of one Party that adversely affect the interests of the other Party

1.   The Parties note that anticompetitive activities may occur within the territory of one Party that, in addition to violating that Party's competition laws, adversely affect important interests of the other Party. The Parties agree that it is in both their interests to address anticompetitive activities of this nature.

2.   If a Party believes that anticompetitive activities carried out on the territory of the other Party are adversely affecting its important interests, the first Party may notify the other Party and may request that the other Party's competition authorities initiate appropriate enforcement activities. The notification shall be as specific as possible about the nature of the anticompetitive activities and their effects on the interests of the notifying Party, and shall include an offer of such further information and other cooperation as the notifying Party is able to provide.

3.   Upon receipt of a notification under paragraph 2, and after such other discussion between the Parties as may be appropriate and useful in the circumstances, the competition authorities of the notified Party will consider whether or not to initiate enforcement activities, or to expand ongoing enforcement activities, with respect to the anticompetitive activities identified in the notification. The notified Party will advise the notifying Party of its decision. If enforcement activities are initiated, the notified Party will advise the notifying Party of their outcome and, to the extent possible, of significant interim developments.

4.   Nothing in this Article limits the discretion of the notified Party under its competition laws and enforcement policies as to whether or not to undertake enforcement activities with respect to the notified anticompetitive activities, or precludes the notifying Party from undertaking enforcement activities with respect to such anticompetitive activities.

Article VI

Avoidance of conflicts over enforcement activities

Within the framework of its own laws and to the extent compatible with its important interests, each Party will seek, at all stages in its enforcement activities, to take into account the important interests of the other Party. Each Party shall consider important interests of the other Party in decisions as to whether or not to initiate an investigation or proceeding, the scope of an investigation or proceeding, the nature of the remedies or penalties sought, and in other ways, as appropriate. In considering one another's important interests in the course of their enforcement activities, the Parties will take account of, but will not be limited to, the following principles:

1.   While an important interest of a Party may exist in the absence of official involvement by the Party with the activity in question, it is recognized that such interests would normally be reflected in antecedent laws, decisions or statements of policy by its competent authorities.

2.   A Party's important interests may be affected at any stage of enforcement activity by the other Party. The Parties recognize, however, that as a general mater the potential for adverse impact on one Party's important interests arising from enforcement activity by the other Party is

less at the investigative stage and greater at the stage at which conduct is prohibited or penalized, or at which other forms of remedial orders are imposed.

3.   Where it appears that one Party's enforcement activities may adversely affect important interests of the other Party, the Parties will consider the following factors, in addition to any other factors that appear relevant in the circumstances, in seeking an appropriate accommodation of the competing interests:

(a)   the relative significance to the anticompetitive activities involved of conduct within the enforcing Party's territory as compared to conduct within the other Party's territory;

(b)   the presence or absence of a purpose on the part of those engaged in the anticompetitive activities to affect consumers, suppliers, or competitors within the enforcing Party's territory;

(c)   the relative significance of the effects of the anticompetitive activities on the enforcing Party's interests as compared to the effects on the other Party's interests;

(d)   the existence or absence of reasonable expectations that would be furthered or defeated by the enforcement activities;

(e)   the degree of conflict or consistency between the enforcement activities and the other Party's laws or articulated economic policies; and

(f)   the extent to which enforcement activities of the other Party with respect to the same persons, including judgments or undertakings resulting from such activities, may be affected.

Article VII

Consultation

1.   Each Party agrees to consult promptly with the other Party in response to a request by the other Party for consultations regarding any matter related to this Agreement and to attempt to conclude consultations expeditiously with a view to reaching mutually satisfactory conclusions. Any request for consultations shall include the reasons therefor and shall state whether procedural time limits or other considerations require the consultations to be expedited. These consultations shall take place at the appropriate level, which may include consultations between the heads of the competition authorities concerned.

2.   In each consultation under paragraph 1, each Party shall take into account the principles of cooperation set forth in this Agreement and shall be prepared to explain to the other Party the specific results of its application of those principles to the issue that is the subject of consultation.

Article VIII

Confidentiality of information

1. Notwithstanding any other provision of this Agreement, neither Party is required to provide information to the other Party if disclosure of that information to the requesting Party (a) is prohibited by the law of the Party possessing the information, or (b) would be incompatible with important interests of the Party possessing the information.

2. Each Party agrees to maintain, to the fullest extent possible, the confidentiality of any information provided to it in confidence by the other Party under this Agreement and to oppose, to the fullest extent possible, any application for disclosure of such information by a third party that is not authorized by the Party that supplied the information.

Article IX

Existing law

Nothing in this Agreement shall be interpreted in a manner inconsistent with the existing laws, or as requiring any change in the laws, of the United States of America or the European Communities or of their respective States or Member States.

Article X

Communications under this Agreement

Communications under this Agreement, including notifications under Articles II and V, may be carried out by direct oral, telephonic, written or facsimile communication from one Party's competition authority to the other Party's authority. Notifications under Articles II, V and XI, and requests under Article VII, shall be confirmed promptly in writing through diplomatic channels.

Article XI

Entry into force, termination and review

1. This Agreement shall enter into force upon signature.

2. This Agreement shall remain in force until 60 days after the date on which either Party notifies the other Party in writing that it wishes to terminate the Agreement.

3. The Parties shall review the operation of this Agreement not more than 24 months from the date of its entry into force, with a view to assessing their cooperative activities, identifying additional areas in which they could usefully cooperate and identifying any other ways in which the Agreement could be improved. The Parties agree that this review will include, among other things, an analysis of actual or potential cases to determine whether their interests could be better served through closer cooperation.

IN WITNESS WHEREOF, the undersigned, being duly authorized, have signed this Agreement.

DONE at Washington, in duplicate, this twenty third day of September, 1991, in the English language.

FOR THE COMMISSION OF THE EUROPEAN COMMUNITIES

FOR THE GOVERNMENT OF THE UNITED STATES OF AMERICA

*   *   *

AGREEMENT BETWEEN THE EUROPEAN COMMUNITIES AND THE GOVERNMENT OF THE UNITED STATES OF AMERICA ON THE APPLICATION OF POSITIVE COMITY PRINCIPLES IN THE ENFORCEMENT OF THEIR COMPETITION LAWS[*]

THE EUROPEAN COMMUNITY AND THE EUROPEAN COAL AND STEEL COMMUNITY of the one part (hereinafter 'the European Communities`), and   THE GOVERNMENT OF THE UNITED STATES OF AMERICA of the other part,

Having regard to the 23 September 1991 Agreement between the European Communities and the Government of the United States of America regarding the application of their competition laws, and the exchange of interpretative letters dated 31 May and 31 July 1995 in relation to that Agreement (together hereinafter 'the 1991 Agreement`),

Recognising that the 1991 Agreement has contributed to coordination, cooperation, and avoidance of conflicts in competition law enforcement,

Noting in particular Article V of the 1991 Agreement, commonly referred to as the 'positive comity' Article, which calls for cooperation regarding anti-competitive activities occurring in the territory of one Party that adversely affect the interests of the other Party,

Believing that further elaboration of the principles of positive comity and of the implementation of those principles would enhance the 1991 Agreement's effectiveness in relation to such conduct, and

Noting that nothing in this Agreement or its implementation shall be construed as prejudicing either Party's position on issues of competition law jurisdiction in the international context,

---

[*] *Source*: European Communities (1998). "Agreement between the European Communities and the Government of the United States of America on the Application of Positive Comity Principles in the Enforcement of their Competition Laws", *Official Journal of the European Communities*, L 173, 18 June 1998, pp. 28-31; available also on the Internet (http://www.europa.eu.int/eur-lex/en/lif/dat/1998/en_298A0618_01.html). [Note added by the editor.]

HAVE AGREED AS FOLLOWS:

Article I

Scope and purpose of this Agreement

1. This Agreement applies where a Party satisfies the other that there is reason to believe that the following circumstances are present:

   (a) anti-competitive activities are occurring in whole or in substantial part in the territory of one of the Parties and are adversely affecting the interests of the other Party; and

   (b) the activities in question are impermissible under the competition laws of the Party in the territory of which the activities are occurring.

2. The purposes of this Agreement are to:

   (a) help ensure that trade and investment flows between the Parties and competition and consumer welfare within the territories of the parties are not impeded by anti-competitive activities for which the competition laws of one or both Parties can provide a remedy, and

   (b) establish cooperative procedures to achieve the most effective and efficient enforcement of competition law, whereby the competition authorities of each Party will normally avoid allocating enforcement resources to deal with anti-competitive activities that occur principally in and are directed principally towards the other Party's territory, where the competition authorities of the other Party are able and prepared to examine and take effective sanctions under their law to deal with those activities.

Article II

Definitions

As used in this Agreement:

1. 'Adverse effects' and 'adversely affected' mean harm caused by anti-competitive activities to:

   (a) the ability of firms in the territory of a Party to export to, invest in, or otherwise compete in the territory of the other Party; or

   (b) competition in a Party's domestic or import markets.

2. 'Requesting Party' means a Party that is adversely affected by anti-competitive activities occurring in whole or in substantial part in the territory of the other Party.

3. 'Requested Party' means a Party in the territory of which such anti-competitive activities appear to be occurring.

4.   'Competition law(s)' means

(a)   for the European Communities, Articles 85, 86, and 89 of the Treaty establishing the European Community (EC), Articles 65 and 66(7) of the Treaty establishing the European Coal and Steel Community (ECSC), and their implementing instruments, to the exclusion of Council Regulation (EEC) No 4064/89 on the control of concentrations between undertakings; and

(b)   for the United States of America, the Sherman Act (15 U.S.C. §§ 1-7), the Clayton Act (15 U.S.C. §§ 12-27, except as it relates to investigations pursuant to Title II of the Hart-Scott-Rodino Antitrust Improvements Act of 1976, 15 U.S.C. § 18a), the Wilson Tariff Act (15 U.S.C. §§ 8-11), and the Federal Trade Commission Act (15 U.S.C. §§ 41-58, except as these sections relate to consumer protection functions);

as well as such other laws or regulations as the Parties shall jointly agree in writing to be a 'competition law' for the purposes of this Agreement.

5.   'Competition authorities' means:

(a)   for the European Communities, the Commission of the European Communities, as to its responsibilities pursuant to the competition laws of the European Communities, and

(b)   for the United States, the Antitrust Division of the United States Department of Justice and the Federal Trade Commission.

6.   'Enforcement activities' means any application of competition law by way of investigation or proceeding conducted by the competition authorities of a Party.

7.   'Anti-competitive activities' means any conduct or transaction that is impermissible under the competition laws of a Party.

Article III

Positive comity

The competition authorities of a Requesting Party may request the competition authorities of a Requested Party to investigate and, if warranted, to remedy anti-competitive activities in accordance with the Requested Party's competition laws. Such a request may be made regardless of whether the activities also violate the Requesting Party's competition laws, and regardless of whether the competition authorities of the Requesting Party have commenced or contemplate taking enforcement activities under their own competition laws.

Article IV

Deferral or suspension of investigations in reliance on enforcement activity by the Requested Party

1.   The competition authorities of the Parties may agree that the competition authorities of the Requesting Party will defer or suspend pending or contemplated enforcement activities during the pendency of enforcement activities of the Requested Party.

2.   The competition authorities of a Requesting Party will normally defer or suspend their own enforcement activities in favour of enforcement activities by the competition authorities of the Requested Party when the following conditions are satisfied:

(a)   the anti-competitive activities at issue:

    (i)   do not have a direct, substantial and reasonably foreseeable impact on consumers in the Requesting Party's territory; or

    (ii)   where the anti-competitive activities do have such an impact on the Requesting Party's consumers, they occur principally in and are directed principally towards the other Party's territory;

(b)   the adverse effects on the interests of the Requesting Party can be and are likely to be fully and adequately investigated and, as appropriate, eliminated or adequately remedied pursuant to the laws, procedures, and available remedies of the Requested Party. The Parties recognise that it may be appropriate to pursue separate enforcement activities where anti-competitive activities affecting both territories justify the imposition of penalties within both jurisdictions; and

(c)   the competition authorities of the Requested Party agree that in conducting their own enforcement activities, they will:

    (i)   devote adequate resources to investigate the anti-competitive activities and, where appropriate, promptly pursue adequate enforcement activities;

    (ii)   use their best efforts to pursue all reasonably available sources of information, including such sources of information as may be suggested by the competition authorities of the Requesting Party;

    (iii)   inform the competition authorities of the Requesting Party, on request or at reasonable intervals, of the status of their enforcement activities and intentions, and where appropriate provide to the competition authorities of the Requesting Party relevant confidential information if consent has been obtained from the source concerned. The use and disclosure of such information shall be governed by Article V;

    (iv)   promptly notify the competition authorities of the Requesting Party of any change in their intentions with respect to investigation or enforcement;

(v)   use their best efforts to complete their investigation and to obtain a remedy or initiate proceedings within six months, or such other time as agreed to by the competition authorities of the Parties, of the deferral or suspension of enforcement activities by the competition authorities of the Requesting Party;

(vi)   fully inform the competition authorities of the Requesting Party of the results of their investigation, and take into account the views of the competition authorities of the Requesting Party, prior to any settlement, initiation of proceedings, adoption of remedies, or termination of the investigation; and

(vii)   comply with any reasonable request that may be made by the competition authorities of the Requesting Party.

When the above conditions are satisfied, a Requesting Party which chooses not to defer or suspend its enforcement activities shall inform the competition authorities of the Requested Party of its reasons.

3.   The competition authorities of the Requesting Party may defer or suspend their own enforcement activities if fewer than all of the conditions set out in paragraph 2 are satisfied.

4.   Nothing in this Agreement precludes the competition authorities of a Requesting Party that choose to defer or suspend independent enforcement activities from later initiating or such activities. In such circumstances, the competition authorities of the Requesting Party will promptly inform the competition authorities of the Requested Party of their intentions and reasons. If the competition authorities of the Requested Party continue with their own investigation, the competition authorities of the two Parties shall, where appropriate, coordinate their respective investigations under the criteria and procedures of Article IV of the 1991 Agreement.

Article V

Confidentiality and use of information

Where pursuant to this Agreement the competition authorities of one Party provide information to the competition authorities of the other Party for the purpose of implementing this Agreement, that information shall be used by the latter competition authorities only for that purpose. However, the competition authorities that provided the information may consent to another use, on condition that where confidential information has been provided pursuant to Article IV(2)(c)(iii) on the basis of the consent of the source concerned, that source also agrees to the other use. Disclosure of such information shall be governed by the provisions of Article VIII of the 1991 Agreement and the exchange of interpretative letters dated 31 May and 31 July 1995.

Article VI

Relationship to the 1991 Agreement

This Agreement shall supplement and be interpreted consistently with the 1991 Agreement, which remains fully in force.

Article VII

Existing law

Nothing in this Agreement shall be interpreted in a manner inconsistent with the existing laws, or as requiring any change in the laws, of the European Communities or the United States of America or of their respective Member States or states.

Article VIII

Entry into force and termination

1.   This Agreement shall enter into force upon signature.

2.   This Agreement shall remain in force until 60 days after the date on which either Party notifies the other Party in writing that it wishes to terminate the Agreement.

IN WITNESS WHEREOF, the undersigned, being duly authorised, have signed this Agreement.

DONE at Brussels and Washington, in duplicate, in the English language.

For the European Community and for the European Coal and Steel Community

For the Government of the United States of america

*   *   *

ASEAN FRAMEWORK AGREEMENT ON SERVICES[*]

(ASSOCIATION OF SOUTHEAST ASIAN NATIONS)

The ASEAN Framework Agreement on Services was signed during the Fifth ASEAN Summit in Bangkok on 15 December 1995 and entered into force on 19 September 1998. As of 24 October 1999, the following countries had signed or acceded to this Agreement: Brunei Darussalam, Cambodia, Indonesia, Lao People's Democratic Republic, Malaysia, Myanmar, the Philippines, Singapore, Thailand and Viet Nam.

The Governments of Brunei Darussalam, the Republic of Indonesia, Malaysia, the Republic of the Philippines, the Republic of Singapore, the Kingdom of Thailand, and the Socialist Republic of Vietnam, Member States of the Association of South East Asian Nations (hereinafter referred to as "ASEAN");

RECOGNISING the Singapore Declaration of 1992 which provides that ASEAN shall move towards a higher plane of economic cooperation to secure regional peace and prosperity;

RECALLING that the Heads of Government, at the Fourth Summit held in Singapore on 27-28 January 1992 declared that an ASEAN Free Trade Area (AFTA) shall be established in the region;

NOTING that the Framework Agreement on Enhancing ASEAN Economic Cooperation signed in Singapore on 28 January 1992 provides that ASEAN Member States shall explore further measures on border and non-border areas of cooperation to supplement and complement the liberalisation of trade;

RECOGNISING that intra-ASEAN economic cooperation will secure a liberal trading framework for trade in services which would strengthen and enhance trade in services among ASEAN Member States;

DESIRING to mobilise the private sector in the realisation of economic development of ASEAN Member States in order to improve the efficiency and competitiveness of their service industry sector;

REITERATING their commitments to the rules and principles of the General Agreement on Trade in Services (hereinafter referred to as "GATS") and noting that Article V of GATS permits the liberalising of trade in services between or among the parties to an economic integration agreement;

[*]*Source*: Association of Southeast Asian Nations (1996). "ASEAN Framework Agreement on Services", *International Legal Materials*, vol. 35 (1996), pp. 1077-1080. [Note added by the editor.]

43

AFFIRMING that ASEAN Member States shall extend to one another preference in trade in services;

HAVE AGREED AS FOLLOWS:

Article I. Objectives

The objectives of the Member States under the ASEAN Framework Agreement on Services (hereinafter referred to as "this Framework Agreement") are:

(a)   to enhance cooperation in services amongst Member States in order to improve the efficiency and competitiveness, diversify production capacity and supply and distribution of services of their service suppliers within and outside ASEAN;

(b)   to eliminate substantially restrictions to trade in services amongst Member States; and

(c)   to liberalise trade in services by expanding the depth and scope of liberalisation beyond those undertaken by Member States under the GATS with the aim to realising a free trade area in services.

Article II. Areas of Cooperation

1.   All Member States shall participate in the cooperation arrangements under this Framework Agreement. However, taking cognizance of paragraph 3 of Article I of this Framework Agreement on Enhancing ASEAN Economic Cooperation, two or more Member States may proceed first if other Member States are not ready to implement these arrangements.

2.   Member States shall strengthen and enhance existing cooperation efforts in service sectors and develop cooperation in sectors that are not covered by existing cooperation arrangements, through inter alia:

(a)   establishing or improving infrastructural facilities;

(b)   joint production, marketing and purchasing arrangements;

(c)   research and development; and

(d)   exchange of information.

3.   Member States shall identify sectors for cooperation and formulate Action Plans, Programmes and Understandings that shall provide details on the nature and extent of cooperation.

Article III. Liberalisation

Pursuant to Article 1 (c), Member States shall liberalise trade in services in a substantial number of sectors within a reasonable time-frame by:

(a) eliminating substantially all existing discriminatory measures and market access limitations amongst Member States; and

(b) prohibiting new or more discriminatory measures and market access limitations.

Article IV. Negotiation of Specific Commitments

1. Member States shall enter into negotiations on measures affecting trade in specific service sectors. Such negotiations shall be directed towards achieving commitments which are beyond those inscribed in each Member State's schedule of specific commitments under the GATS and for which Member States shall accord preferential treatment to one another on an MFN basis.

2. Each Member State shall set out in a schedule, the specific commitments it shall undertake under paragraph 1 .

3. The provisions of this Framework Agreement shall not be so construed as to prevent any Member State from conferring or according advantages to adjacent countries in order to facilitate exchanges limited to contiguous frontier zones of services that are both locally produced and consumed.

Article V. Mutual Recognition

1. Each Member State may recognise the education or experience obtained, requirements met, or licenses or certifications granted in another Member State, for the purpose of licensing or certification of service suppliers. Such recognition may be based upon an agreement or arrangement with the Member State concerned or may be accorded autonomously.

2. Nothing in paragraph 1 shall be so construed as to require any Member State to accept or to enter into such mutual recognition agreements or arrangements.[1]

Article VI. Denial of Benefits

The benefits of this Framework Agreement shall be denied to a service supplier who is a natural person of a non-Member State or a juridical person owned or controlled by persons of a non-Member State constituted under the laws of a Member State, but not engaged in substantive business operations in the territory of Member State(s).

Article VII. Settlement of Disputes

1. The Protocol on Dispute Settlement Mechanism for ASEAN shall generally be referred to and applied with respect to any disputes arising from, or any differences between Member States concerning the interpretation or application of, this Framework Agreement or any arrangements arising therefrom.

2. A specific dispute settlement mechanism may be established for the purposes of this Framework Agreement which shall form an integral part of this Framework Agreement.

---

[1] These agreements or arrangements are concluded for Member State only. In the event a Member State wishes to join such agreements or arrangements, it should be given equal opportunity to do so at any time.

Article VIII. Supplementary Agreements or Arrangements

Schedules of specific commitments and Understandings arising from subsequent negotiations under this Framework Agreement and any other agreements or arrangements, Action Plans and Programmes arising thereunder shall form an integral part of this Framework Agreement.

Article IX. Other Agreements

1.   This Framework Agreement or any action taken under it shall not affect the rights and obligations of the Member States under any existing agreements[2] to which they are parties.

2.   Nothing in this Framework Agreement shall affect the rights of the Member States to enter into other agreements not contrary to the principles, objectives and terms of this Framework Agreement.

3.   Upon the signing of this Framework Agreement, Member States shall promptly notify the ASEAN Secretariat of any agreements pertaining to or affecting trade in services to which that Member is a signatory.

Article X. Modification of Schedules of Specific Commitments

1.   A Member State may modify or withdraw any commitment in its schedule of specific commitments, at any time after three years from the date on which that commitment entered into force provided:

    (a)   that it notifies other Member States and the ASEAN Secretariat of the intent to modify or withdraw a commitment three months before the intended date of implementation of the modification or withdrawal; and

    (b)   that it enters into negotiations with an affected Member State to agree to necessary compensatory adjustment.

2.   In achieving a compensatory adjustment, Member States shall ensure that the general level of mutually advantageous commitment is not less favourable to trade than that provided for in the schedules of specific commitments prior to such negotiations.

3.   Compensatory adjustment shall be made on an MFN basis to all other Member States.

4.   The SEOM with the endorsement of the AEM may draw up additional procedures to give effect to this Article.

Article XI. Institutional Arrangements

1.   The SEOM shall carry out such functions to facilitate the operation of this Framework Agreement and further its objectives, including the organisation of the conduct of negotiations, review and supervision of the implementation of this Framework Agreement.

---

[2] Existing Agreements are not affected as these have been notified in the MFN Exemption List of the GATS.

2.   The ASEAN Secretariat shall assist SEOM in carrying out its functions, including providing the support for supervising, coordinating and reviewing the implementation of this Framework Agreement.

Article XII. Amendments

The provisions of this Framework Agreement may be amended through the consent of all the Member States and such amendments shall become effective upon acceptance by all Member States.

Article XIII. Accession of New Members

New Members of ASEAN shall accede to this Framework Agreement on terms and conditions agreed between them and signatories to this Framework Agreement.

Article XIV. Final Provision

1.   The terms and definitions and other provisions of the GATS shall be referred to and applied to matters arising under this Framework Agreement for which no specific provision has been made under it.

2.   This Framework Agreement shall be deposited with the Secretary-General of ASEAN, who shall promptly furnish a certified copy thereof to each Member State.

3.   This Framework Agreement shall enter into force upon the deposit of instruments of ratification or acceptance by all signatory governments with the Secretary-General of ASEAN.

IN WITNESS WHEREOF, the undersigned, being duly authorised by their respective Governments, have signed the ASEAN Framework Agreement on Services.

DONE at Bangkok, this 15th day of December 1995 in a single copy in the English Language.

*   *   *

INTER-AMERICAN CONVENTION AGAINST CORRUPTION[*]

(ORGANIZATION OF AMERICAN STATES)

The Inter-American Convention against Corruption was adopted at the Third Plenary Session of the Organization of American States, in Caracas (Venezuela), on 29 March 1996. The countries signatories of the Convention were: Argentina, Bahamas, Bolivia, Brazil, Canada, Chile, Colombia, Costa Rica, Dominican Republic, Ecuador, El Salvador, Guatemala, Guyana, Haiti, Honduras, Jamaica, Mexico, Nicaragua, Panama, Paraguay, Peru, Suriname, Trinidad and Tobago, United States of America, Uruguay and Venezuela. The Convention entered into force on 6 March 1997. As of 21 September 1999, the following countries had ratified, accepted or acceded to the Convention: Argentina, Bolivia, Chile, Colombia, Costa Rica, Dominican Republic, Ecuador, El Salvador, Honduras, Mexico, Nicaragua, Panama, Paraguay, Peru, Trinidad and Tobago, Uruguay and Venezuela.

THE MEMBER STATES OF THE ORGANIZATION OF AMERICAN STATES,

CONVINCED that corruption undermines the legitimacy of public institutions and strikes at society, moral order and justice, as well as at the comprehensive development of peoples;

CONSIDERING that representative democracy, an essential condition for stability, peace and development of the region, requires, by its nature, the combating of every form of corruption in the performance of public functions, as well as acts of corruption specifically related to such performance;

PERSUADED that fighting corruption strengthens democratic institutions and prevents distortions in the economy, improprieties in public administration and damage to a society's moral fiber;

RECOGNIZING that corruption is often a tool used by organized crime for the accomplishment of its purposes;

CONVINCED of the importance of making people in the countries of the region aware of this problem and its gravity, and of the need to strengthen participation by civil society in preventing and fighting corruption;

RECOGNIZING that, in some cases, corruption has international dimensions, which requires coordinated action by States to fight it effectively;

---

[*] *Source* : Organization of American States (OAS) (1996). "Inter American Convention against Corruption"; available on the Internet (http://www.oas.org/en/juridico/english/Treaties/b-58.html). [Note added by the editor.]

CONVINCED of the need for prompt adoption of an international instrument to promote and facilitate international cooperation in fighting corruption and, especially, in taking appropriate action against persons who commit acts of corruption in the performance of public functions, or acts specifically related to such performance, as well as appropriate measures with respect to the proceeds of such acts;

DEEPLY CONCERNED by the steadily increasing links between corruption and the proceeds generated by illicit narcotics trafficking which undermine and threaten legitimate commercial and financial activities, and society, at all levels;

BEARING IN MIND the responsibility of States to hold corrupt persons accountable in order to combat corruption and to cooperate with one another for their efforts in this area to be effective; and

DETERMINED to make every effort to prevent, detect, punish and eradicate corruption in the performance of public functions and acts of corruption specifically related to such performance,

HAVE AGREED

to adopt the following

INTER-AMERICAN CONVENTION AGAINST CORRUPTION

Article I
Definitions

For the purposes of this Convention:

"Public function" means any temporary or permanent, paid or honorary activity, performed by a natural person in the name of the State or in the service of the State or its institutions, at any level of its hierarchy.

"Public official", "government official", or "public servant" means any official or employee of the State or its agencies, including those who have been selected, appointed, or elected to perform activities or functions in the name of the State or in the service of the State, at any level of its hierarchy.

"Property" means assets of any kind, whether movable or immovable, tangible or intangible, and any document or legal instrument demonstrating, purporting to demonstrate, or relating to ownership or other rights pertaining to such assets.

Article II
Purposes

The purposes of this Convention are:

1.   To promote and strengthen the development by each of the States Parties of the mechanisms needed to prevent, detect, punish and eradicate corruption; and

2.   To promote, facilitate and regulate cooperation among the States Parties to ensure the effectiveness of measures and actions to prevent, detect, punish and eradicate corruption in the performance of public functions and acts of corruption specifically related to such performance.

Article III
Preventive Measures

For the purposes set forth in Article II of this Convention, the States Parties agree to consider the applicability of measures within their own institutional systems to create, maintain and strengthen:

1.   Standards of conduct for the correct, honorable, and proper fulfillment of public functions. These standards shall be intended to prevent conflicts of interest and mandate the proper conservation and use of resources entrusted to government officials in the performance of their functions. These standards shall also establish measures and systems requiring government officials to report to appropriate authorities acts of corruption in the performance of public functions. Such measures should help preserve the public's confidence in the integrity of public servants and government processes.

2.   Mechanisms to enforce these standards of conduct.

3.   Instruction to government personnel to ensure proper understanding of their responsibilities and the ethical rules governing their activities.

4.   Systems for registering the income, assets and liabilities of persons who perform public functions in certain posts as specified by law and, where appropriate, for making such registrations public.

5.   Systems of government hiring and procurement of goods and services that assure the openness, equity and efficiency of such systems.

6.   Government revenue collection and control systems that deter corruption.

7.   Laws that deny favorable tax treatment for any individual or corporation for expenditures made in violation of the anticorruption laws of the States Parties.

8.   Systems for protecting public servants and private citizens who, in good faith, report acts of corruption, including protection of their identities, in accordance with their Constitutions and the basic principles of their domestic legal systems.

9.   Oversight bodies with a view to implementing modern mechanisms for preventing, detecting, punishing and eradicating corrupt acts.

10.   Deterrents to the bribery of domestic and foreign government officials, such as mechanisms to ensure that publicly held companies and other types of associations maintain books and records which, in reasonable detail, accurately reflect the acquisition and disposition of assets, and have sufficient internal accounting controls to enable their officers to detect corrupt acts.

11.   Mechanisms to encourage participation by civil society and nongovernmental organizations in efforts to prevent corruption.

12.   The study of further preventive measures that take into account the relationship between equitable compensation and probity in public service.

Article IV
Scope

This Convention is applicable provided that the alleged act of corruption has been committed or has effects in a State Party.

Article V
Jurisdiction

1.   Each State Party shall adopt such measures as may be necessary to establish its jurisdiction over the offenses it has established in accordance with this Convention when the offense in question is committed in its territory.

2.   Each State Party may adopt such measures as may be necessary to establish its jurisdiction over the offenses it has established in accordance with this Convention when the offense is committed by one of its nationals or by a person who habitually resides in its territory.

3.   Each State Party shall adopt such measures as may be necessary to establish its jurisdiction over the offenses it has established in accordance with this Convention when the alleged criminal is present in its territory and it does not extradite such person to another country on the ground of the nationality of the alleged criminal.

4.   This Convention does not preclude the application of any other rule of criminal jurisdiction established by a State Party under its domestic law.

Article VI
Acts of Corruption

1.   This Convention is applicable to the following acts of corruption:

   a.   The solicitation or acceptance, directly or indirectly, by a government official or a person who performs public functions, of any article of monetary value, or other benefit, such as a gift, favor, promise or advantage for himself or for another person or entity, in exchange for any act or omission in the performance of his public functions;

   b.   The offering or granting, directly or indirectly, to a government official or a person who performs public functions, of any article of monetary value, or other benefit, such as a gift, favor, promise or advantage for himself or for another person or entity, in exchange for any act or omission in the performance of his public functions;

c. Any act or omission in the discharge of his duties by a government official or a person who performs public functions for the purpose of illicitly obtaining benefits for himself or for a third party;

d. The fraudulent use or concealment of property derived from any of the acts referred to in this article; and

e. Participation as a principal, coprincipal, instigator, accomplice or accessory after the fact, or in any other manner, in the commission or attempted commission of, or in any collaboration or conspiracy to commit, any of the acts referred to in this article.

2. This Convention shall also be applicable by mutual agreement between or among two or more States Parties with respect to any other act of corruption not described herein.

Article VII
Domestic Law

The States Parties that have not yet done so shall adopt the necessary legislative or other measures to establish as criminal offenses under their domestic law the acts of corruption described in Article VI(1) and to facilitate cooperation among themselves pursuant to this Convention.

Article VIII
Transnational Bribery

Subject to its Constitution and the fundamental principles of its legal system, each State Party shall prohibit and punish the offering or granting, directly or indirectly, by its nationals, persons having their habitual residence in its territory, and businesses domiciled there, to a government official of another State, of any article of monetary value, or other benefit, such as a gift, favor, promise or advantage, in connection with any economic or commercial transaction in exchange for any act or omission in the performance of that official's public functions.

Among those States Parties that have established transnational bribery as an offense, such offense shall be considered an act of corruption for the purposes of this Convention. Any State Party that has not established transnational bribery as an offense shall, insofar as its laws permit, provide assistance and cooperation with respect to this offense as provided in this Convention.

Article IX
Illicit Enrichment

Subject to its Constitution and the fundamental principles of its legal system, each State Party that has not yet done so shall take the necessary measures to establish under its laws as an offense a significant increase in the assets of a government official that he cannot reasonably explain in relation to his lawful earnings during the performance of his functions.

Among those States Parties that have established illicit enrichment as an offense, such offense shall be considered an act of corruption for the purposes of this Convention.

Any State Party that has not established illicit enrichment as an offense shall, insofar as its laws permit, provide assistance and cooperation with respect to this offense as provided in this Convention.

Article X
Notification

When a State Party adopts the legislation referred to in paragraph 1 of articles VIII and IX, it shall notify the Secretary General of the Organization of American States, who shall in turn notify the other States Parties. For the purposes of this Convention, the crimes of transnational bribery and illicit enrichment shall be considered acts of corruption for that State Party thirty days following the date of such notification.

Article XI
Progressive Development

1.   In order to foster the development and harmonization of their domestic legislation and the attainment of the purposes of this Convention, the States Parties view as desirable, and undertake to consider, establishing as offenses under their laws the following acts:

   a.   The improper use by a government official or a person who performs public functions, for his own benefit or that of a third party, of any kind of classified or confidential information which that official or person who performs public functions has obtained because of, or in the performance of, his functions;

   b.   The improper use by a government official or a person who performs public functions, for his own benefit or that of a third party, of any kind of property belonging to the State or to any firm or institution in which the State has a proprietary interest, to which that official or person who performs public functions has access because of, or in the performance of, his functions;

   c.   Any act or omission by any person who, personally or through a third party, or acting as an intermediary, seeks to obtain a decision from a public authority whereby he illicitly obtains for himself or for another person any benefit or gain, whether or not such act or omission harms State property; and

   d.   The diversion by a government official, for purposes unrelated to those for which they were intended, for his own benefit or that of a third party, of any movable or immovable property, monies or securities belonging to the State, to an independent agency, or to an individual, that such official has received by virtue of his position for purposes of administration, custody or for other reasons.

2.   Among those States Parties that have established these offenses, such offenses shall be considered acts of corruption for the purposes of this Convention.

3.   Any State Party that has not established these offenses shall, insofar as its laws permit, provide assistance and cooperation with respect to these offenses as provided in this Convention.

Article XII
Effect on State Property

For application of this Convention, it shall not be necessary that the acts of corruption harm State property.

Article XIII
Extradition

1.   This article shall apply to the offenses established by the States Parties in accordance with this Convention.

2.   Each of the offenses to which this article applies shall be deemed to be included as an extraditable offense in any extradition treaty existing between or among the States Parties. The States Parties undertake to include such offenses as extraditable offenses in every extradition treaty to be concluded between or among them.

3.   If a State Party that makes extradition conditional on the existence of a treaty receives a request for extradition from another State Party with which it does not have an extradition treaty, it may consider this Convention as the legal basis for extradition with respect to any offense to which this article applies.

4.   States Parties that do not make extradition conditional on the existence of a treaty shall recognize offenses to which this article applies as extraditable offenses between themselves.

5.   Extradition shall be subject to the conditions provided for by the law of the Requested State or by applicable extradition treaties, including the grounds on which the Requested State may refuse extradition.

6.   If extradition for an offense to which this article applies is refused solely on the basis of the nationality of the person sought, or because the Requested State deems that it has jurisdiction over the offense, the Requested State shall submit the case to its competent authorities for the purpose of prosecution unless otherwise agreed with the Requesting State, and shall report the final outcome to the Requesting State in due course.

7.   Subject to the provisions of its domestic law and its extradition treaties, the Requested State may, upon being satisfied that the circumstances so warrant and are urgent, and at the request of the Requesting State, take into custody a person whose extradition is sought and who is present in its territory, or take other appropriate measures to ensure his presence at extradition proceedings.

Article XIV
Assistance and Cooperation

1.   In accordance with their domestic laws and applicable treaties, the States Parties shall afford one another the widest measure of mutual assistance by processing requests from authorities that, in conformity with their domestic laws, have the power to investigate or prosecute the acts of corruption described in this Convention, to obtain evidence and take other necessary action to facilitate legal proceedings and measures regarding the investigation or prosecution of acts of corruption.

2.   The States Parties shall also provide each other with the widest measure of mutual technical cooperation on the most effective ways and means of preventing, detecting, investigating and punishing acts of corruption. To that end, they shall foster exchanges of experiences by way of agreements and meetings between competent bodies and institutions, and shall pay special attention to methods and procedures of citizen participation in the fight against corruption.

Article XV
Measures Regarding Property

1.   In accordance with their applicable domestic laws and relevant treaties or other agreements that may be in force between or among them, the States Parties shall provide each other the broadest possible measure of assistance in the identification, tracing, freezing, seizure and forfeiture of property or proceeds obtained, derived from or used in the commission of offenses established in accordance with this Convention.

2.   A State Party that enforces its own or another State Party's forfeiture judgment against property or proceeds described in paragraph 1 of this article shall dispose of the property or proceeds in accordance with its laws. To the extent permitted by a State Party's laws and upon such terms as it deems appropriate, it may transfer all or part of such property or proceeds to another State Party that assisted in the underlying investigation or proceedings.

Article XVI
Bank Secrecy

1.   The Requested State shall not invoke bank secrecy as a basis for refusal to provide the assistance sought by the Requesting State. The Requested State shall apply this article in accordance with its domestic law, its procedural provisions, or bilateral or multilateral agreements with the Requesting State.

2.   The Requesting State shall be obligated not to use any information received that is protected by bank secrecy for any purpose other than the proceeding for which that information was requested, unless authorized by the Requested State.

ARTICLE XVII
Nature of the Act

For the purposes of articles XIII, XIV, XV and XVI of this Convention, the fact that the property obtained or derived from an act of corruption was intended for political purposes, or that it is alleged that an act of corruption was committed for political motives or purposes, shall not suffice in and of itself to qualify the act as a political offense or as a common offense related to a political offense.

Article XVIII
Central Authorities

1.   For the purposes of international assistance and cooperation provided under this Convention, each State Party may designate a central authority or may rely upon such central authorities as are provided for in any relevant treaties or other agreements.

2.   The central authorities shall be responsible for making and receiving the requests for assistance and cooperation referred to in this Convention.

3.   The central authorities shall communicate with each other directly for the purposes of this Convention.

Article XIX
Temporal Application

Subject to the constitutional principles and the domestic laws of each State and existing treaties between the States Parties, the fact that the alleged act of corruption was committed before this Convention entered into force shall not preclude procedural cooperation in criminal matters between the States Parties. This provision shall in no case affect the principle of non-retroactivity in criminal law, nor shall application of this provision interrupt existing statutes of limitations relating to crimes committed prior to the date of the entry into force of this Convention.

Article XX
Other Agreements or Practices

No provision of this Convention shall be construed as preventing the States Parties from engaging in mutual cooperation within the framework of other international agreements, bilateral or multilateral, currently in force or concluded in the future, or pursuant to any other applicable arrangement or practice.

Article XXI
Signature

This Convention is open for signature by the Member States of the Organization of American States.

Article XXII
Ratification

This Convention is subject to ratification. The instruments of ratification shall be deposited with the General Secretariat of the Organization of American States.

Article XXIII
Accession

This Convention shall remain open for accession by any other State. The instruments of accession shall be deposited with the General Secretariat of the Organization of American States.

Article XXIV
Reservations

The States Parties may, at the time of adoption, signature, ratification, or accession, make reservations to this Convention, provided that each reservation concerns one or more specific provisions and is not incompatible with the object and purpose of the Convention.

Article XXV
Entry Into Force

This Convention shall enter into force on the thirtieth day following the date of deposit of the second instrument of ratification. For each State ratifying or acceding to the Convention after the deposit of the second instrument of ratification, the Convention shall enter into force on the thirtieth day after deposit by such State of its instrument of ratification or accession.

Article XXVI
Denunciation

This Convention shall remain in force indefinitely, but any of the States Parties may denounce it. The instrument of denunciation shall be deposited with the General Secretariat of the Organization of American States. One year from the date of deposit of the instrument of denunciation, the Convention shall cease to be in force for the denouncing State, but shall remain in force for the other States Parties.

Article XXVII
Additional Protocols

Any State Party may submit for the consideration of other States Parties meeting at a General Assembly of the Organization of American States draft additional protocols to this Convention to contribute to the attainment of the purposes set forth in Article II thereof.

Each additional protocol shall establish the terms for its entry into force and shall apply only to those States that become Parties to it.

Article XXVIII
Deposit of Original Instrument

The original instrument of this Convention, the English, French, Portuguese, and Spanish texts of which are equally authentic, shall be deposited with the General Secretariat of the Organization of American States, which shall forward an authenticated copy of its text to the Secretariat of the United Nations for registration and publication in accordance with Article 102 of the United Nations Charter. The General Secretariat of the Organization of American States shall notify its Member States and the States that have acceded to the Convention of signatures, of the deposit of instruments of ratification, accession, or denunciation, and of reservations, if any.

* * *

Protocol to Amend the Agreement among the Governments of Brunei Darussalam, the Republic of Indonesia, Malaysia, the Republic of the Philippines, the Republic of Singapore and the Kingdom of Thailand for the Promotion and Protection of Investments[*]

(Association of Southeast Asian Nations)

The Protocol to Amend the Agreement among the Governments of Brunei Darussalam, the Republic of Indonesia, the Republic of the Philippines, the Republic of Singapore and the Kingdom of Thailand for the Promotion and Protection of Investments (signed in Manila, the Philippines, on 15 December 1987) (see *volume II* of this *Compendium*), was signed in Jakarta on 12 September 1996. With the adoption of the 1996 Protocol, the 1987 Agreement is referred to as "The ASEAN Agreement for the Protection and Promotion of Investments". The Protocol added the following elements to the existing commitments of the member countries: (a) endeavour to simplify and streamline investments procedures and approval process to facilitate investment flows; (b) ensure the provision of up-to-date information on all laws and regulations pertaining to direct investment and take appropriate measures to ensure that such information be made as transparent, timely and publicly accessible as possible; and (c) include the ASEAN Dispute Settlement Mechanism as an alternative modality for the settlement of investment disputes. Cambodia, Lao People's Democratic Republic, Myanmar and Viet Nam acceded to the ASEAN Agreement for the Promotion and Protection of Investment as they became members of ASEAN.

The Governments of Brunei Darussalam, the Republic of Indonesia, Malaysia, the Republic of the Philippines, the Republic of Singapore, the Kingdom of Thailand, and the Socialist Republic of Vietnam;

REFERRING to Article XII of the Agreement among the Governments of Brunei Darussalam, the Republic of Indonesia, Malaysia, the Republic of the Philippines, the Republic of Singapore, and the Kingdom of Thailand for the Promotion and Protection of Investments signed on 15 December 1987 in Manila, hereinafter refereed to as "the Agreement";

RECALLING the Framework Agreement on Enhancing ASEAN Economic Cooperation signed in Singapore on 28 January 1992 which acknowledged the importance of sustaining economic growth and development in all Member States through joint efforts in liberalising trade and promoting intra-ASEAN trade and investment flows;

MINDFUL of the agreement to establish an ASEAN Free Trade Area (AFTA) with the aim to encourage greater investment flows into the region;

* *Source*: Association of Southeast Asian Nations (1996). "Protocol to Amend the Agreement among the Governments of Brunei Darussalam, the Republic of Indonesia, Malaysia, the Republic of the Philippines, the Republic of Singapore and the Kingdom of Thailand for the Promotion and Protection of Investments", *Handbook of Investment Agreements in ASEAN* (Jakarta: ASEAN Secretariat), pp 25-30; available also on the Internet (http://www.asean.or.id/economic/agrfin96.htm). [Note added by the editor.]

BEARING IN MIND the decision of the Fifth ASEAN Summit held on 15 December 1995 and the subsequent work within ASEAN to establish an ASEAN Investment Area (AIA) in order to enhance the area's attractiveness and competitiveness for promoting direct investment, as well as to implement, among other investment measures, an ASEAN Plan of Action on Cooperation and Promotion of Foreign Direct Investment and Intra-ASEAN Investment;

NOTING that the Government of the Socialist Republic of Vietnam had become a member of ASEAN on 28 July 1995 and had agreed to subscribe or accede, as the case may be, to all Declarations, Treaties and Agreements in ASEAN, and that the Socialist Republic of Vietnam had, on 16 August 1996, acceded to the Agreement by depositing its instrument of accession with the Secretary-General of ASEAN and thereby became a party to the Agreement;

RECOGNISING the need to update the Agreement to reflect the rapid development in the global investment environment and the commitment which Member Countries had offered under the various international and regional investment agreements; and

ACKNOWLEDGING the importance of investment as a source of finance for sustaining the pace of economic, industrial and technological development of the region;

HAVE AGREED ON FOLLOWS:

ARTICLE 1

The title of the Agreement shall be amended to read as "The ASEAN Agreement for the Promotion and Protection of Investments."

ARTICLE 2

The following shall be inserted after Article III as a new Article III-A to the Agreement:

"Simplification of Investment Procedures and Approval Process

Each Contracting Party shall endeavour to simplify and streamline its investment procedures and approval process to facilitate investment flows."

ARTICLE 3

The following shall be inserted after the new Article III-A as a new Article III-B to the Agreement:

"Transparency and Predictability

Each Contracting Party shall ensure the provision of up-to-date information on all laws and regulations pertaining to foreign investment in its territory and shall take appropriate measures to ensure that such information be made as transparent, timely and publicly accessible as possible."

ARTICLE 4

Article IX of the Agreement shall be substituted with the following:

"Dispute Between the Contracting Parties

The provisions of the ASEAN Dispute Settlement Mechanism shall apply to the settlement of disputes under the agreement."

ARTICLE 5

Article X of the Agreement shall be renamed as "Dispute Between Contracting Parties and Investors of Other Contracting Parties."

ARTICLE 6

The following shall be inserted after Article XI as a new Article XI-A to the Agreement:

"Accession of New Members

New Members of ASEAN shall accede to the Agreement by depositing their instruments of accession with the Secretary-General of ASEAN. For new Members of ASEAN who accede to the Agreement, it shall enter into force on the date of the deposit of the instrument of accession."

ARTICLE 7

This Protocol shall enter into force on the date of deposit of the instruments of ratification or acceptance by all signatory governments with the Secretary-General of ASEAN.
This Protocol shall be deposited with the Secretary-General of ASEAN, who shall promptly furnish a certified copy thereof to each Member Country.

IN WITNESS THEREOF, the undersigned, being duly authorised thereto by their respective Governments, have signed the Protocol to Amend the Agreement among the Governments of Brunei Darussalam, the Republic of Indonesia, Malaysia, the Republic of the Philippines, the Republic of Singapore, and the Kingdom of Thailand for the Promotion and Protection of Investments.

DONE at Jakarta, this 12th day of September 1996 in a single copy in the English Language.

*   *   *

PROTOCOL FOR THE PROTECTION OF COMPETITION IN MERCOSUR[*]

(COMMON MARKET OF THE SOUTHERN CONE)

The Protocol for the Protection of Competition in MERCOSUR was adopted by Decision 17/96 on 17 December 1996 by the countries members of the Common Market of the Southern Cone (MERCOSUR), created by the Agreement of Asunción on 16 March 1991. The member countries of MERCOSUR are Argentina, Brazil, Paraguay and Uruguay. The Protocol contains the main provisions related to competition policy in MERCOSUR. As of 31 October 1999 this Protocol was pending congressional approval by each member to become enforceable as national law.

The Republic of Argentina, The Federal Republic of Brazil, the Republic of Paraguay, the Eastern Republic of Uruguay, henceforth designated as the States Parties

CONSIDERING

that the free movement of goods and services between the States Parties renders essential that adequate conditions of competition be assured in order to contribute to the strengthening of the Custom Union;

that States Parties must assure, in the exercise of their economic rights within their territories, equal conditions of free competition;

that balanced and harmonious growth of intra-zonal trade relations, as well as increased competitiveness among the States Parties will depend in large part upon the consolidation of a competitive environment in the integrated framework of the MERCOSUR;

that it is urgent that directives be established in order to provide guidance to States Parties and the enterprises situated within them in the defense of competition in the MERCOSUR, as an instrument capable of assuring free market access and a balanced distribution of the benefits of the process of economic integration.

RESOLVE:

---

[*] *Source:* Organization of American States (1996). "Protocol for the Protection of Competition in MERCOSUR"; available on the Internet (http://www.sice.oas.org/cp_comp/english/cpa/cpa3_e.stm#mercosur). [Note added by the editor.]

CHAPTER I

THE PURPOSE AND THE SCOPE OF APPLICATION

ARTICLE 1

The purpose of the present Protocol is the defense of competition in the framework of the MERCOSUR.

ARTICLE 2

The rules of this Protocol apply to actions taken by natural and legal persons under public and private law, and other entities whose purpose is to influence or to bring influence to bear upon competition in the framework of the MERCOSUR and consequently to influence trade between the States Parties;

Single Paragraph - Among the legal entities referred to in the preceding paragraph are included those enterprises which exercise a State monopoly, insofar as the rules of this Protocol do not prevent the regular exercise of their legal attributions.

ARTICLE 3

The regulation of the acts carried out within their respective territory by natural persons or legal entities or by any other entity domiciled therein, and whose influence on competition is limited to same, falls within the exclusive competence of each State.

CHAPTER II

REGARDING THE RESTRICTIVE CONDUCT AND PRACTICES OF COMPETITION

ARTICLE 4

Constitute an infringement of the rules of the present Protocol, regardless of guilt, individual or concerted acts, of whatever kind, the purpose or final effect of which is to restrict, limit, falsify or distort competition or access to the market or which constitute an abuse of a dominant position in the relevant goods or services market in the framework of the MERCOSUR, and which affect trade between the States Parties.

ARTICLE 5

Mere market conquest resulting from the natural process of the most efficient economic agent among competitors does not constitute any violation of competition.

ARTICLE 6

The following forms of conduct, inter alia, insofar as they embody the hypotheses advanced in article 4, constitute practices which limit competition;

I.   to fix, impose or practice, directly or indirectly, in collaboration with competitors or individually, in any form, the prices and conditions of the purchase or sale of goods, the providing of services or production;

II.   to procure or to contribute to the adoption of uniform business practices or concerted action by competitors;

III.   to regulate goods or service markets, entering into agreements to limit or control research and technological development, the production of goods or the supply of services, or to hinder investments intended for the production of goods or services or their distribution.

IV.   to divide up the markets of finished or semifinished goods or services, or the supply source of raw materials and intermediate products.

V.   to limit or prevent access of new enterprises to the market;

VI.   to agree on prices or advantages which may affect competition in public bids;

VII.   to adopt, with regard to third parties, unequal conditions for equivalent services, thus placing them at a competitive disadvantage;

VIII.   to subordinate the sale of one good to the purchase of another good or to the use of a service, or to subordinate the supply of a service to the use of another or to the purchase of a good;

IX.   to prevent the access of competitors to raw materials, investment goods or technologies, as well as to distribution channels;

X.   to require or to grant exclusivity with respect to the dissemination of publicity in the communication media;

XI.   to subordinate buying or selling to the condition of not using or acquiring, selling or supplying goods or services which are produced, processed, distributed or marketed by a third party;

XII.   to sell merchandise, for reasons unfounded on business practices, at prices below the cost price;

XIII.   to reject without good reason the sale of goods or the supply of services;

XIV.   to interrupt or to reduce production on a large scale, without any justifiable cause;

XV.   to destroy, render useless or accumulate raw materials, intermediate or finished goods, as well as to destroy, render useless or obstruct the functioning of equipment designed to produce, transport or distribute them.

XVI.   to abandon, cause to be abandoned or destroy crops and plantations without just cause.

XVII.   to manipulate the market in order to impose prices.

CHAPTER III

ON THE CONTROL OF ACTS AND CONTRACTS

ARTICLE 7

The States Parties shall adopt, for the purpose of their incorporation in the regulations of the MERCOSUR, within the period of two years, common rules for the control of acts and contracts, of any kind, which may limit or in any way cause prejudice to free trade, or result in the domination of the relevant regional market of goods and services, including which result in economic concentration, with a view to preventing their possible anti-competitive effects in the framework of the MERCOSUR.

CHAPTER IV

ON THE ENFORCEMENT BODIES

ARTICLE 8

Application of the present Protocol is applied by the Trade Commission of the MERCOSUR, in accordance with the terms of article 19 of the Protocol of Ouro Preto, and by the Committee for the Defense of Competition.

Single Paragraph - The Committee for the Defense of Competition, an organ of intergovernmental nature, shall be constituted by the national organs for the application of the present Protocol in each State Party.

ARTICLE 9

The Committee for the Defense of Competition shall submit the rules of procedure of the present Protocol to the Trade Commission for approval;

CHAPTER V

ON THE ENFORCEMENT PROCEDURE

ARTICLE 10

The national organs of application shall initiate the procedure provided through the present Protocol ex officio or through reasoned presentation by the legitimately concerned party, which should appear before the Committee for the Defense of Competition and present a preliminary technical evaluation;

ARTICLE 11

The Committee for the Defense of Competition, following a preliminary technical analysis, shall initiate an inquiry or, ad referendum of the Trade Commission of MERCOSUR, shelve the case.

ARTICLE 12

The Committee for the Defense of Competition shall regularly submit reports on the state of negotiations on the cases under consideration to the Trade Commission of the MERCOSUR.

ARTICLE 13

In case of emergency or threat of irreparable damage to competition, the Committee for the Defense of Competition of the MERCOSUR shall determine, ad referendum of the Trade Commission of the MERCOSUR, the application of preventive measures, including the immediate cessation of the practice subject to inquiry, and the reestablishment of the prior situation or other measures which it deems necessary.

1.   In case of non observance of the preventive measure, the Committee for the Defense of Competition may define, ad referendum of the Trade Commission of the MERCOSUR, application of a fine of the infringing party.

2.   Application of the preventive measure or of the fine shall be effected by the national organ of application of the State in the territory of which the defendant is domiciled.

ARTICLE 14

The Committee for the Defense of Competition shall establish, in each case investigated, guidelines for the definition of, among other aspects, the relevant market structure, the evidence regarding conduct and analytical criteria of the economic effects of the investigated practice.

ARTICLE 15

The national organ of application of the State in the territory of which the defendant is domiciled shall carry out the investigation of the restrictive practice of competition, bearing in mind the guidelines set forth in article 14.

1.   The national enforcement bodies undertaking the investigation shall disseminate regular reports on its activities.

2.   The exercise of the right of defense shall be guaranteed to the defendant.

ARTICLE 16

The national organs of application of the other States Parties are responsible for assistance to the national enforcement body responsible for the investigation through contribution of information, documentation and other means considered essential to the correct execution of the investigation procedures.

ARTICLE 17

In case of differences regarding the application of procedures set forth in this Protocol, the Committee for the Defense of Competition may request MERCOSUR Trade Commission for an opinion on the matter.

ARTICLE 18

Once the process of investigation has en concluded the national body responsible for the investigation shall present a conclusive ruling on the matter to the Committee for the Defense of Competition.

ARTICLE 19

The Committee for the Defense of Competition, taking into account the ruling of the national enforcement bodies, ad referendum of the Trade Commission of the MERCOSUR, shall decide on the infringing practices and shall establish the sanctions to be imposed or any other appropriate measures.

Single Paragraph -If the Committee for the Defense of Competition should not arrive at a consensus, it shall bring its conclusions before the Trade Commission of the MERCOSUR, noting existing differences.

ARTICLE 20

The Trade Commission of the MERCOSUR, taking into account the ruling or the conclusions of the Committee for the Defense of Competition, shall make a ruling through adoption of a Directive, setting forth the sanctions to be applied to the infringing party or other appropriate measures.

1.   The sanctions shall be applied by the national enforcement bodies of the State Party whose territory the infringing party is domiciled.

2.   If a consensus were not reached, MERCOSUR Trade Commission shall bring the different proposed solutions before the Common Market Group.

ARTICLE 21

The Common Market Group shall make a ruling upon the matter through adoption of a resolution.

Single Paragraph -If the Common Market Group should not arrive at a consensus, the interested State Party could resort directly to the procedure set forth in chapter IV of the Brasilia Protocol on the Settlement of Disputes.

CHAPTER VI

UNDERTAKING OF CESSATION

ARTICLE 22

At any stage of the procedure, the Committee for the Defense of Competition may ratify, ad referendum of MERCOSUR Trade Commission, an undertaking of cessation of the practice under investigation, which shall not imply a confession as to the facts nor recognition of the illicit nature of the conduct under analysis.

ARTICLE 23

The Undertaking of Cessation shall necessarily include the following paragraphs:

a)   the obligations of the defendant, in the sense of the cessation of the practice being investigated within the established period.

b)   the value of the daily fine to be imposed in case of noncompliance with the Undertaking of Cessation.

c)   the obligation of the defendant to submit regular reports on his activities in the market, keeping the national enforcement bodies informed of eventual changes in the company's structure, control, activities and location.

ARTICLE 24

The procedure shall be suspended when compliance with the Undertaking of Cessation has been reached and will be shelved upon conclusion of the established period, if all the conditions listed in the Undertaking are complied with.

ARTICLE 25

The MERCOSUR Committee for the Defense of Competition may ratify modifications of the Undertaking of Cessation if the latter should prove to be an excessive burden for the defendant, and if the new situation should not constitute any infringement of competition.

ARTICLE 26

The Undertaking of Cessation, changes in the Undertaking and the sanction referred to in the present Chapter shall be executed by the national enforcement bodies of the State Party in the territory of which the defendant is domiciled.

CHAPTER VII

ON SANCTIONS

ARTICLE 27

The Committee for the Defense of Competition, ad referendum of the MERCOSUR Trade Commission, shall determine the definitive cessation of the infringing practice within a period of time to be specified.

1.   In case of noncompliance with the order of cessation, the daily fine to be determined by the Committee for the Defense of Competition, ad referendum of the MERCOSUR Trade Commission.

2.   The order of cessation as well as imposition of the fine shall be executed by the national organ of application of the State Party in the territory of which the infringing party is domiciled.

ARTICLE 28

In case of violation of the rules of procedure of the present Protocol the following sanctions shall be applied, either cumulatively or alternatively:

I.   a fine, based on the earnings obtained from commission of the infringing practice, gross revenues or the assets involved which would be paid to the national enforcement bodies of the State Party in the territory of which the infringing party is domiciled.

II.   prohibition to participate in the systems of public procurement in any of the States Parties, for a period of time to be determined.

III.   prohibition to enter into contracts with public financial institutions of any of the States Parties, for a period of time to be determined.

    1.   The Committee for the Defense of Competition, ad referendum of the Trade Commission of the MERCOSUR, may recommend to the competent authorities of the States Parties that no incentives of any kind or terms of payment of tax obligations be granted to the infringing party.

    2.   The penalties set forth in this article shall be executed by the national enforcement bodies of the State Party in the territory of which the infringing party is domiciled.

ARTICLE 29

As regards the levels of the sanctions established in the present Protocol, the seriousness of the fact of the case and the significance of the damage caused to competition in the framework of the MERCOSUR should be considered.

CHAPTER X

ON COOPERATION

ARTICLE 30

In order to ensure application of the present Protocol, the States Parties shall, through the respective national enforcement bodies, adopt mechanisms of cooperation and of technical consultation, so as:

a)   to systematize and strengthen cooperation between the national organs and authorities responsible for the perfecting of the national systems and of the joint defense instruments of competition, through a program of the exchange, as well as of the joint investigation of the practices harmful to competition, through a program of exchange of information and experience, of the training of technicians and the accumulation of case law relative to the defense of competition, as well as of the joint investigation of practices harmful to competition in the MERCOSUR.

b)   to identify and mobilize, by means of agreements of technical cooperation in the area of the defense of competition with other States or regional groups, the necessary resources for the implementation of programs of cooperation referred to in the preceding paragraph.

CHAPTER IX

ON THE SETTLEMENT OF DISPUTES

ARTICLE 31

To the settlement of differences regarding the application, interpretation or nonobservance of the provisions contained in the present Protocol, the provisions of the Protocol of Brasilia and of the General Procedure for Complaints before the Trade Commission of the MERCOSUR set forth in the Annex to the Protocol of Ouro Preto shall applied.

CHAPTER X

FINAL AND TRANSITORIAL PROVISIONS

ARTICLE 32

The States Parties undertake, within a two year period following entry into force of the present Protocol, and for purposes of their incorporation in this instrument, to draft joint standards and mechanisms which shall govern State aid which is susceptible to limit, restrict, falsify or distort competition and to affect trade between the States Parties.

To this end, progress made on the subject of public policies which distort competitiveness and the relevant standards of the WTO shall be taken into consideration.

ARTICLE 33

The present Protocol, as an integral part of the Treaty of Asuncion, shall enter into force thirty days after the second instrument of ratification has been deposited, with respect to the first two States Parties ratifying it and, in the case of the other signatories, on the thirtieth day after the respective instrument of ratification has been deposited.

ARTICLE 34

No provision of the present Protocol shall apply to the restrictive practices of competition the study of which has been initiated by the competent authority of a State Party before the entry into force provided in Article 33.

ARTICLE 35

The present Protocol may be revised of common accord, on the proposal of one of the States Parties.

ARTICLE 36

Adherence on the part of a State to the Treaty of Asuncion shall imply, ipso iure, adherence to the present Protocol.

ARTICLE 37

The Government of the Republic of Paraguay shall be the depository of the present Protocol and of the instruments of ratification, and shall send duly authenticated copies of same to the Governments of the other States Parties.

Similarly, the Government of the Republic of Paraguay shall notify the Government of the other States Parties of the date of entry into force of the present Protocol, as well as of the date of deposit of the instruments of ratification.

Done in the city of Fortaleza, on the seventeenth day of the month of December of 1996, in one original in the Spanish and Portuguese languages, both these texts being equally authentic.

MERCOSUR/CMC/DEC No. 2/97

ANNEX TO THE PROTOCOL FOR THE PROTECTION OF COMPETITION IN MERCOSUR

HAVING SEEN: The Asuncion Treaty, the Ouro Preto Protocol, Decisions No. 21/94 and 18/96 of the Common Market Council, Resolution No. 129/94 of the Common Market Group, and the Minutes of the Twenty-first Meeting of the MERCOSUR Trade Committee,

CONSIDERING:

The importance of establishing criteria for quantifying the amount of fines provided for in the Protocol for the Protection of Competition in MERCOSUR, approved by Decision CMC No. 18/96,

The Common Market Council Decides:

Art. 1. - To approve the following Annex to the Protocol for the Protection of Competition in MERCOSUR:

"ANNEX TO THE PROTOCOL FOR THE PROTECTION OF COMPETITION IN MERCOSUR":

Art. 1. The fines provided for in the present Protocol shall be equivalent to up to 150% of the profits obtained through the illegal practice; up to 100% of the value of the assets involved; or up to 30% of the value of the company's gross billing for its previous financial year, net of tax. Such fines may not be less than the advantage obtained, if quantifiable.

Art. 2. In the specific cases referred to in Articles 13.1, 23.b, and 27.1 of the present Protocol, a daily fine of up to 1% of the company's gross billing for the previous financial period.

XII CMC - ASUNCIÓN, 18/VI/97

*   *   *

PROTOCOL AMENDING THE TREATY ESTABLISHING THE CARIBBEAN COMMUNITY (PROTOCOL II : ESTABLISHMENT, SERVICES, CAPITAL)*
[excerpts]

(CARIBBEAN COMMUNITY)

The Protocol Amending the Treaty Establishing the Caribbean Community (Protocol II: Establishment, Services, and Capital) was opened for signature on 1 July 1997 and entered into provisional application on 4 July 1998, pending ratification by all parties. The Protocol was signed by the member States of the Caribbean Community (CARICOM), namely, Antigua and Barbuda, Barbados, Belize, Dominica, Grenada, Guyana, Jamaica, Monserrat, Saint Kitts and Nevis, Saint Lucia, Saint Vincent and the Grenadines, Trinidad and Tobago, and by Suriname. The Bahamas, a member of the Caribbean Community, is not a party to this protocol.

The States Parties to the Treaty Establishing the Caribbean Community (hereinafter referred to as " the Member States"):

Recalling the Declaration of Grand Anse and other decisions of the Conference of Heads of Government of the Caribbean Community expressing their commitment to the deepening of the regional economic integration process;

Conscious of the need to promote in the Caribbean Community the highest level of efficiency in the production of goods and services especially with a view to maximising foreign exchange earnngs on the basis of international competitiveness, attaining food security, achieving structural diversification and improving the standard of living of their peoples;

Recognising that optimal production by economic enterprises in the Community requires the structured integration of production in the Region, and particularly the unrestricted movement of capital, labour and technology;

Determined to establish conditions which would facilitate access by their nationals to the collective resources of the Region on a non-discriminatory basis;

Desirous of achieving sustained expansion and continuing integration of economic activities, the benefits of which shall be equitably shared taking into account the need to provide special opportunities for disadvantaged countries;

Conscious of the special needs and circumstances of the Less Developed Countries;

Have Agreed as follows:

---

* *Source*: The Caribbean Community secretariat (1997). "Protocol Amending the Treaty Establishing the Caribbean Community (Protocol II: Establishment, Services, Capital)"; available on the Internet (http://www.caricom.org/expframes.htm). [Note added by the editor.]

ARTICLE II . Amendment

The provisions of this Protocol shall replace Articles 28, 35, 36, 37, 38 and 43 of the Caribbean Common Market Annex to the Treaty and take effect as hereinafter provided.

ARTICLE III

Replace the title to Chapter V of the Caribbean Common Market Annex with the following:

CHAPTER V

Rights of Establishment, Provision of Services and Movement of Capital

ARTICLE IV

Replace Article 35 of the Caribbean Common Market Annex with the following:

ARTICLE 35

Scope of Application

1.   Save as otherwise provided in this Article and Article 35a, the provisions of this Chapter shall apply to the right of establishment, the right to provide services and the right to move capital in the Community.

2.   Activities in a Member State involving the exercise of governmental authority shall, in so far as that Member State is concerned, be excluded from the operation of this Chapter.

3.   For the purposes of this Chapter, "activities involving the exercise of governmental authority" means activities conducted neither on a commercial basis nor in competition with one or more economic enterprises, and includes:

    (a)   activities conducted by a central bank or monetary authority or any other public entity, in pursuit of monetary or exchange rate policies;

    (b)   activities forming part of a statutory system of social security or public retirement plans;

    (c)   activities forming part of a system of national security or for the establishment or maintenance of public order; and

    (d)   other activities conducted by a public entity for the account of or with the guarantee or using financial resources of the government.

ARTICLE 35a

Treatment of Monopolies

1.   Member States may determine that the public interest requires the exclusion or restriction of the right of establishment in any industry or in a particular sector of an industry.

2.   Where such a determination has been made:

(a)   if the determination results in the continuation or establishment of a government monopoly, the Member State shall adopt appropriate measures to ensure that the monopoly does not discriminate between nationals of Member States, save as otherwise provided in this Treaty, and is subject to the agreed rules of competition established for Community economic enterprises;

(b)   if the determination results in the establishment of a private sector monopoly, the Member State shall, subject to the provisions of this Treaty, adopt appropriate measures to ensure that national treatment is accorded to nationals of other Member States in terms of participating in its operations.

ARTICLE 35b

Prohibition of New Restrictions on the Right of Establishment

1.   Upon the entry into force of this Protocol, Member States shall not introduce in their territories any new restrictions relating to the right of establishment of nationals of other Member States save as otherwise provided in this Treaty.

2.   Upon the entry into force of this Protocol, Member States shall notify the Council for Trade and Economic Development of existing restrictions on the right of establishment in respect of nationals of other Member States.

3.   (1)   The right of establishment within the meaning of this Chapter shall include the right to:

(a)   engage in any non-wage-earning activities of a commercial, industrial, professional or artisanal nature;

(b)   create and manage economic enterprises referred to in paragraph 5 (c) of this Article.

4.   For the purposes of this Chapter "non-wage earning activities" means activities undertaken by self-employed persons.

5.   The Community Council may, with the approval of the Conference and upon the recommendation of the Council for Trade and Economic Development or the Council for Finance and Planning, as the case may be, enlarge the body of rights provided in paragraph 3 of this Article. The competent Organ shall establish basic criteria for Member States in order to safeguard against manipulation or abuse of such rights so as to gain an unfair advantage against

other Member States, for example, in the areas of nationality criteria and in the operation of companies.

6.   For the purposes of this Chapter:

(a)   a person shall be regarded as a national of a Member State if such person:

(i)   is a citizen of that State;

(ii)   has a connection with that State of a kind which entitles him to be regarded as belonging to or, if it be so expressed, as being a native or resident of the State for the purposes of the laws thereof relating to immigration; or

(iii)   is a company or other legal entity constituted in the Member State in conformity with the laws thereof and which that State regards as belonging to it, provided that such company or other legal entity has been formed for gainful purposes and has its registered office and central administration, and carries on substantial activity, within the Community and which is substantially owned and effectively controlled by persons mentioned in sub-paragraphs (i) and (ii) of this paragraph.

7.   "economic enterprises" includes any type of organisation for the production of or trade in goods or the provision of services (other than a non-profit organisation) owned or controlled by any person or entity mentioned in sub-paragraph (a) of this paragraph.

8.   a company or other legal entity is:

(i)   substantially owned if more than 50 per cent of the equity interest therein is beneficially owned by nationals mentioned in sub-paragraph (a) (i) or (ii) of this paragraph;

(ii)   effectively controlled if nationals mentioned in sub-paragraph (a) of this paragraph have the power to name a majority of its directors or otherwise legally to direct its actions.

ARTICLE 35c

Removal of Restrictions on the Right of Establishment

1.   Subject to the provisions of Article 38a and Article 38b, Member States shall remove restrictions on the right of establishment of nationals of a Member State in the territory of another Member State.

2.   The removal of restrictions on the right of establishment mentioned in paragraph 1 of this Article shall also apply to restrictions on the setting up of agencies, branches or subsidiaries by nationals of a Member State in the territory of another Member State.

3.   Subject to the approval of the Conference, the Council for Trade and Economic Development, in consultation with the Council on Human and Social Development and the

Council for Finance and Planning, shall, within one year from the entry into force of this Protocol, establish a programme providing for the removal of restrictions on the right of establishment of nationals of a Member State in the territory of another Member State. The programme shall, inter alia:

(a)   identify the activities in respect of which the right of establishment shall not apply;

(b)   establish the conditions under which the right of establishment is to be achieved; and

(c) set out the conditions, stages and time-frames for the removal of restrictions on the right of establishment.

(c)   The Community Council may authorise a Member State whose nationals have been aggrieved by the violation of obligations set out in this Article, Article 35b, Article 36 and Article 36a to take such measures as may be provided for in this Treaty.

ARTICLE 35d

Management of Removal of Restrictions on the Right of Establishment

In performing its tasks set out in Article 35c, the Council for Trade and Economic Development shall, inter alia:

(a)   accord priority to the removal of restrictions on activities in respect of which the right of establishment encourages the development of:

(i)   the production or trade in goods;

(ii)   the provision of services;

which generate foreign exchange earnings;

(b)   require Member States to remove administrative practices and procedures, the maintenance of which impede the exercise of the right of establishment;

(c)   require Member States to remove all restrictions on the movement of managerial, technical and supervisory staff of economic enterprises and on establishing agencies, branches and subsidiaries of companies and other entities established in the Community;

(d)   establish measures to ensure the removal of restrictions on the right of establishment in respect of activities accorded priority treatment pursuant to paragraph (a) of this Article as they relate to:

(i)   the establishment, in the territories of Member States, of agencies, branches or subsidiaries belonging to an economic enterprise; and

        (ii)   conditions governing the entry of managerial, technical or supervisory personnel employed in such agencies, branches and subsidiaries, including the spouses and immediate dependent family members of such personnel;

(e)   take appropriate measures to ensure close collaboration among competent national authorities in order to improve their knowledge of the particular situation regarding the relevant activities within the Community;

(f)   require Member States to ensure that nationals of one Member State may have access to land, buildings and other property situated in the territory of another Member State, other than for speculative purposes or for a purpose potentially destabilising to the economy, on a non-discriminatory basis, bearing in mind the importance of agriculture for many national economies;

(g)   ensure concordance in Member States regarding the protection afforded the interests of partners, members and other persons with financial interests in companies and other entities.

ARTICLE V

Replace Article 36 of the Caribbean Common Market Annex with the following:

ARTICLE 36

Prohibition of New Restrictions on the Provision of Services

1.   Upon the entry into force of this Protocol, Member States shall not introduce any new restrictions on the provision of services in the Community by nationals of other Member States except as otherwise provided in this Treaty.

2.   Without prejudice to the provisions relating to the right of establishment, persons providing services may, in order to provide such services, temporarily engage in approved activities in the Member State where the services are to be provided under the same conditions enjoyed by nationals of that Member State.

3.   Upon the entry into force of this Protocol, Member States shall notify the Council for Trade and Economic Development of existing restrictions on the provision of services in respect of nationals of other Member States.

4.   For the purposes of this Chapter, "services" means services provided against remuneration other than wages in any approved sector and "the provision of services" means the supply of services:

(a)   from the territory of one Member State into the territory of another Member State;

(b)   in the territory of one Member State to the service consumer of another Member State;

(c)   by a service supplier of one Member State through commercial presence in the territory of another Member State; and

(d)   by a service supplier of one Member State through the presence of natural persons of a Member State in the territory of another Member State.

ARTICLE 36a

Removal of Restrictions on the Provision of Services

1.   Subject to the provisions of this Treaty, Member States shall remove discriminatory restrictions on the provision of services within the Community in respect of Community nationals.

2.   Subject to the approval of the Conference, the Council for Trade and Economic Development, in consultation with other competent Organs, shall, within one year from the entry into force of this Protocol, establish a programme for the removal of restrictions on the provision of such services in the Community by Community nationals.

3.   In establishing the programme mentioned in paragraph 2 of this Article, the Council for Trade and Economic Development shall:

(a)   accord priority to services which directly affect production costs or facilitate the trade in goods and services which generate foreign exchange earnings;

(b)   require Member States to remove administrative practices and procedures, the maintenance of which impede the exercise of the right to provide services;

(c)   establish measures to ensure the removal of restrictions on the right to provide services in respect of activities accorded priority treatment in accordance with sub-paragraph (a) of this paragraph, both in terms of conditions for the provision of services in the territories of Member States as well as the conditions governing the entry of personnel, including their spouses and immediate dependent family members, for the provision of services;

(d)   take appropriate measures to ensure close collaboration among competent national authorities in order to improve their knowledge of the conditions regarding relevant activities within the Community, and

(e)   require Member States to ensure that nationals of one Member State have on a non-discriminatory basis, access to land, buildings and other property situated in the territory of another Member State for purposes directly related to the provision of services, bearing in mind the importance of agriculture for many national economies.

ARTICLE 36b

Banking, Insurance and Other Financial Services

1.   Subject to the provisions of this Chapter, Member States shall remove discriminatory restrictions in respect of Community nationals, on banking, insurance and other financial services.

2.   Subject to the approval of the Conference, the Council for Finance and Planning, in consultation with other competent Organs of the Community, may exclude certain financial services from the operation of the provisions of this Article.

ARTICLE VI

Replace Articles 37 and 43 of the Caribbean Common Market Annex with the following:

ARTICLE 37

Prohibition of New Restrictions on Movement of Capital and Current Transactions

Upon the entry into force of this Protocol, Member States shall not introduce any new restrictions on the movement of capital and payments connected with such movement and on current payments and transfers, nor render more restrictive existing regulations except as provided in Article 37c (bis) and Article 38a.

ARTICLE 37a

Removal of Restrictions on Movement of Capital and Current Transactions

1.   After the entry into force of this Protocol, Member States shall, in order to ensure the proper functioning of the Single Market and Economy, remove among themselves:

   (a)   restrictions on the movement of capital payments;

   (b)   restrictions on all current payments including payments for goods and services and other current transfers.

2.   The Council for Finance and Planning shall, subject to the approval of the Conference, establish in collaboration with the Committee of Central Bank Governors a programme for the removal of the restrictions mentioned in paragraph 1 of this Article.

3.   For the purpose of this Article, capital and related payments and transfers include:

   (a)   equity and portfolio investments;

   (b)   short-term bank and credit transactions;

   (c)   payment of interest on loans and amortization;

   (d)   dividends and other income on investments after taxes;

   (e)   repatriation of proceeds from the sale of assets; and

   (f)   other transfers and payments relating to investment flows.

ARTICLE 37b

Authorisation to Facilitate Movement of Capital

1.   Upon entry into force of this Protocol, Member States shall, where necessary and subject to paragraph 2 of this Article, grant the authorisations required for the movement of capital mentioned in Article 37a on a non-discriminatory basis.

2.   A loan intended for State purposes may require prior notification to the State in which it is being issued or placed.

ARTICLE VII

Replace Article 28 of the Caribbean Common Market Annex with the following:

ARTICLE 37c (bis)

Restrictions to Safeguard Balance-of-Payments

1.   In the event of serious balance-of-payments and external financial difficulties or threat thereof, a Member State may, consistent with its international obligations and subject to paragraph 5 of this Article, adopt or maintain restrictions to address such difficulties.

2.   The restrictions which may be adoted or maintained pursuant to paragraph 1 of this Article may include quantitative restrictions on imports, restrictions on the right of establishment, restrictions on the right to provide services, restrictions on the right to move capital or on payments and transfers for transactions connected therewith. However, such restrictions:

(a)   shall, subject to the provisions of this Treaty, not discriminate among Member States or against Member States in favour of third States;

(b)   shall at all times seek to minimise damage to the commercial, economic or financial interests of any other Member State;

(c)   shall not exceed those necessary to deal with the circumstances described in paragraph 1 of this Article; and

(d)   shall be temporary but in any event not longer than a period of eighteen (18) months and be phased out progressively as the situation described in paragraph 1 improves.

3.   In determining the incidence of such restrictions, the Member State concerned may accord priority to activities which are essential to its economic stability. Such restrictions shall not be adopted or maintained for the purpose of protecting a particular sector in contravention of the relevant provisions of this Treaty, due regard being paid in either case to any special factors which may be affecting the reserves of such Member State or its need for reserves.

4.   Restrictions adopted or maintained pursuant to paragraph 1 of this Article, or any changes therein, shall be notified within three (3) working days to the Council for Finance and

Planning and to the Council for Trade and Economic Development, and, in any event, the Member State concerned shall immediately consult with the competent Organ if and when requested.

5.   The Council for Finance and Planning shall establish procedures for periodic consultations including, where possible and desirable, prior consultations with the objective of making recommendations to the Member State concerned for the removal of the restrictions.

6.   The consultations referred to in paragraph 5 of this Article shall:

(a)   be designed to assist the Member State concerned to overcome its balance-of-payments and external financial difficulties;

(b)   assess the balance-of-payments situation of the Member State concerned and the restrictions adopted or maintained under this Article, taking into account, inter alia:

(i)   the nature and extent of the balance-of-payments and the external financial difficulties;

(ii)   the external economic and trading environment of the Member State applying the restrictions; and

(iii)   alternative corrective measures which may be available.

7.   The consultations shall address the compliance of any restrictions with paragraph 2 of this Article and, in particular, the progressive phase-out of restrictions in accordance with paragraph 2(d).

8.   In such consultations, all findings of statistical and other facts presented by the Committee of Central Bank Governors relating to foreign exchange, monetary reserves and balance-of-payments, shall be accepted and conclusions shall be based on the assessment by the Committee of the balance-of-payments and the external financial situation of the Member State concerned.

ARTICLE VIII

ARTICLE 38

Non-Discrimination

1.   Within the scope of application of this Treaty and without prejudice to any special provisions contained therein, any discrimination on grounds of nationality only shall be prohibited.

2.   The Community Council shall, after consultation with the competent Organs, establish rules to prohibit any such discrimination.

ARTICLE 38 (bis)

Measures to Facilitate Establishment, Provision of Services and Movement of Capital

1.   In order to facilitate the exercise of the rights provided for in this Chapter, the Council for Trade and Economic Development and the Council for Finance and Planning shall, subject to the approval of the Conference, adopt appropriate measures for:

(a)   the establishment of market intelligence and information systems in the Community;

(b)   harmonised legal and administrative requirements for the operation of partnerships, companies, or other entities;

(c)   abolition of exchange controls in the Community, and free convertibility of the currencies of Member States;

(d)   the establishment of an integrated capital market in the Community;

(e)   convergence of macro-economic performance and policies through the co-ordination or harmonisation of monetary and fiscal policies, including, in particular, policies relating to interest rates, exchange rates, tax structures and national budgetary deficits;

(f)   the establishment of economical and efficient land, sea and air transport services throughout the Community, and

(g)   the establishment of efficient communication services.

2.   The Council for Finance and Planning and the Council for Trade and Economic Development shall establish a comprehensive set of rules in respect of the areas listed in paragraph 1 of this Article for approval by the Conference.

ARTICLE 38a

Restrictions to Resolve Difficulties or Hardships Arising from the Exercise of Rights

1.   Where the exercise of rights granted under this Chapter creates serious difficulties in any sector of the economy of a Member State or occasions economic hardships in a region of the Community, a Member State adversely affected thereby may, subject to the provisions of this Article, apply such restrictions on the exercise of the rights as it considers appropriate in order to resolve the difficulties or alleviate the hardships.

2.   Where a Member State:

(a)   intends to apply restrictions in accordance with paragraph 1 of this Article, it shall, prior to applying those restrictions, notify the competent Organ of that intention and the nature of the restrictions;

(b)　　is unable to comply with sub-paragraph (a) of this paragraph, it shall, upon applying the restrictions in accordance with paragraph 1, immediately notify the competent Organ of the application and nature of the restrictions.

3.　　The Member State shall, at the time of application of the restrictions mentioned in paragraph 1, submit to the Council for Trade and Economic Development or the Council for Finance and Planning, as the case may require, a programme setting out the measures to be taken by that Member State to resolve the difficulties or to alleviate the hardships.

4.　　The competent Organ shall give its earliest consideration to the programme, and:

(a)　　make a determination in respect of the appropriateness of the restrictions and whether they shall be continued ; and

(b)　　where it decides that the restrictions shall be continued, determine:

(i)　　the adequacy of the programme; and

(ii)　　the period for which the restrictions should continue.

The competent Organ, in making a determination under sub-paragraph (b) of this paragraph, may impose such conditions as it considers necessary.

5.　　Restrictions applied by a Member State pursuant to paragraph 1 of this Article shall be confined to those necessary:

(a)　　to resolve the difficulties in affected sectors;

(b)　　to alleviate economic hardships in a particular region;

(c)　　to minimise damage to the commercial or economic interests of any other Member State; or

(d)　　to prevent the unreasonable exercise of rights granted under this Chapter, the exclusion of which could impair the development of the Single Market and Economy.

6.　　Member States, in applying restrictions pursuant to paragraph 1 of this Article, shall not discriminate and:

(a)　　shall progressively relax them as relevant conditions improve;

(b)　　may maintain them only to the extent that conditions mentioned in paragraph 1 of this Article continue to justify their application.

7.　　If the Council for Trade and Economic Development is not satisfied that Member States applying restrictions are acting in accordance with the provisions of paragraph 6 of this Article, it may recommend to Member States adversely affected thereby alternative arrangements to the same end.

ARTICLE 38b

Waiver of Obligations to Grant Rights

1.   Notwithstanding any provision in this Chapter, a Member State may apply to the Community Council for a waiver of the requirement to grant any of the rights mentioned in paragraph 1 of Article 35 in respect of any industry, sector or enterprise.

2.   An application for a waiver within the meaning of paragraph 1 of this Article shall:

    (a)   be made prior to the establishment of the relevant programme for the removal of restrictions on the rights mentioned in paragraph 1;

    (b)   identify the rights in respect of which the waiver is required;

    (c)   set out the circumstances justifying the grant of the waiver; and

    (d)   indicate the period for which the waiver is required.

3.   The Community Council may require the applicant to furnish such additional information as the Council may specify.

4.   Where the Community Council is satisfied that the waiver should be granted, it shall grant a waiver for a period not exceeding five years, subject to such terms and conditions as the Community Council may determine.

5.   A Member State which has been granted a waiver within the meaning of paragraph 1 of this Article:

    (a)   shall not, while the waiver is in force, be entitled to espouse a claim on behalf of its nationals against another Member State in respect of the rights for which the waiver was granted;

    (b)   shall:

        (i)   at the termination of the period of the waiver, remove the restrictions and notify the Community Council; or

        (ii)   where the Member State removes the restrictions before the end of the period of the waiver, notify the Community Council accordingly.

ARTICLE 38b (bis)

General Exceptions

1.   Subject to the requirement that such measures are not applied in a manner which would constitute a means of arbitrary or unjustifiable discrimination between Member States where like conditions prevail, or a disguised restriction on the rights provided for in this Treaty, nothing in this Chapter shall be construed as preventing the adoption or enforcement by any Member State of measures necessary:

(a)   to protect public morals or to maintain public order and safety;

(b)   to protect human, animal or plant life or health;

(c)   to secure compliance with laws or regulations which are not inconsistent with the provisions of the Treaty including those relating to:

   (i)   the prevention of deceptive and fraudulent practices, and the effects of a default on contracts;

   (ii)   the protection of the privacy of individuals in relation to the processing and dissemination of personal data and the protection of confidentiality of individual records and accounts; and

(d)   to give effect to international obligations including treaties on the avoidance of double taxation.

2.   The Community Council shall take appropriate measures to co-ordinate applicable legislation, regulations and administrative practices established in accordance with Article 38 (bis).

ARTICLE 38b (ter)

Security Exceptions

Nothing in this Treaty shall be construed:

(a)   as requiring any Member State to furnish information, the disclosure of which it considers contrary to its essential security interests;

(b)   as preventing any Member State from taking any action which it considers necessary for the protection of its essential security interests:

   (i)   relating to the supply of services carried out directly or indirectly for the purpose of provisioning a military establishment;

   (ii)   in time of war or other emergency in international relations; or

(c)   as preventing any Member State from taking any action in pursuance of its obligations for the maintenance of international peace and security.

ARTICLE 38c

Special Provisions for Less Developed Countries

Where in this Chapter, Member States or competent Organs are required to remove restrictions on the exercise of the rights mentioned in paragraph 1 of Article 35 the special needs and circumstances of the Less Developed Countries shall be taken into account.

ARTICLE 38d

Implementation

Nothing in this Chapter shall be construed as precluding Member States from adopting measures to remove restrictions on the right of establishment, the right to provide services or the right to move capital within the Community earlier than is required by these provisions.

ARTICLE IX

Signature

This Protocol shall be open for signature on the ……………... day of July 1997 by any State mentioned in paragraph 1 (a) of Article 2 of the Treaty and Suriname.

*   *   *

CONVENTION ON COMBATING BRIBERY OF FOREIGN PUBLIC OFFICIALS IN INTERNATIONAL BUSINESS TRANSACTIONS[*]

(ORGANISATION FOR ECONOMIC CO-OPERATION AND DEVELOPMENT)

The Convention on Combating Bribery of Foreign Public Officials in International Business Transactions was adopted by the member countries of the Organisation for Economic Co-operation and Development and five non-member countries, namely, Argentina, Brazil, Bulgaria, Chile and the Slovak Republic. The Convention, which was opened to signature in Paris on 17 December 1997, entered into force on 15 February 1999. As of 21 October 1999, the following countries had ratified the Convention: Australia, Austria, Belgium, Bulgaria, Canada, Finland, Germany, Greece, Hungary, Iceland, Japan, the Republic of Korea, Mexico, Norway, the Slovak Republic, Sweden, the United Kingdom and the United States. The Convention is also open to accession by any non-signatory which is a member of the OECD or has become a full participant in the Working Group on Bribery in International Business Transactions or any successor to its functions. The annex to the Convention on Statistics on OECD Exports is not included in this volume.

Preamble

The Parties,

Considering that bribery is a widespread phenomenon in international business transactions, including trade and investment, which raises serious moral and political concerns, undermines good governance and economic development, and distorts international competitive conditions;

Considering that all countries share a responsibility to combat bribery in international business transactions;

Having regard to the Revised Recommendation on Combating Bribery in International Business Transactions, adopted by the Council of the Organisation for Economic Co-operation and Development (OECD) on 23 May 1997, C(97)123/FINAL, which, inter alia, called for effective measures to deter, prevent and combat the bribery of foreign public officials in connection with international business transactions, in particular the prompt criminalisation of such bribery in an effective and co-ordinated manner and in conformity with the agreed common elements set out in that Recommendation and with the jurisdictional and other basic legal principles of each country;

---

[*] *Source*: Organisation for Economic Co-operation and Development (1998). "Convention on Combating Bribery of Foreign Public Officials in International Business Transactions", document DAFFE/IME/BR(97)20, 8 April 1998; available on the Internet (http://www.oecd.org//daf/nocorruption/20nov1e.htm). [Note added by the editor.]

Welcoming other recent developments which further advance international understanding and co-operation in combating bribery of public officials, including actions of the United Nations, the World Bank, the International Monetary Fund, the World Trade Organisation, the Organisation of American States, the Council of Europe and the European Union;

Welcoming the efforts of companies, business organisations and trade unions as well as other non-governmental organisations to combat bribery;

Recognising the role of governments in the prevention of solicitation of bribes from individuals and enterprises in international business transactions;

Recognising that achieving progress in this field requires not only efforts on a national level but also multilateral co-operation, monitoring and follow-up;

Recognising that achieving equivalence among the measures to be taken by the Parties is an essential object and purpose of the Convention, which requires that the Convention be ratified without derogations affecting this equivalence;

Have agreed as follows:

Article 1 - The Offence of Bribery of Foreign Public Officials

1.   Each Party shall take such measures as may be necessary to establish that it is a criminal offence under its law for any person intentionally to offer, promise or give any undue pecuniary or other advantage, whether directly or through intermediaries, to a foreign public official, for that official or for a third party, in order that the official act or refrain from acting in relation to the performance of official duties, in order to obtain or retain business or other improper advantage in the conduct of international business.

2.   Each Party shall take any measures necessary to establish that complicity in, including incitement, aiding and abetting, or authorisation of an act of bribery of a foreign public official shall be a criminal offence. Attempt and conspiracy to bribe a foreign public official shall be criminal offences to the same extent as attempt and conspiracy to bribe a public official of that Party.

3.   The offences set out in paragraphs 1 and 2 above are hereinafter referred to as "bribery of a foreign public official".

4.   For the purpose of this Convention:

a.   "foreign public official" means any person holding a legislative, administrative or judicial office of a foreign country, whether appointed or elected; any person exercising a public function for a foreign country, including for a public agency or public enterprise; and any official or agent of a public international organisation;

b.   "foreign country" includes all levels and subdivisions of government, from national to local;

c.   "act or refrain from acting in relation to the performance of official duties" includes any use of the public official's position, whether or not within the official's authorised competence.

Article 2 - Responsibility of Legal Persons

Each Party shall take such measures as may be necessary, in accordance with its legal principles, to establish the liability of legal persons for the bribery of a foreign public official.

Article 3 - Sanctions

1.   The bribery of a foreign public official shall be punishable by effective, proportionate and dissuasive criminal penalties. The range of penalties shall be comparable to that applicable to the bribery of the Party's own public officials and shall, in the case of natural persons, include deprivation of liberty sufficient to enable effective mutual legal assistance and extradition.

2.   In the event that, under the legal system of a Party, criminal responsibility is not applicable to legal persons, that Party shall ensure that legal persons shall be subject to effective, proportionate and dissuasive non-criminal sanctions, including monetary sanctions, for bribery of foreign public officials.

3.   Each Party shall take such measures as may be necessary to provide that the bribe and the proceeds of the bribery of a foreign public official, or property the value of which corresponds to that of such proceeds, are subject to seizure and confiscation or that monetary sanctions of comparable effect are applicable.

4.   Each Party shall consider the imposition of additional civil or administrative sanctions upon a person subject to sanctions for the bribery of a foreign public official.

Article 4 - Jurisdiction

1.   Each Party shall take such measures as may be necessary to establish its jurisdiction over the bribery of a foreign public official when the offence is committed in whole or in part in its territory.

2.   Each Party which has jurisdiction to prosecute its nationals for offences committed abroad shall take such measures as may be necessary to establish its jurisdiction to do so in respect of the bribery of a foreign public official, according to the same principles.

3.   When more than one Party has jurisdiction over an alleged offence described in this Convention, the Parties involved shall, at the request of one of them, consult with a view to determining the most appropriate jurisdiction for prosecution.

4.   Each Party shall review whether its current basis for jurisdiction is effective in the fight against the bribery of foreign public officials and, if it is not, shall take remedial steps.

Article 5 - Enforcement

Investigation and prosecution of the bribery of a foreign public official shall be subject to the applicable rules and principles of each Party. They shall not be influenced by considerations of national economic interest, the potential effect upon relations with another State or the identity of the natural or legal persons involved.

Article 6 - Statute of Limitations

Any statute of limitations applicable to the offence of bribery of a foreign public official shall allow an adequate period of time for the investigation and prosecution of this offence.

Article 7 - Money Laundering

Each Party which has made bribery of its own public official a predicate offence for the purpose of the application of its money laundering legislation shall do so on the same terms for the bribery of a foreign public official, without regard to the place where the bribery occurred.

Article 8 - Accounting

1. In order to combat bribery of foreign public officials effectively, each Party shall take such measures as may be necessary, within the framework of its laws and regulations regarding the maintenance of books and records, financial statement disclosures, and accounting and auditing standards, to prohibit the establishment of off-the-books accounts, the making of off-the-books or inadequately identified transactions, the recording of non-existent expenditures, the entry of liabilities with incorrect identification of their object, as well as the use of false documents, by companies subject to those laws and regulations, for the purpose of bribing foreign public officials or of hiding such bribery.

2. Each Party shall provide effective, proportionate and dissuasive civil, administrative or criminal penalties for such omissions and falsifications in respect of the books, records, accounts and financial statements of such companies.

Article 9 - Mutual Legal Assistance

1. Each Party shall, to the fullest extent possible under its laws and relevant treaties and arrangements, provide prompt and effective legal assistance to another Party for the purpose of criminal investigations and proceedings brought by a Party concerning offences within the scope of this Convention and for non-criminal proceedings within the scope of this Convention brought by a Party against a legal person. The requested Party shall inform the requesting Party, without delay, of any additional information or documents needed to support the request for assistance and, where requested, of the status and outcome of the request for assistance.

2. Where a Party makes mutual legal assistance conditional upon the existence of dual criminality, dual criminality shall be deemed to exist if the offence for which the assistance is sought is within the scope of this Convention.

3. A Party shall not decline to render mutual legal assistance for criminal matters within the scope of this Convention on the ground of bank secrecy.

Article 10 - Extradition

1.   Bribery of a foreign public official shall be deemed to be included as an extraditable offence under the laws of the Parties and the extradition treaties between them.

2.   If a Party which makes extradition conditional on the existence of an extradition treaty receives a request for extradition from another Party with which it has no extradition treaty, it may consider this Convention to be the legal basis for extradition in respect of the offence of bribery of a foreign public official.

3.   Each Party shall take any measures necessary to assure either that it can extradite its nationals or that it can prosecute its nationals for the offence of bribery of a foreign public official. A Party which declines a request to extradite a person for bribery of a foreign public official solely on the ground that the person is its national shall submit the case to its competent authorities for the purpose of prosecution.

4.   Extradition for bribery of a foreign public official is subject to the conditions set out in the domestic law and applicable treaties and arrangements of each Party. Where a Party makes extradition conditional upon the existence of dual criminality, that condition shall be deemed to be fulfilled if the offence for which extradition is sought is within the scope of Article 1 of this Convention.

Article 11 - Responsible Authorities

For the purposes of Article 4, paragraph 3, on consultation, Article 9, on mutual legal assistance and Article 10, on extradition, each Party shall notify to the Secretary-General of the OECD an authority or authorities responsible for making and receiving requests, which shall serve as channel of communication for these matters for that Party, without prejudice to other arrangements between Parties.

Article 12 - Monitoring and Follow-up

The Parties shall co-operate in carrying out a programme of systematic follow-up to monitor and promote the full implementation of this Convention. Unless otherwise decided by consensus of the Parties, this shall be done in the framework of the OECD Working Group on Bribery in International Business Transactions and according to its terms of reference, or within the framework and terms of reference of any successor to its functions, and Parties shall bear the costs of the programme in accordance with the rules applicable to that body.

Article 13 - Signature and Accession

1.   Until its entry into force, this Convention shall be open for signature by OECD members and by non-members which have been invited to become full participants in its Working Group on Bribery in International Business Transactions.

2.   Subsequent to its entry into force, this Convention shall be open to accession by any non-signatory which is a member of the OECD or has become a full participant in the Working Group on Bribery in International Business Transactions or any successor to its functions. For

each such non-signatory, the Convention shall enter into force on the sixtieth day following the date of deposit of its instrument of accession.

Article 14 - Ratification and Depositary

1.   This Convention is subject to acceptance, approval or ratification by the Signatories, in accordance with their respective laws.

2.   Instruments of acceptance, approval, ratification or accession shall be deposited with the Secretary-General of the OECD, who shall serve as Depositary of this Convention.

Article 15 - Entry into Force

1.   This Convention shall enter into force on the sixtieth day following the date upon which five of the ten countries which have the ten largest export shares (see annex), and which represent by themselves at least sixty per cent of the combined total exports of those ten countries, have deposited their instruments of acceptance, approval, or ratification. For each signatory depositing its instrument after such entry into force, the Convention shall enter into force on the sixtieth day after deposit of its instrument.

2.   If, after 31 December 1998, the Convention has not entered into force under paragraph 1 above, any signatory which has deposited its instrument of acceptance, approval or ratification may declare in writing to the Depositary its readiness to accept entry into force of this Convention under this paragraph 2. The Convention shall enter into force for such a signatory on the sixtieth day following the date upon which such declarations have been deposited by at least two signatories. For each signatory depositing its declaration after such entry into force, the Convention shall enter into force on the sixtieth day following the date of deposit.

Article 16 - Amendment

Any Party may propose the amendment of this Convention. A proposed amendment shall be submitted to the Depositary which shall communicate it to the other Parties at least sixty days before convening a meeting of the Parties to consider the proposed amendment. An amendment adopted by consensus of the Parties, or by such other means as the Parties may determine by consensus, shall enter into force sixty days after the deposit of an instrument of ratification, acceptance or approval by all of the Parties, or in such other circumstances as may be specified by the Parties at the time of adoption of the amendment.

Article 17 - Withdrawal

A Party may withdraw from this Convention by submitting written notification to the Depositary. Such withdrawal shall be effective one year after the date of the receipt of the notification. After withdrawal, co-operation shall continue between the Parties and the Party which has withdrawn on all requests for assistance or extradition made before the effective date of withdrawal which remain pending.

*   *   *

RECOMMENDATION OF THE COUNCIL CONCERNING EFFECTIVE ACTION AGAINST HARD CORE CARTELS[*]

(ORGANISATION FOR ECONOMIC CO-OPERATION AND DEVELOPMENT)

The Recommendation of the Council Concerning Effective Action against Hard Core Cartels was adopted by the Council of the Organisation for Economic Co-operation and Development on 25 March 1998.

THE COUNCIL,

Having regard to Article 5 b) of the Convention on the Organisation for Economic Co-operation and Development of 14th December 1960;

Having regard to previous Council Recommendations recognition that "effective application of competition policy plays a vital role in promoting world trade by ensuring dynamic national markets and encouraging the lowering or reducing of entry barriers to imports" [C(86)65(Final)]; and that "anticompetitive practices may constitute an obstacle to the achievement of economic growth, trade expansion, and other economic goals of Member countries" [C(95)130/FINAL];

Having regard to the Council Recommendation that exemptions from competition laws should be no broader than necessary [C(79)155(Final)] and to the agreement in the Communiqué of the May 1997 meeting of the Council at Ministerial level to "work towards eliminating gaps in coverage of competition law, unless evidence suggests that compelling public interests cannot be served in better ways" [C/MIN(97)10];

Having regard to the Council's long-standing position that closer co-operation is necessary to deal effectively with anticompetitive practices in one country that affect other countries and harm international trade, and its recommendation that when permitted by their laws and interests, Member countries should co-ordinate investigations of mutual concern and should comply with each other's requests to share information from their files and to obtain and share information obtained from third parties [C(95)130/FINAL];

Recognising that benefits have resulted from the ability of competition authorities of some Member countries to share confidential investigatory information with a foreign competition authority in cases of mutual interest, pursuant to multilateral and bilateral treaties and agreements, and considering that most competition authorities are currently not authorised to share investigatory information with foreign competition authorities;

---

[*] *Source*: Organisation for Economic Co-operation and Development (1998). "Recommendation of the Council Concerning Effective Action Against Hard Core Cartels", *OECD News Releases*, document [C (98)35/FINAL]; available also on the Internet (http://www.oecd.org//daf/clp/rec9com.htm). [Note added by the editor.]

Recognising also that co-operation through the sharing of confidential information presupposes satisfactory protection against improper disclosure or use of shared information and may require resolution of other issues, including potential difficulties relating to differences in the territorial scope of competition law and in the nature of sanctions for competition law violations;

Considering that hard core cartels are the most egregious violations of competition law and that they injure consumers in many countries by raising prices and restricting supply, thus making goods and services completely unavailable to some purchasers and unnecessarily expensive for others; and

Considering that effective action against hard core cartels is particularly important from an international perspective -- because their distortion of world trade creates market power, waste, and inefficiency in countries whose markets would otherwise be competitive -- and particularly dependent upon co-operation -- because they generally operate in secret, and relevant evidence may be located in many different countries;

I.   RECOMMENDS as follows to Governments of Member countries:

A.   CONVERGENCE AND EFFECTIVENESS OF LAWS PROHIBITING HARD CORE CARTELS

1.   Member countries should ensure that their competition laws effectively halt and deter hard core cartels. In particular, their laws should provide for:

   a)   effective sanctions, of a kind and at a level adequate to deter firms and individuals from participating in such cartels; and

   b)   enforcement procedures and institutions with powers adequate to detect and remedy hard core cartels, including powers to obtain documents and information and to impose penalties for non-compliance.

2.   For purposes of this Recommendation:

   a)   a "hard core cartel" is an anticompetitive agreement, anticompetitive concerted practice, or anticompetitive arrangement by competitors to fix prices, make rigged bids (collusive tenders), establish output restrictions or quotas, or share or divide markets by allocating customers, suppliers, territories, or lines of commerce;

   b)   the hard core cartel category does not include agreements, concerted practices, or arrangements that (i) are reasonably related to the lawful realisation of cost-reducing or output-enhancing efficiencies, (ii) are excluded directly or indirectly from the coverage of a Member country's own laws, or (iii) are authorised in accordance with those laws. However, all exclusions and authorisations of what would otherwise be hard core cartels should be transparent and should be reviewed periodically to assess whether they are both necessary and no broader than necessary to achieve their overriding policy objectives. After the issuance of this Recommendation, Members should provide the Organisation annual notice of any new or extended exclusion or category of authorisation.

B. INTERNATIONAL CO-OPERATION AND COMITY IN ENFORCING LAWS PROHIBITING HARD CORE CARTELS

1. Member countries have a common interest in preventing hard core cartels and should co-operate with each other in enforcing their laws against such cartels. In this connection, they should seek ways in which co-operation might be improved by positive comity principles applicable to requests that another country remedy anticompetitive conduct that adversely affects both countries, and should conduct their own enforcement activities in accordance with principles of comity when they affect other countries' important interests.

2. Co-operation between or among Member countries in dealing with hard core cartels should take into account the following principles:

   a) the common interest in preventing hard core cartels generally warrants co-operation to the extent that such co-operation would be consistent with a requested country's laws, regulations, and important interests;

   b) to the extent consistent with their own laws, regulations, and important interests, and subject to effective safeguards to protect commercially sensitive and other confidential information, Member countries' mutual interest in preventing hard core cartels warrants co-operation that might include sharing documents and information in their possession with foreign competition authorities and gathering documents and information on behalf of foreign competition authorities on a voluntary basis and when necessary through use of compulsory process;

   c) a Member country may decline to comply with a request for assistance, or limit or condition its co-operation on the ground that it considers compliance with the request to be not in accordance with its laws or regulations or to be inconsistent with its important interests or on any other grounds, including its competition authority's resource constraints or the absence of a mutual interest in the investigation or proceeding in question;

   d) Member countries should agree to engage in consultations over issues relating to co-operation.

In order to establish a framework for their co-operation in dealing with hard core cartels, Member countries are encouraged to consider entering into bilateral or multilateral agreements or other instruments consistent with these principles.

3. Member countries are encouraged to review all obstacles to their effective co-operation in the enforcement of laws against hard core cartels and to consider actions, including national legislation and/or bilateral or multilateral agreements or other instruments, by which they could eliminate or reduce those obstacles in a manner consistent with their important interests.

4. The co-operation contemplated by this Recommendation is without prejudice to any other co-operation that may occur in accordance with prior Recommendations of the Council, pursuant to any applicable bilateral or multilateral agreements to which Member countries may be parties, or otherwise.

II.   INSTRUCTS the Competition Law and Policy Committee:

1.   to maintain a record of such exclusions and authorisations as are notified to the Organisation pursuant to Paragraph I. A 2b);

2.   to serve, at the request of the Member countries involved, as a forum for consultations on the application of the Recommendation; and

3.   to review Member countries' experience in implementing this Recommendation and report to the Council within two years on any further action needed to improve co-operation in the enforcement of competition law prohibitions of hard core cartels.

III.   INVITES non-Member countries to associate themselves with this Recommendation and to implement it.

*   *   *

RECOMMENDATION OF THE COUNCIL ON COUNTERACTING HARMFUL TAX COMPETITION[*]

(ORGANISATION FOR ECONOMIC CO-OPERATION AND DEVELOPMENT)

In May 1996, Ministers of the OECD member countries called upon the OECD to develop measures to counter the distorting effects of harmful tax competition on investment and financing decisions, and the consequences for national tax bases, and report back in 1998. In response to that request, the OECD Committee on Fiscal Affairs prepared a report defining the factors to be used in identifying harmful tax practices and made 19 wide-ranging recommendations to counteract such practices. On 9 April 1998, the OECD Council adopted the Recommendation on Harmful Tax Competition and instructed the Committee on Fiscal Affairs to continue to pursue its work in this area and to develop a dialogue with non-member countries. Luxembourg and Switzerland abstained on the adoption of the Recommendation.

THE COUNCIL,

Having regard to Article 5 b) of the Convention on the Organisation for Economic Co-operation and Development of 14 December 1960;

Having regard to the Recommendation of the Council dated 23 October 1997 concerning Model Tax Convention on Income and Capital;

Having regard to the Revised Recommendations of the Council dated 24 July 1997 on the Determination of Transfer Pricing between Associated Enterprises;

Having regard to the Ministerial Communiqué issued on the 22 May 1996 which calls upon the Organisation to "develop measures to counter the distorting effects of harmful tax competition on investment and financing decisions and the consequences for national tax bases, and report back in 1998";

Having regard to the Report entitled "Harmful Tax Competition: An Emerging Global Issue" adopted by the Committee on Fiscal Affairs on 20 January 1998 (hereinafter referred to as "the Report");

Recognising the OECD's role in promoting an open, multilateral trading system and the need to promote the "level playing field" which is essential to the continued expansion of global economic growth;

---

[*] *Source*: Organisation for Economic Co-operation and Development (1998). "Recommendation of the Council on Counteracting Harmful Tax Competition", *Harmful Tax Competition: An Emerging Global Issue* (Paris: OECD), Annex I, pp. 65-69; available also on the Internet (http://www.oecd.org//daf/fa/TAX_COMP/r_htp.htm). [Note added by the editor.]

Recognising that the process of globalisation and the development of new technologies has brought about prosperity for many citizens around the world, but also raises challenges for governments to minimise tax induced distortions in investment and financing decisions and to maintain their tax base in this new global environment;

Considering that if governments do not intensify their co-operation, a part of the tax burden will shift from income on mobile activities to taxes on labour, consumption and non mobile activities and such a shift would make tax systems less equitable and may have a negative impact on employment;

On the proposal of the Committee on Fiscal Affairs:

I.   RECOMMENDS that Member countries implement the recommendations, including the Guidelines for dealing with harmful Preferential Tax Regimes, which are set out in an Appendix to this Recommendation, of which it forms an integral part.

II.   INSTRUCTS the Committee on Fiscal Affairs:

1.   to establish a Forum on Harmful Tax Practices;

2.   to implement the relevant measures identified in the attached Appendix;

3.   to report periodically to the Council on the results of its work in these matters together with any relevant proposals for further improvements in the co-operation to counter harmful tax practices;

4.   to develop its dialogue with non-member countries, consistently with the policy of the Organisation, with the aim of assisting these countries to become familiar with the analysis and conclusions of the Report and, where appropriate, to encourage them to associate themselves with the recommendations set out in the Report.

ANNEX

Recommendations and Guidelines for dealing with Harmful Tax Practices

I.   Recommendations concerning domestic legislation and practices

1.   *Recommendation concerning Controlled Foreign Corporations (CFC) or equivalent rules*: that countries that do not have such rules consider adopting them and that countries that have such rules ensure that they apply in a fashion consistent with the desirability of curbing harmful tax practices.

2.   *Recommendation concerning foreign investment fund or equivalent rules*: that countries that do not have such rules consider adopting them and that countries that have such rules consider applying them to income and entities covered by practices considered to constitute harmful tax competition.

3.   *Recommendation concerning restrictions on participation exemption and other systems of exempting foreign income in the context of harmful tax competition*: that countries that

apply the exemption method to eliminate double taxation of foreign source income consider adopting rules that would ensure that foreign income that has benefited from tax practices deemed as constituting harmful tax competition do not qualify for the application of the exemption method.

4. *Recommendation concerning foreign information reporting rules*: that countries that do not have rules concerning reporting of international transactions and foreign operations of resident taxpayers consider adopting such rules and that countries exchange information obtained under these rules.

5. *Recommendation concerning rulings*: that countries, where administrative decisions concerning the particular position of a taxpayer may be obtained in advance of planned transactions, make public the conditions for granting, denying or revoking such decisions.

6. *Recommendation concerning transfer pricing rules*: that countries follow the principles set out in the OECD's 1995 Guidelines on Transfer Pricing and thereby refrain from applying or not applying their transfer pricing rules in a way that would constitute harmful tax competition.

7. *Recommendation concerning access to banking information for tax purposes*: in the context of counteracting harmful tax competition, countries should review their laws, regulations and practices which govern access to banking information with a view to removing impediments to the access to such information by tax authorities.

II.   Recommendations concerning tax treaties

8. *Recommendation concerning greater and more efficient use of exchanges of information*: that countries should undertake programs to intensify exchange of relevant information concerning transactions in tax havens and preferential tax regimes constituting harmful tax competition.

9. *Recommendation concerning the entitlement to treaty benefits*: that countries consider including in their tax conventions provisions aimed at restricting the entitlement to treaty benefits for entities and income covered by measures constituting harmful tax practices and consider how the existing provisions of their tax conventions can be applied for the same purpose; that the Model Tax Convention be modified to include such provisions or clarifications as are needed in that respect.

10. *Recommendation concerning the clarification of the status of domestic anti-abuse rules and doctrines in tax treaties*: that the Commentary on the Model Tax Convention be clarified to remove any uncertainty or ambiguity regarding the compatibility of domestic anti-abuse measures with the Model Tax Convention.

11. *Recommendation concerning a list of specific exclusion provisions found in treaties*: that the Committee prepare and maintain a list of provisions used by countries to exclude from the benefits of tax conventions certain specific entities or types of income and that the list be used by Member countries as a reference point when negotiating tax conventions and as a basis for discussions in the Forum.

12. *Recommendation concerning tax treaties with tax havens*: that countries consider terminating their tax conventions with tax havens and consider not entering into tax treaties with such countries in the future.

13. *Recommendation concerning co-ordinated enforcement regimes* (joint audits; co-ordinated training programmes, etc.): that countries consider undertaking co-ordinated enforcement programs (such as simultaneous examinations, specific exchange of information projects or joint training activities) in relation to income or taxpayers benefiting from practices constituting harmful tax competition.

14. *Recommendation concerning assistance in recovery of tax claims*: that countries be encouraged to review the current rules applying to the enforcement of tax claims of other countries and that the Committee pursue its work in this area with a view to drafting provisions that could be included in tax conventions for that purpose.

III. Recommendations to intensify international co-operation in response to harmful tax competition

15. *Recommendation for Guidelines and a Forum on Harmful Tax Practices*: that the Member countries endorse the Guidelines on harmful preferential tax regimes set out in the following Box and establish a Forum to implement the Guidelines and other Recommendations in this Report.

* * *

MULTILATERAL AGREEMENT ON INVESTMENT

DRAFT NEGOTIATING TEXT AS OF 24 APRIL 1998[*]

(ORGANISATION FOR ECONOMIC CO-OPERATION AND DEVELOPMENT)

The negotiations on a Multilateral Agreement on Investment (MAI) in the Organisation for Economic Co-operation and Development (OECD) began in 1995. The MAI was intended to provide a broad multilateral framework for international investment with high standards for the liberalization of investment regimes, the protection of investment, and effective dispute settlement procedures. Between September 1995 and early 1997, the negotiating process was mostly of a technical nature. Since early 1997, the negotiations began to encounter significant difficulties and, at the OECD Council meeting at the ministerial level on 28 April 1998, the ministers agreed to have a six-month pause in order to reflect and consult on the negotiations. The pause lasted until October 1998 and, on 3 December 1998, the OECD announced that the negotiations on the MAI were no longer taking place. The text of the MAI reproduced in this volume reflects the status of the negotiations as of 24 April 1998. It consolidates the texts of the agreement considered in the course of the MAI negotiations as a result mainly of the work of expert groups. It is presented with footnotes and proposals that were still under consideration at the time when the negotiations were discontinued.

TABLE OF CONTENTS

I. GENERAL PROVISIONS

Preamble

II. SCOPE AND APPLICATION

Definitions
Geographical Scope of Application
Application to Overseas Territories

III. TREATMENT OF INVESTORS AND INVESTMENTS

National Treatment and Most Favoured Nation Treatment
Transparency

---

[*] *Source*: Organisation for Economic Co-operation and Development (OECD) (1998). "The Multilateral Agreement on Investment: The MAI Negotiating Text as of 24 April 1998", DAFFE/MAI/NM(98)2/REV1; available on the Internet (http://www.oecd.org/daf/cmis/mai/negtext.htm). [Note added by the editor.]

Membership of Self-regulatory Bodies and Associations
Payments and Clearing Systems/Lender of Last Resort
Dispute Settlement
Definition of Financial Services

VIII. TAXATION

IX. COUNTRY SPECIFIC EXCEPTIONS

Lodging of Country Specific Exceptions

X. RELATIONSHIP TO OTHER INTERNATIONAL AGREEMENTS

Obligations under the Articles of Agreement of
the International Monetary Fund
The OECD Guidelines for Multinational Enterprises

XI. IMPLEMENTATION AND OPERATION

The Preparatory Group
The Parties Group

XII. FINAL PROVISIONS

Signature
Acceptance and Entry Into Force
Accession
Non-Applicability
Review
Amendment
Revisions to the OECD Guidelines for Multinational Enterprises
Withdrawal
Depositary
Status of Annexes
Authentic Texts
Denial of Benefits

ANNEX 1

COUNTRY SPECIFIC PROPOSALS FOR DRAFT TEXTS

Scope
Geographical Scope
Application to Overseas Territories and Non-applicability
Scope of Application
Government Procurement of Services
Substantive Approach to the Respect Clause

Respect Clause
Regional Economic Integration Organisations
Regional Economic Integration Organisations
Additional Environmental Proposals
Conflicting Requirements
Secondary Investment Boycotts
Culture
Subnational measures
The Svalbard Treaty
Labour Market Integration Agreements
Sami People
Dispute Settlement
Dispute Settlement
Dispute Settlement: Response to Non-compliance
Maintaining the Overall Level of Liberalisation

ANNEX 2

**CHAIRMAN'S PROPOSALS ON ENVIRONMENT AND RELATED
MATTERS AND ON LABOUR**

I. GENERAL PROVISIONS

PREAMBLE

The Contracting Parties to this Agreement,[1] [2] [3]

Desiring to strengthen their ties of friendship and to promote greater economic co-operation between them;

Considering that international investment has assumed great importance in the world economy and has considerably contributed to the development of their countries;

Recognising that agreement upon the treatment to be accorded to investors and their investments will contribute to the efficient utilisation of economic resources, the creation of employment opportunities and the improvement of living standards;

Emphasising that fair, transparent and predictable investment regimes complement and benefit the world trading system;[4]

[Wishing that this Agreement enhances international co-operation with respect to investment and the development of world-wide rules on foreign direct investment in the framework of the world trading system as embodied in the World Trade Organization;][5]

Wishing to establish a broad multilateral framework for international investment with high standards for the liberalisation of investment regimes and investment protection and with effective dispute settlement procedures;

[Recognising that investment, as an engine of economic growth, can play a key role in ensuring that economic growth is sustainable, when accompanied by appropriate environmental policies to ensure it takes place in an environmentally sound manner] [Recognising that appropriate environmental policies can play a key role in ensuring that economic development, to

---

[1] One delegation, with the support of another delegation, proposes that the Preamble include the following language on natural resources: "Reaffirming the sovereignty and sovereign rights of States over natural resources within the limits of national jurisdiction".

[2] Three delegations continue to oppose any reference to labour in the Preamble. One delegation is willing to consider preambular language on the environment as part of the entire package on labour and environment. Another delegation also opposes any reference to the environment unless its concerns are met.

[3] It is the strong feeling of many delegations that preambular reference to the environment be limited to one paragraph and that it be as short as possible. Similarly, it was the feeling of many delegations that preambular reference to labour be limited to one paragraph and that it be as short as possible.

[4] Some delegations propose an explicit reference to the World Trade Organisation. One delegation proposes the addition immediately after the words "world trading system" of: "encompassing multilateral and bilateral investment instruments as well as agreements of the World Trade Organisation". This proposal would need some refinement to ensure that it does not limit the scope of the phrase "world trading system" by excluding, for example, regional agreements.

[5] One delegation proposes this language. Some delegations oppose the inclusion of such language because they believe that it would prejudge, and be prejudicial to, future work on investment in the World Trade Organisation.

which investment contributes, is sustainable][6], and resolving to [desiring to][7] implement this agreement [in accordance with international environmental law and][8] in a manner consistent with sustainable development, as reflected in the Rio Declaration on Environment and Development and Agenda 21, [including the protection and preservation of the environment and principles of the polluter pays and the precautionary approach][9];[10] [11] [12]

---

[6] There is about even support for each "recognising" formulation.

[7] Four delegations object to "resolving to" and would prefer "desiring to".

[8] This phrase raises the questions whether the MAI intends to set a presumption that multilateral environmental agreements have precedence and over it, and, if so, whether a preambular reference establishes that presumption. One delegation is strongly opposed to the inclusion of this phrase because it is impossible to define precisely.

[9] While a majority favour explicit mention of these two principles, a number of delegations prefer a more general reference to Rio Declaration and Agenda 21 principles without specifics. One delegation would explicitly mention two additional principles: "public participation and the right of communities to have access to information, and the avoidance of relocation and transfer of activities causing severe environmental degradation or found to be harmful to human health".

[10] One delegation proposes additional language: "and recognising that such environmental policies shall not constitute a means of disguised restriction on international trade and investment;". Some delegations support this proposal in concept but wonder if it belonged in the Preamble or in a more general anti-abuse clause in the MAI.

[11] One delegation, supported by another delegation, would insert four additional tirets from its alternative for the Preamble:

> Convinced of the need for optimal use of the world's resources in accordance with the objective of sustainable development;

> Recognising that investment can result in changes in the scale and structure of economic activity within countries, with potential effects on health and the environment;

> Recognising the interdependent nature of their environments;

> Encouraging the protection, conservation, preservation and enhancement of the environment;

[12] One delegation believes that the proposal for two paragraphs of preambular language on the environment as set out in the report by DG3 reflected broadly shared ideas of substance and was prepared to continue work on the basis of that text. Bracketed text in that proposal related primarily to nuance. The paragraph now contained in the text has lost or weakened at least two concepts that had been broadly shared by the group. This delegation would like to know why a number of delegations appear to find it a preferred basis on which to continue work. The two key concepts that have been lost and the substance of this delegation's concern are set out below:

1. The commitment (or desire) of Parties to implement the agreement in a manner consistent with environmental protection and conservation has been omitted. In the current text this idea is expressed only as a subsidiary notion to the Rio declaration when in fact environmental protection and conservation should be a generally affirmed principle that is not limited to the provisions of Rio.

2. A clear statement of reaffirmation of commitment to the Rio Declaration, writ large, is not clearly made. In the current text, parties resolve to implement the agreement in a manner consistent only with specific ideals (sustainable development and/or international environmental law) as reflected in the Rio Declaration; they do not reaffirm a commitment to the Rio Declaration as a whole. Furthermore, the new text adds the idea of implementing the agreement in accordance with the specified concepts of Rio; this is an idea that has not been explicitly discussed by the group.

Therefore, based on the report by DG3, and in addition to the position set out in footnote 8 above, the proposal of this delegation is:

> Resolving to implement this agreement in a manner consistent with environmental protection and conservation;

> Reaffirming their commitment to the RIO Declaration on Environment and Development and Agenda 21, including to sustainable development as reflected therein, and recognising that investment, as an engine

Renewing their commitment to the Copenhagen Declaration of the World Summit on Social Development[13] and to observance of internationally recognised core labour standards, i.e. freedom of association, the right to organise and bargain collectively, prohibition of forced labour, the elimination of exploitative forms of child labour, and non-discrimination in employment, and noting that the International Labour Organisation is the competent body to set and deal with core labour standards world-wide.[14] [15]

Affirming their decision to create a free-standing Agreement open to accession by all countries;[16]

[Noting] [Affirming their support for] the OECD Guidelines for Multinational Enterprises and emphasising that implementation of the Guidelines, which are non-binding and which are observed on a voluntary basis, will promote mutual confidence between enterprises and host countries and contribute to a favourable climate for investment; [17]

---

of economic growth, can play a key role in ensuring that growth is sustainable, when accompanied by appropriate environmental policies to ensure it takes place in an environmental sound manner;

Noting that the Rio Declaration principles of relevance to investment include, *inter alia*, the polluter pays, the precautionary approach, public participation and the right of communities to have access to information, and the avoidance of relocation and transfer of activities causing severe environmental degradation or found to be harmful to human health;

[13] A number of delegations maintain a scrutiny reserve to consider whether there should also be explicit mention of the Singapore WTO Ministerial.

[14] One delegation could not support a reference to labour in the preamble if it included explicit statement of basic principles of core labour standards.

[15] One delegations would insert three additional tirets from its alternative for the Preamble:

Recognising that development of economic and business ties can promote respect for core labour standards;

Resolved to foster investment with due regard for the importance of labour laws and core labour standards;

Noting that, as members of the International Labour Organisation, they have endorsed the Tripartite Declaration of Principles concerning Multilateral Enterprises and Social Policy, and agreeing to renew their support for that voluntary instrument.

[16] Some delegations propose that the statement that the Agreement is open to accession by all countries be strengthened.

[17] One delegation proposes that the Preamble state that the Guidelines include, in particular, recommendations on employment and industrial relations and environmental protection; other delegations are of the view that the text introducing the Guidelines as an annex should specify the eight subject areas, including those just mentioned, on which the Guidelines make recommendations (see Section III below). In addition, one delegation would like to add words to the effect that the Contracting Parties consider the Guidelines to be "a valuable part of the framework for the consideration of issues of investment and multilateral enterprises."

HAVE AGREED AS FOLLOWS:

II.   SCOPE AND APPLICATION

DEFINITIONS

1.   Investor means:

  (i)   a natural person having the nationality of, or who is permanently residing in, a Contracting Party in accordance with its applicable law; or

  (ii)   a legal person or any other entity constituted or organised under the applicable law of a Contracting Party, whether or not for profit, and whether private or government owned or controlled, and includes a corporation, trust, partnership, sole proprietorship, joint venture, association or organisation.

2.   Investment means:

Every kind of asset owned or controlled, directly or indirectly, by an investor, including:[18, 19]

  (i)   an enterprise (being a legal person or any other entity constituted or organised under the applicable law of the Contracting Party, whether or not for profit, and whether private or government owned or controlled, and includes a corporation, trust, partnership, sole proprietorship, branch, joint venture, association or organisation);

  (ii)   shares, stocks or other forms of equity participation in an enterprise, and rights derived therefrom;

  (iii)   bonds, debentures, loans and other forms of debt, and rights derived therefrom;

  (iv)   rights under contracts, including turnkey, construction, management, production or revenue-sharing contracts;

  (v)   claims to money and claims to performance;

  (vi)   intellectual property rights;

  (vii)   rights conferred pursuant to law or contract such as concessions, licenses, authorisations, and permits;

---

[18] The Negotiating Group agrees that this broad definition of investment calls for further work on appropriate safeguard provisions. In addition, the following issues require further work to determine their appropriate treatment in the MAI: indirect investment, intellectual property, concessions, public debt and real estate.

[19] For greater certainty, an interpretative note will be required to indicate that, in order to qualify as an investment under the MAI, an asset must have the characteristics of an investment, such as the commitment of capital or other resources, the expectation of gain or profit, or the assumption of risk.

(viii) any other tangible and intangible, movable and immovable property, and any related property rights, such as leases, mortgages, liens and pledges.

GEOGRAPHICAL SCOPE OF APPLICATION [20]

This Agreement shall apply in:

(a) the land territory, internal waters, and the territorial sea of a Contracting Party, and, in the case of a Contracting Party which is an archipelagic state, its archipelagic waters; and

(b) the maritime areas beyond the territorial sea with respect to which a Contracting Party exercises sovereign rights or jurisdiction in accordance with international law, as reflected particularly in the 1982 United Nations Convention on the Law of the Sea.[21]

APPLICATION TO OVERSEAS TERRITORIES[22]

1. A State may at any time declare in writing to the Depositary that this Agreement shall apply to all or to one or more of the territories for the international relations of which it is responsible.[23] Such declaration, made prior to or upon ratification, accession or acceptance, shall take effect upon entry into force of this Agreement for that State. A subsequent declaration shall take effect with respect to the territory or territories concerned on the ninetieth day following receipt of the declaration by the Depositary.

2. A Party may at any time declare in writing to the Depositary, that this Agreement shall cease to apply to all or to one or more of the territories for the international relations of which it is responsible. Such declaration shall take effect upon the expiry of one year from the date of receipt of the declaration by the Depositary, with the same effect regarding existing investment as withdrawal of a Party.

---

[20] A number of EG1 delegations were of the view that rather than an article on geographical scope, an article should define the "territory" or "area" of a Contracting Party to which the MAI would be applicable and in that case, it could be included in a general definitions part of the agreement. Some delegations had serious misgivings about the feasibility of embarking on this approach.

[21] EG1 agreed that an alternative text of subparagraph (b) illustrating the "functional" approach supported by some delegations should be included in order to preserve the approach for future consideration if the Negotiating Group were to decide to pursue that option further. An alternative subparagraph (b), could read:

"..................investments beyond the territorial sea under the jurisdiction of a Contracting Party in accordance with international law as reflected in the 1982 United Nations Convention on the Law of the Sea."

[22] One delegation has submitted an alternative draft text concerning this article (see Annex 1).

[23] In case such a declaration of application were to be accompanied by reservations or exceptions beyond those of the declaring state, these would be subject to acceptance of the other Parties.

III. TREATMENT OF INVESTORS AND INVESTMENTS

NATIONAL TREATMENT AND MOST FAVOURED NATION TREATMENT

1.   Each Contracting Party shall accord to investors of another Contracting Party and to their investments, treatment no less favourable than the treatment it accords [in like circumstances] to its own investors and their investments with respect to the establishment, acquisition, expansion, operation, management, maintenance, use, enjoyment and sale or other disposition of investments.

2.   Each Contracting Party shall accord to investors of another Contracting Party and to their investments, treatment no less favourable than the treatment it accords [in like circumstances] to investors of any other Contracting Party or of a non-Contracting Party, and to the investments of investors of any other Contracting Party or of a non-Contracting Party, with respect to the establishment, acquisition, expansion, operation, management, maintenance, use, enjoyment, and sale or other disposition of investments.

3.   Each Contracting Party shall accord to investors of another Contracting Party and to their investments the better of the treatment required by Articles 1.1 and 1.2, whichever is the more favourable to those investors or investments.

TRANSPARENCY

1.   Each Contracting Party shall promptly publish, or otherwise make publicly available, its laws, regulations, procedures and administrative rulings and judicial decisions of general application as well as international agreements which may affect the operation of the Agreement. Where a Contracting Party establishes policies which are not expressed in laws or regulations or by other means listed in this paragraph but which may affect the operation of the Agreement, that Contracting Party shall promptly publish them or otherwise make them publicly available.[24]

2.   Each Contracting Party shall promptly respond to specific questions and provide, upon request, information to other Contracting Parties on matters referred to in Article 2.1.

3.   Nothing in this Agreement shall prevent a Contracting Party from requiring an investor of another Contracting Party, or its investment, to provide routine information concerning that investment solely for information or statistical purposes. Nothing in this Agreement requires a Contracting Party to furnish or allow access to:

      a)   information related to the financial affairs and accounts of individual customers of particular investors or investments, or

      b)   any confidential or proprietary information, including information concerning particular investors or investments, the disclosure of which would impede law

---

[24] The Chairman of the Negotiating Group proposes to keep this sentence without brackets, noting that several delegations could go along with this proposal provided that there was a satisfactory explanatory statement in the commentary.

enforcement or be contrary to its laws[25] protecting confidentiality or prejudice legitimate commercial interests of particular enterprises.

TEMPORARY ENTRY, STAY AND WORK OF INVESTORS AND KEY PERSONNEL[26]

1.   Subject to the application of Contracting Parties' national laws, regulations and procedures affecting the entry, stay and work of natural persons

    (a)   Each Contracting Party shall grant temporary entry, stay and authorisation to work[27] and provide any necessary confirming documentation to a natural person of another Contracting Party who is:

        (i)   an investor who seeks to establish, develop, administer or provide advice or essential technical services to the operation of an enterprise[28] in the territory of the former Contracting Party to which the investor has committed, or is in the process of committing, a substantial amount of capital, or

        (ii)   an employee employed by an enterprise referred to in (i) above, or by an investor[29], [who may be required to have been employed for a specified minimum period, for example one year],[30] in a capacity of executive, manager or specialist and who is essential to the enterprise;

    so long as that person continues to meet the requirements of this Article;[31]

    (b)   (i)   Each Contracting Party shall grant temporary entry and stay and provide any necessary confirming documentation to the spouse and minor children of a natural person who has been granted temporary entry, stay and authorisation

---

[25] Two delegations propose to insert after "laws", the terms "policies, or practices". One delegation can only support the proposed text for paragraph 3 of the Transparency article if these terms are inserted.

[26] Whether there should be an anti-abuse clause, its precise wording, as well as its specific placement is to be decided.

[27] Interpretative note: "The granting of an "authorisation to work" may imply that a natural person may have to meet specific professional qualifications required in order to carry out particular activities. Professional qualification criteria that may be applicable are outside the scope of this Article."

[28] "Enterprise" under this Article would have the same meaning as under the MAI definition of "investment."

[29] It is recalled that the MAI definition of an "investor" includes both natural and legal persons. It is understood that the national authorities may impose on investors some requirements under domestic immigration laws regulations and procedures given the content of the chapeau of paragraph 1.

[30] The phrase *"who may be required to have been employed for a specified minimum period, for example one year"* reproduces an amendment proposed by one delegation. It is generally agreed, however, that legally speaking, it is not necessary to clarify in the text that specific minimum periods, for example one year, are allowed by the chapeau of paragraph 1. Some delegations consider, however, the retention of this language to be a political necessity.

[31] Interpretative note: "It is understood that the national authorities may periodically verify continued eligibility under this paragraph."

to work in accordance with subparagraph (a) above. The spouse and minor children shall be admitted for the period of the stay of that person.

(ii)   Each Contracting Party is encouraged[32] to grant authorisation to work to the spouse of the person who has been granted temporary entry, stay and authorisation to work in accordance with subparagraph (a) above·

2.   No Contracting Party may deny entry and stay as provided for by this Article, or authorisation to work as provided for by paragraph 1(a) of this Article, for reasons relating to labour market or other economic needs tests or numerical restrictions in national laws, regulations, and procedures[33]

3.   For the purposes of this Article:

Natural person of another Contracting Party means a natural person having the nationality of [or who is permanently residing in] [34] another Contracting Party in accordance with its applicable law;

Executive means a natural person who primarily directs the management of an enterprise or establishes goals and policies for the enterprise or a major component or function of the enterprise, exercises wide latitude in decision-making and receives only general supervision or direction from higher-level executives, the board of directors, or stockholders of the enterprise;

Manager means a natural person who directs the management of an enterprise, or department, or subdivision of the enterprise, supervises and controls the work of other supervisory, professional or managerial employees, has the authority to hire and fire or recommend hiring, firing, or other personnel actions and exercises discretionary authority over day-to-day operations at a senior level; and

Specialist means a natural person who possesses knowledge at an advanced level of expertise and who may be required to possess specific or proprietary knowledge of the enterprise's product, service, research equipment, techniques, or management.

---

[32] Some countries prefer "shall endeavour" and may need to refer to capitals before agreeing to deletion.

[33] There is no substantive disagreement about making it clear in an interpretative note that "numerical restrictions referred to in this paragraph are restrictions on the maximum number of natural persons who can enter, stay or work in the Contracting Party." A number of delegations maintain a scrutiny reserve on the wording of this interpretative note.

[34] Several delegations have concerns with extending the benefits of the MAI Key Personnel provisions to permanent residents of another Contracting Party. As a result of the Negotiating Group discussion on 23-25 April 1997, the Chairman proposed that at least for the purposes of investors, nationals and permanent residents should be covered. Delegations should reflect further on the inclusion of permanent residents as concerns the categories of executive, manager, or specialist.

NATIONALITY REQUIREMENTS FOR EXECUTIVES, MANAGERS AND MEMBERS OF BOARDS OF DIRECTORS

No Contracting Party may require that an enterprise of that Contracting Party that is an investment of an investor of another Contracting Party appoint as executives, managers[35] and members of boards of directors[36] individuals of any particular nationality.

EMPLOYMENT REQUIREMENTS[37]

A Contracting Party shall permit investors of another Contracting Party and their investments to employ any natural person of the investor's or the investment's choice regardless of nationality and citizenship provided that such person is holding a valid permit of sejour and work delivered by the competent authorities of the former Contracting Party and that the employment concerned conforms to the terms, conditions and time limits of the permission granted to such person.

---

[35] The definitions of "Executive" and "Manager" are the same as those provided by the article on Temporary Entry, Stay and Work of Investors and Key Personnel in section I of the report. The placement of these definitions in the Agreement could be considered at a later stage. It is understood that technical differences between MAI definitions and national definitions of these terms could be highlighted in country specific reservations.

[36] Three delegations reserve on the coverage of membership in boards of directors. Given the diversity of corporate governance rules across countries, it is proposed that the MAI rely on national definitions.

[37] It is understood that this article would not interfere with domestic anti-discrimination and labour laws.

PERFORMANCE REQUIREMENTS[38] [39]

1.   A Contracting Party shall not, in connection with the establishment, acquisition, expansion, management, operation, maintenance, use, enjoyment, sale or other disposition[40] of an investment in its territory of an investor of a Contracting Party or of a non-Contracting Party,

---

[38] One delegation reserves its position on all obligations on performance requirements that go beyond those in the TRIMS Agreement and the Energy Charter Treaty. Another delegation maintains a reserve on the prohibition of requirements listed in paragraph 1(a) through (e), when linked to an advantage. Another delegation maintains a reserve on the scope of the article. One delegation reserves its position on the scope of paragraphs 3 to 5 of this article.

[39] At the February 1998 consultations, One delegation proposed the following interpretative note to paragraph 1 of the Performance Requirements article as a possible solution to the concerns raised in footnotes 26,27, 29-32 and 37-39. This interpretative note could do away with the need for paragraphs 4 and 5(c) (both alternatives) and lead to the deletion of footnotes 26, 29-32 and 37-39. This proposal reads:

> *"The Contracting Parties agree that the Performance Requirements Article relates to requirements, undertakings and commitments which are directly imposed on or made by investors and/or their investments in connection with the investment. It does not intend to cover provisions applicable as the general law of the land governing in particular customs, trade or environment matters such as duties (including anti-dumping duties, preferential rates, origin rules) quantitative restrictions, safeguard measures, trade sanctions, measures necessary to protect human, animal or plant life or health or the conservation of living or non-living exhaustible natural resources.*
>
> *The Article is without prejudice to the rights and obligations of Contracting Parties under the WTO rules".*

Delegations agree to consider this proposal further. Some delegations expressed concern that use of the terms "in particular" and "such as" could result in an uncertain and overbroad carve out, which would undermine the article's coverage, perhaps even exempting any law of general application. Several delegations state their preference for recording this understanding in the form of an interpretative note rather than in a separate article since, in their view, an interpretative note would be more enlightening for arbitrators about the real intentions of negotiators. It would be very difficult, on the other hand, to draft an article that would translate faithfully this intention into legal text. A number of delegations wonder whether *"environment matters"* and *"measures necessary to protect human, animal or plant life or health or the conservation of living or non-living exhaustible natural resources"* should be covered by this note. This also relates to how these subjects would be treated elsewhere under the MAI (see also footnote 29). Some delegations propose the deletion of the phrase "intend to" at the beginning of the second sentence of this delegation's text to give greater precision to the proposed interpretative note.

One delegation restates its position that the Performance Requirements article should not apply to conditions imposed on an investment which are linked to cross-border trade (such as refunds, preferential rates, rules of origin, and anti-dumping duties). This could be made it clear in a separate indent to paragraph 2 (see footnote 27).

---

[40] A large majority of delegations consider that the enumeration of activities in the chapeau should closely follow the list of activities in the National Treatment/MFN articles to avoid any confusion over the meaning of any differences in the lists. They consider furthermore that there are no substantive grounds for the deletion of the terms "maintenance, use, enjoyment" since the implications for intellectual property rights are taken care of by the proposed carve-out in paragraph 1(f) and the consequences of keeping them as regards land assets are immaterial. It is noted that these are also arguments for not mentioning these terms in the chapeau. One delegation favours the deletion of these terms. Two delegations question the relevancy of the terms "sale or other disposition".

impose, enforce or maintain[41] any of the following requirements, or enforce any commitment or undertaking[42]:

    (a)   to export a given level or percentage of goods or services;

    (b)   to achieve a given level or percentage of domestic content;

    (c)   to purchase, use or accord a preference to goods produced or services[43] provided in its territory, or to purchase goods or services from persons in its territory;

    (d)   to relate in any way the volume or value of imports to the volume or value of exports or to the amount of foreign exchange inflows associated with such investment;

    (e)   to restrict sales of goods or services in its territory that such investment produces or provides by relating such sales to the volume or value of its exports or foreign exchange earnings;

    (f)   to transfer technology, a production process or other proprietary knowledge to a natural or legal person in its territory, except when the requirement

---

[41] One delegation reserves its position on the inclusion of the word "maintain". This delegation suggests that the use of this word could oblige Contracting Parties to undertake the burdensome task of having to expunge all possible non-conforming requirements from existing laws, regulations, contracts, etc. It should be sufficient, and less burdensome, for a Contracting Party to be obliged not to "impose" and "enforce" such requirements.

[42] One delegation presented an explanatory note on the formulation of NAFTA article 1106 which, in its view, is significantly clearer than the proposed MAI article on Performance Requirements. In order to improve on the MAI articles, this delegation proposes that the following phrase be added at the end of the chapeau of this paragraph: "or condition the receipt or continued receipt of an advantage on compliance with any of the following requirements". This addition is intended to make clear that the performance requirements article applies in two basic circumstances: *i)* when linked to the establishment, expansion, etc. of an investment; and *ii)* when linked to the granting of an advantage.

According to this delegation, unless expressly stated (as proposed) in paragraph 1, there may always be some uncertainty as to whether the article would apply in cases of granting an advantage. This delegation considers this addition necessary to provide greater certainty. As was the intention in the development of a "one list" approach in the MAI article, the proposed addition would, in the second case (linked to an advantage), limit prohibitions to "requirements" imposed by governments. Extending the prohibitions to only certain (but not all) "commitments and undertakings" would, according to this delegation, unduly interfere with government practices regarding "voluntary" commitments in exchange for an advantage and could result in a significant burden on Contracting Parties on lodging reservations for government-firm agreements containing "prohibited" voluntary undertakings.

The other delegations feel, however, that there is no need to modify the structure of the Article.

[43] It is understood that item (c) is not meant to cover the provision of cross-border services as defined under the GATS. It is felt that this understanding could be recorded by using the following language: *"This provision does not obligate a Contracting Party to permit cross-border trade in services beyond the obligations it has undertaken pursuant to GATS."* This understanding could also be part of a general provision in the Agreement concerning the relationship between the MAI and the GATS. One delegation reserves its position on the inclusion of "services" in 1(c) with respect to requirements associated with the granting of an advantage. It is noted that the relationship between the MAI and the GATS is an issue that could be addressed in a number of ways, including by way of individual footnotes.

-- is imposed or the commitment or undertaking is enforced by a court, administrative tribunal or competition authority to remedy an alleged violation of competition laws, or

-- concerns the transfer of intellectual property and is undertaken in a manner not inconsistent with the TRIPS Agreement;[44]

(g) to locate its headquarters for a specific region or the world market in the territory of that Contracting Party;[45]

(h) to supply one or more of the goods that it produces or the services that it provides to a specific region or the world market exclusively from the territory of that Contracting Party;

(i) to achieve a given level or value of research and development in its territory;[46]

(j) to hire a given level of nationals;[47]

(k) to establish a joint venture with domestic participation;[48] or

---

[44] The wording of this tiret is being elaborated in consultations with intellectual property experts. These experts have not agreed whether the current wording covers future IPRS and moral rights. It remains to be seen how the article will relate to other agreements such as the Rome and Berne Conventions. Paragraphs 1(b) and 1(c) may also have implications for IPRs. Some delegations note that a general provision for interpreting MAI obligations in a manner consistent with other obligations under international agreements would avoid the need for specific language for IPRs. It is understood that the concept of "proprietary knowledge" has a broader coverage than that of "trade secrets" or "undisclosed information" (see TRIPS Article 39) and can include information collected by an investor from publicly available sources by "the sweat of the brow".

[45] One delegation reserves its position on paragraph (g) and notes that the inclusion of (g) may inadvertently oblige Contracting Parties to lodge reservations in respect of basic business incorporation laws in so far as such laws oblige the establishment and/or maintenance of representative or head offices for legal purposes. It is noted that the prohibition is intended to apply to head offices or headquarters and not to the establishment of other offices.

[46] Two delegations maintain a scrutiny reserve on this paragraph while two other delegations maintain the view that paragraph (i) should be deleted.

[47] There is wide agreement to retain paragraph (j) with the inclusion of the following footnote with the same legal standing as the paragraph itself:

"Nothing in this paragraph shall be construed as interfering with programmes targeted at disadvantaged regions/persons or other equally legitimate employment policy programmes. It is also understood that permanent residency requirements are not inconsistent with this paragraph."

It is confirmed that this provision will not overlap with the MAI article on Employment Requirements since it is meant to cover specific performance requirements expressed in terms of given numbers or percentages of employees while the article on employment requirements addresses problems of discrimination among natural persons holding a valid permit of sejour and work in a given Contracting Party.

Two delegations continue to favour the deletion of paragraph (j).

[48] Paragraph (k) includes joint ventures even if not covered by paragraph 1(l) because they do not involve equity participation. It allows, however, joint venture requirements, not involving a requirement of domestic participation, which may be motivated by an economic concern to spread risk.

Some delegations, maintain a scrutiny reserve on paragraph (k) and (l) on the basis that they are covered by the National Treatment provision of the MAI.

(l)   to achieve a minimum level of domestic equity participation other than nominal qualifying shares for directors or incorporators of corporations. [49]

2.   A Contracting Party is not precluded by paragraph 1 from conditioning the receipt or continued receipt of an advantage, in connection with an investment in its territory of a Contracting Party or of a non-Contracting Party, on compliance with any of the requirements, commitments or undertakings set forth in paragraphs 1(f) through 1(l).[50] [51]

Some delegations point out to the difficulty of defining "joint-ventures". It is agreed to clarify in an interpretative note that *"Paragraphs 1(k) and (l) do not prevent a Contracting Party from establishing a joint venture in which it is the domestic participant itself"*. Italy points outs out it is most unlikely that the Contracting Party would be the participant in a joint venture and proposes the phrase *"a Contracting Party, a state agency or a state enterprise"*. It is also noted that Paragraph 2 of the Privatisation article states that "Nothing in this Agreement" shall be construed as imposing an obligation to privatise.

[49] The phrase "other than nominal qualifying shares for directors or incorporators of corporations" clarifies that this performance requirement will not be breached merely because members of boards of directors and those who establish a corporation (incorporators) may be required by domestic law, as a condition of that position, to hold a small equity participation in the corporation.

[50] It is understood that the receipt or continued receipt of an advantage with respect to paragraphs (k) and (l) will need to be granted on a non-discriminatory basis (provided that no country reservation has been lodged).

Several delegations consider that the concerns that paragraph 5(abis) intends to cover in respect of rights and obligations under the WTO agreements would better be addressed by the reinsertion of paragraph 1(a) in paragraph 2. This would avoid, in particular, confusion and overlap with respect to the dispute settlement provision of the MAI and the WTO. In that regard, some delegations note, in particular, a concern that if the extent of paragraph 1(a)'s disciplines were defined, [as proposed in one of the alternatives to paragraph, 5(a bis) (see footnote 34)], by reference to WTO Disciplines, then if paragraph 1(a) were to become a subject of MAI dispute settlement, the MAI arbital panel would have to determine whether a WTO violation had occurred, which would be an inappropriate role for it to undertake. Two delegations would also support a reference to paragraphs 1(b) and 1(c) in paragraph 2 to exclude the coverage of advantages associated with services from paragraph 1. Some delegations view adding paragraphs 1(b) and 1(c) to paragraph 2 as an undesirable "TRIMs-minus" solution because TRIMs covers paragraphs 1(b) and 1(c) with respect to goods in all circumstances. Other delegations consider that the reinsertion of any of these items would result in too much of a carve-out from paragraph 1 because this carve-out would apply across the board to all sectors or economic activities and not limited to the exclusions allowed under the WTO provisions. They favour instead a solution in the context of paragraph 5(a bis).

At the February 1998 consultations, a majority of delegations reiterated their preference for a solution along the more limited parameters of paragraph 5(a bis).

[51] In February 1998 , one delegation considered that the concerns with respect to paragraphs 4 and 5 could better be addressed by the addition of a second indent to paragraph 2. This indent could read:

" Requirements or obligations expressed in laws, regulations and other government measures of a general application concerning conditions of, or incentives linked to, cross-border trade on goods or services are not covered by paragraph 1. "

This provision could also be relevant for the understanding recorded in footnote 19 about the coverage of paragraph 1(c). Several delegations reserved their judgement on this proposal. It was recognised, however, that it could provide a way to avoid a problematic overlap between the dispute settlement procedures of the MAI and WTO which has been associated with an earlier proposal outlined in footnote 35. On the other hand, this would still constitute a limitation to investor-to-state dispute settlement.

---

3.   [ ]⁵²

4.⁵³   [Provided that such measures are not applied in an arbitrary or unjustifiable manner, or do not constitute a disguised restriction on investment, nothing in paragraphs 1(b) and 1(c) shall be construed to prevent any Contracting Party from adopting or maintaining measures, including environmental measures:

   (a)   necessary to secure compliance with laws and regulations that are not inconsistent with the provisions of this Agreement;

   (b)   necessary to protect human, animal or plant life or health;

   (c)   necessary for the conservation of living or non-living exhaustible natural resources.]^{54 55}

---

[52] It is agreed to transform the previous paragraph 3 in the special topics report into an interpretative footnote to paragraph 1 with the same legal standing and which reads:

"For the avoidance of doubt, nothing in paragraph 1(a), 1(b), 1(c), 1(d) and 1(e) shall be construed to prevent a Contracting Party from conditioning the receipt or continued receipt of an advantage, in connection with an investment in its territory of an investor of a Contracting Party or of a non-Contracting Party, on compliance with a requirement, commitment or undertaking to locate production, provide particular services, train or employ personnel, construct or expand particular facilities, or carry out research and development in its territory."

One delegation notes that the question of the status of footnotes and interpretative notes for the MAI remains to be determined.

[53] A majority of delegations see no need for paragraph 4. They consider that the proposed text is too broad, especially that of paragraph 4(a). Some delegations also wonder whether there is a need for an interpretative note. If there is such a need, a majority of delegations consider that it should be along the line proposed by one delegation which reads as follows:

"Provided that such measures are not applied in an arbitrary or unjustifiable manner, or do not constitute a disguised restriction on investment, nothing in paragraphs 1(b) and 1(c) shall be construed to prevent any Contracting Party from adopting or maintaining measures necessary to secure compliance with environmental laws and regulations [that are not otherwise inconsistent with the provisions of this Agreement and] that are necessary for the conservation of living or non-living resources, [or that are necessary to protect human, animal or plant life or health.]"

It is recognised that the Negotiating Group's general deliberations on environmental issues would provide guidance with regard to a solution regarding this paragraph. The retention of this paragraph may also depend on the final position of delegations concerning the proposals by two delegations outlined in footnotes 16 and 28 respectively.

[54] One delegation would like the words "within its jurisdiction" to be added to paragraph 4(c) to make it clear that this provision has no extra-territorial ramifications.

[55] One delegation believes that paragraph 4 is properly framed and that its scope should not be limited to environmental measures, which would be the consequence of another delegation's proposal. It suggests replacing the words "necessary for" by "relating to", which are used in article XX of GATT 1994. One delegation has withdrawn the example it provided in footnote 29 in the special topics report; the example did not describe a situation that would be disciplined by this article .

One delegation favours the retention of paragraph 4.

It is confirmed that no other general exceptions covered by Article XX of GATT 1994 would need to be covered by the proposed paragraph 4. The same confirmation is given with respect to Article XI of GATT 1994 on the General Elimination of Quantitative Restrictions.

5.[56] (a) Paragraphs 1(a), 1(b), and 1(c) do not apply to qualification requirements for goods or services with respect to export promotion[57] and foreign aid programmes;

[(a *bis*) Paragraph 1(a), 1(b), and 1(c) do not apply to:[58]

---

[56] Prior to the submission of its proposal in footnote 15, one delegation favoured the inclusion of the following header to paragraph 5: "Without prejudice to rights and obligations under the WTO" to ensure that the WTO obligations are not modified by the provision.

[57] One delegation suggests adding the word "and investment" after the word "export". It also suggests clarifying by means of an interpretative note the meaning of "promotion" for the purposes of this article.

[58] The obligations of the Performance Requirements article relate to requirements, undertakings and commitments that are directly imposed on or made by investors and their investments. In addition, they are not intended to discipline "advantages" as such. It is recognised that the performance requirements article raises questions about the relationship with the WTO Agreements, notably relating to agriculture, services and government procurement.

In this connection, it is agreed that the performance requirements article should not undo or undermine the Contracting Parties obligations under any WTO Agreements. It is also generally recognised that this article should not interfere with WTO rights and obligations in the agricultural sector. Some delegations consider in addition that the MAI should not attempt to discipline subsidies relating to services since this matter is presently being addressed in the WTO.

Paragraph 5(a bis) has been proposed as a way of addressing these concerns. Discussions on this proposal focused on: a) the need of specific reference to measures covered by WTO Agreements; b) the coverage of such a reference; and c) whether it could be a viable alternative to the inclusion of a reference of paragraph 1(a), and possibly paragraphs 1(b) and 1(c) in paragraph 2.

One delegation questions the need for subparagraph (5 abis) since the underlying problems could be addressed in country specific exceptions. One delegation questions the exclusion of the agriculture sector with respect to export performance requirements not linked to an advantage. It also wonders whether paragraph 5(a bis) would provide an exception for duty drawback programs outside the agriculture sector (e.g., chemicals).

Two delegations have proposed the following language as a possible alternative to paragraph 5(a bis):

"*Paragraphs 1(a), 1(b) and 1(c) do not apply to measures consistent with rights and obligations under the WTO Agreements.*" One delegation also proposes to limit the scope of this wording by adding the phrase "*if linked to an advantage*" at the end of this sentence.

While some delegations recognise that the proposals by these two delegations presented above could provide a technical solution, several delegations remain concerned about the reference to WTO disciplines which, as noted in footnote 27, could lead a MAI panel to pass judgement on WTO provisions. There is general agreement that a MAI panel should not be put in a situation of interpreting WTO disciplines. One delegation notes that under the safeguard provisions of the MAI, the IMF would be consulted in any MAI dispute settlement case involving a measure that the IMF approved or found to be consistent with the MAI. This delegation suggests that a similar solution could be found in the dispute settlement provisions of the MAI where it could be stated that WTO provisions can only be interpreted by WTO.

The following examples were provided to focus discussion on which cases should or should not be covered by the Performance Requirements article, so that the article's exclusions (paragraph 2) and exceptions (paragraph 5) can be drafted appropriately.

1. A Contracting Party screens investments:

(a) In connection with the establishment of a widget manufacturing plant, a Contracting Party imposes a requirement that the investor export 100 percent of the widgets produced.

(b) Same as 1(a), but the investor receives an advantage: no customs duties are imposed on manufacturing equipment or materials.

> > – [measures] [advantages] related to the production, processing and trade of agricultural and processed agricultural products[59];
>
> > – advantages related to trade[60] in services;]

> b) Paragraphs 1(b), 1(c), 1(f), and 1(h) do not apply to procurement by a Contracting Party or an entity that is owned or controlled by a Contracting Party;[61]

> [c] paragraphs 1(b) and 1(c) do not apply to requirements imposed by an importing Party relating to the content of goods necessary to qualify for preferential tariffs or preferential quotas.[62]]

> [c] Paragraphs 1(a), 1(b), 1(c) and 1(d) do not apply to customs duties, exemptions from such duties and preferential tariffs or to any trade measure regulating imports and exports provided that such measures are not applied in an arbitrary or unjustified manner, and do not constitute a disguised restriction on investment.[63]]

---

2. A Contracting Party allows any investor to establish a widget manufacturing plant:

(a) Any widget manufacturer may operate in an "export processing zone" but if it does so, it is required to export 100 per cent of the widgets produced in the zone. No customs duties are imposed on manufacturing equipment or materials that enter the zone.

(b) Any widget manufacturer may operate in an "export processing zone". No customs duties are imposed on manufacturing equipment or materials that enter the zone. Customs duties are imposed on any products produced in the zone that are sold within a Contracting Party's territory.

[59] A number of delegations would prefer the use of the more general term "measures" while other delegations would prefer the term "advantages" which is also used in the TRIMS Agreement. Two delegations question the need to extend the coverage of this indent to the production and processing of agricultural products and to processed agricultural products. One delegation proposes, on the other hand, that the indent also should be extended to apply to fisheries products including processed ones.

[60] One delegation suggests that the second indent of subparagraph 5(a bis) should apply as well to advantages linked to the provision of services and proposes the insertion of the words "the provision and" before the word " trade".

[61] It is agreed to add the following interpretative note:

"The Performance Requirements article does not affect any obligations that may exist under the WTO Government Procurement Agreement."

Two delegations consider that a reference to paragraph 1(i) may be needed if that paragraph is retained.

[62] One delegation provided the following example to illustrate the need for subparagraph (c).

"A French manufacturer of textiles located in the US manufactures and cuts cloth for garments in the US, sends it to a country eligible for the special programme (e.g., Jamaica), to be assembled into finished garments, and then re-imports the garments into the US for retail sale. The tariff rate on the re-imported garments is lower than on garments from other countries. Without the subparagraph 5(c) exception, subparagraphs 1(b) and 1(c) would prevent the US from offering the special access programme, which is consistent with existing international obligations. Many MAI countries have similar programmes."

Several other delegations believe that customs tariff issues fall outside the scope of this article and thus there is no need for the proposed general carve-out in subaragraph 5(c). There may also be a link with the issues raised with respect to paragraph (a).

[63] As indicated in footnote 15, one delegation considers that the Performance Requirements article should not apply to the general law of the land governing customs and trade.

PRIVATISATION[64]

Paragraph 1 (Application of National Treatment/MFN)

1.   The obligation on a Contracting Party to accord National Treatment and MFN treatment as defined in Paragraph XX (NT/MFN) applies to:

>   a)   all kinds of privatisation, irrespective of the method of privatisation (whether by public offering, direct sale or other method)[65]; and

>   b)   subsequent transactions involving a privatised asset.[66]

[Paragraph 1a (voucher schemes)

2.   Notwithstanding paragraph 1, arrangements under which natural persons of a Contracting Party are granted exclusive rights as regards the initial privatisation are acceptable as a method of privatisation under this Agreement provided that the exclusive right as regards the initial privatisation is limited to natural persons only and provided that there is no restriction on subsequent sales].[67]

Paragraph 2 (Right to privatise)

3.   Nothing in this Agreement shall be construed as imposing an obligation on a Contracting Party to privatise.[68]

Paragraph 3 (Special share arrangements)[69] [70]

---

[64] Four delegations reserve their position on all privatisation obligations.

[65] One delegation reserves its position.

[66] Four delegations reserve their position on sub-paragraph (b) as it goes beyond the scope of a privatisation article. Delegations agree that this provision does not apply to the behaviour of private entities (corporate practices). It is understood that the meaning of that provision is to prevent Contracting Parties from imposing rules on such secondary transactions which are inconsistent with NT/MFN. In the light of this, some delegations propose to include language along the lines of "b) measures governing subsequent ...". It is felt useful that legal experts examine the ultimate formulation of this provision on the basis of this understanding.

[67] One delegation is ready to withdraw this proposal if reference to vouchers schemes under paragraph 3, alternative 2, letter d, is deleted.

[68] Two delegations propose to insert "prejudice Contracting Parties' rules governing the system of property ownership or" between the words "shall" and "be".

[69] Work on paragraph 3 has been based on alternative 1, which is supported by a large number of delegations. However, one delegation maintains its preference for alternative 2. It cannot accept the phrase "are compatible with paragraph 1" (Alternative 1, paragraph 3) on the grounds of the implication that such special rules, regardless of how they are exercised, necessarily conform with NT/MFN. The use, application or exercise of such relevant measures under the tirets (alternative 1) may in fact not conform with NT/MFN. One delegation proposes the deletion of paragraph 3.

Alternative 1

4.   Contracting Parties acknowledge that special share arrangements are compatible with Paragraph 1, unless they explicitly or intentionally favour investors or investments of a Contracting Party or discriminate against investors or investments of another Contracting Party on the grounds of their nationality or permanent residency.[71]

Alternative 2[72]

5.   [Special share holding arrangements including, *inter alia*, a) the retention of "golden shares" by Contracting Parties, b) stable shareholder groups assembled by a Contracting Party, c) management/employee buyouts, and d) voucher schemes for members of the public, hold strong potential for discrimination against foreign investors and are, in fact, inconsistent with National Treatment and MFN treatment obligations in many instances.]

Alternative 3[73]

Footnote to paragraph 1

6.   Special share arrangements which explicitly discriminate (i.e. *de jure*) against foreign investors and their investment are contrary to obligations on National Treatment/MFN Treatment. It is also understood that when, in their application, special share arrangements lead to *de facto* discrimination they are also contrary to National Treatment/MFN Treatment.

[Alternative 4[74]

7.   Nothing in this Agreement shall prevent Contracting Parties from using special methods of privatisation or having special rules as regards ownership, management or control of privatised assets such as:

---

[70] It was recalled that the issue of providing the possibility for lodging reservations after the entry into force of the MAI concerning privatisations is under consideration in the Negotiating Group.

[71] One delegation would still prefer the inclusion of an illustrative list, such as contained in the Consolidated Text.

[72] One delegation's proposal, together with the following note: "As with other measures contrary to obligations on National Treatment and MFN treatment, use of special share arrangements should be subject to listing as reservations. Recognising that Contracting Parties may privatise assets in the future, Contracting Parties will be permitted to take precautionary reservations for the use of special share arrangements in those sectors where Contracting Parties generally have state-owned enterprises or government restrictions." This proposal was not discussed by the delegations.

[73] This language is put forward as a compromise. A number of delegations supporting alternative 1 state their willingness to accept this compromise pending the outcome of the discussions in the Negotiating Group on how to handle *de facto* discrimination in the context of lodging country specific reservations. One delegation suggests the insertion, after "investments" on the second line, of the words "on the ground of nationality"; of the word "intentionally" after "arrangements" on the third line; and, "on the ground of nationality", after "discrimination" on the same line. This delegation also suggests the inclusion of an illustrative list.

[74] This proposal by one delegation has not been discussed by delegations.

-- a Contracting Party or any person designated by the Contracting Party maintaining special shareholder rights to influence or veto any decision concerning such assets after the privatisation,

-- arrangements under which managers or other employees of an enterprise are granted special treatment as regards the acquisition of shares of that enterprise,

-- arrangements under which shareholders are required to maintain their share in the capital of the enterprise during a certain period of time,

-- arrangements under which locals of a certain community are granted special treatment as regards the acquisition of this community's property,

unless they explicitly or intentionally favour investors or investments of a Contracting Party or discriminate against investors or investments of another Contracting Party on the grounds of their nationality or permanent residency.]

Paragraph 4 (Transparency) [75]

8.   For the purposes of this Article, each Contracting Party or its designated agency shall promptly publish or otherwise make publicly available the essential features and procedures for participation in each prospective privatisation[76].*

*Footnote

This footnote confirms the application of the Transparency Article YY. This footnote also confirms that the obligations to accord National Treatment and MFN Treatment prohibit discrimination against investors and investments of other Contracting Parties with respect to all arrangements for making public information about a privatisation operation. It is also understood that there can be variance in the methods used to make information available, including in the case of small scale privatisations.

---

[75] One delegation reserves its position on the Transparency article. It considers that a principle of <u>parallelism</u> should guide the treatment of privatisation and that of concessions, which are two connected fields. It also considers the transparency obligations should apply to all levels of government. This delegation therefore conditions its agreement concerning the insertion of a transparency clause for privatisation to the inclusion of a similar clause for concessions.

[76] It is understood that the obligation of this article will be met wherever the information on a privatisation operation is made available. One delegation notes that there is a need for discussion of the potential implications of the proposed transparency provision for legitimate financial market transactions. This delegation proposes the addition of the following interpretative note: "It is understood that paragraph 4 does not place any obligation on a Contracting Party to take actions that could prejudice respect for, or compliance with, the requirements of securities and exchange laws." While several delegations did not need this clarification, they did not oppose that it be added to the Agreement as an interpretative note.

Paragraph 5 (Definition)

9.   Privatisation means the sale by a Contracting Party, in part or in full, of its equity interests[77] in any entity[78] or other disposal having substantially the same effect.*

> *   This definition:
>
> –   does not cover transactions between different levels or entities of the same Contracting Party;
> –   excludes transactions in the normal conduct of business.[79]

MONOPOLIES/STATE ENTERPRISES/CONCESSIONS

A.   Article on Monopolies[80]

1.   Nothing in this Agreement shall be construed to prevent a Contracting Party from maintaining, designating or eliminating a monopoly.[81]

2.   Each Contracting Party shall [endeavour to][82] accord non-discriminatory treatment when designating a monopoly.

---

[77] One delegation considered that the sale of the assets of a state company such as the sale of a division of an entity are to be covered by the definition. It also felt that it was necessary to replace the term "equity interests" by "ownership interests" to clarify the scope of the definition. Another delegation would have preferred to return to the previous definition but could accept the alternative wording "equity or other interests". Another delegation reserved on the phrase "or other disposal having substantially the same effect".

[78] One delegation is of the view that the word "entity" should be qualified by the addition of "it owns or controls through ownership interests."

[79] It is understood that transactions by entities created for the purpose of the sale or other disposal of a Contracting Party's equity interests in an entity are captured by the revised definition in accordance with the MAI Article on entities with delegated governmental authority (See section VIII).

[80] One delegation reserves its position on all obligations on monopolies that go beyond those of the GATT and GATS.

[81] It is understood that paragraph 1 is without prejudice to the article on Expropriation and Compensation. One delegation continues to believe that "Agreement" should be replaced with "Article" but will consider this proposal for an interpretative note that would be an integral part of the Agreement.

[82] Delegations remain divided on the desirability of removing these brackets. One delegation is linking the issue on the inclusion of the inclusion into the MAI of special provisions on concessions; it is also linking it on the definition of monopolies (see footnote 81).

A large part of the discussion in February 1998 focused on a draft alternative text splitting paragraph 2 in the two following paragraphs:

> "2. Each Contracting Party shall endeavour to accord non-discriminatory treatment when designating a publicly-owned monopoly.
>
> 3. Each Contracting Party shall accord non discriminatory treatment when designating a privately-owned monopoly."

Leaving aside the question of the definition of monopolies and the problems of distinguishing between privately-owned and publicly-owned monopolies, several delegations reacted favourably to the proposed

3.   Each Contracting Party shall ensure that any privately-owned monopoly that its national [or subnational] governments [maintain][83] or designate and any public monopoly that its national [or subnational] governments maintain or designate:

Subparagraph a)

a)   provides non-discriminatory treatment to investments of investors of another Contracting Party in its supply of the monopoly good or service in the relevant market;

Subparagraph b)

b)   provides non-discriminatory treatment to investments of investors of another Contracting Party in its purchase of the monopoly good or service in the relevant

---

differentiation in the nature of the obligations for the designation of publicly-owned monopolies (best endeavour) and the designation of privately-owned monopolies. Some delegations feel that paragraph 2 is self-evident and would not therefore be necessary. One delegation indicates that it could agree to a best endeavour undertaking but only for "government monopolies" (for instance the establishment of a government department or entity to provide a new service to the public). It therefore favours a National Treatment obligation for the designation of other types of publicly-owned monopolies (like state enterprises). Italy proposes to replace the words " Contracting Party" by the words "Contracting Party, state agency or state enterprise".

A majority of delegations feel that non-discriminatory treatment should be provided, in any case, when the designation of monopoly involves an investor of a Contracting Party other than the Contracting Party itself (for instance a private investor or public investor of another Contracting Party or another state). In other words, National Treatment should apply when the designation of a monopoly is subject to a competitive process. Delegations were invited to reflect whether the following text would adequately translate this thought:

"Each Contracting Party shall accord non-discriminatory treatment when designating a monopoly, when such designation involves an investor of a Contracting Party other than the Contracting Party itself".

Some delegations are unsure about the meaning of the terms "involves". Other delegations wonder whether "emanations" from the Contracting Party itself should be excluded from the bidding process and whether this should be made explicit in the text. Some other delegations felt that local authorities (such as municipalities) should be allowed to participate in a competitive procedure. Some other delegations considered that the proposal still leaves too much discretion to the government in the designation of public monopolies.

An alternative proposal has since been circulated to delegations.

A few delegations continued to favour a best endeavour clause for both situations (the designation of a publicly-owned and privately-owned monopoly) and proposed the deletion of the brackets in paragraph 2 of the draft text.

[83] One delegation considers that all the provisions of the Monopoly article should not apply to monopolies at subnational levels of government. It also has difficulties with the inclusion of the term "maintains" since this could create disciplines with respect to existing contracts between the government and such privately-owned monopolies and have general ramifications on the rights of existing shareholders. One delegation considers that the disciplines of paragraph 3 should not apply to monopolies designated by subnational authorities. Other delegations consider it essential that monopolies designated by subnational authorities should be covered by the disciplines. They recognise that the reference to national and subnational governments is also related to the coverage of the monopoly definition (see footnote 74) and more broadly to the solution found for the general treatment of subnational entities under the MAI.

---

market. This paragraph does not apply to procurement by governmental agencies of goods or services for government purposes and not with a view to commercial resale or with a view to use in the production of goods or services for commercial sale;[84]

Subparagraph c)

Alternative 1[85]

c)   does not abuse its monopoly position, in a non-monopolised market in its territory, to engage, either directly or indirectly, including through its dealing with its parent company, its subsidiary or other enterprise with common ownership, in anticompetitive practices that adversely affect [an investor or][86] an investment by an investor of another Contracting Party, including through the discriminatory provision of the monopoly good or service, cross-subsidisation or predatory conduct.[87]

Alternative 2:   zero option[88]

[Subparagraph d)[89]

---

[84] One delegation raises the issue of the treatment of sub-contracting of monopoly activities.

[85] This draft article originally proposed by one delegation is supported by several delegations.   Another delegation notes that the reference to "anti-competitive practices" should not be problematic since the GATS contains obligations with respect to anti-competitive practices as an integral part of the GATS agreement on basic telecommunications (cf. GATS Telecoms Reference Paper).

[86] The inclusion of the term "investor" would confirm the application of subparagraph (c) to the pre-establishment phase. Some delegations indicate that their support for Alternative 1 is conditional upon the coverage of the pre-establishment phase. A number of delegations note, however, that this coverage could also create problems with respect to the dispute settlement provisions of the MAI and consider that it should not be retained.

[87] One delegation could agree to the deletion of the phrase "in particular through the abusive use of prices" on the understanding that this practice was covered by the terms "predatory conduct". Another delegation considers that the term "abusive use of prices" has a broader coverage than the concept of anti-competitive practices.

[88] The zero option is supported by some delegations to avoid undue intrusion into the competition policy field. A number of these delegations support, as a fallback position, the inclusion of a subparagraph (c) based on article VIII of the GATS which reads as follows:

"c) which competes, either directly or indirectly, or through an affiliated company, in an economic activity outside the scope of its monopoly rights does not abuse its monopoly position in that activity to act in a manner inconsistent with the obligations of this Agreement;"

One delegation considers that this proposal adds little in substance to the Monopoly article and could even be politically counterproductive.

[89] A large majority of delegations are in favour of the deletion of subparagraph (d) and the following two paragraphs. One delegation is prepared to accept the removal of subparagraph (d) provided that these two paragraphs are maintained as interpretative notes. Two delegations, which are proponents of subparagraph (d) in its entirety, wish to maintain their position for inclusion in the article.

One delegation provides a number of explanations in favour of the inclusion of subparagraph (d). In its view, sub-paragraph (d) would present the advantage of increasing transparency: non-commercial considerations must be both non-discriminatory [as indicated in (a), and (b)] and must be clearly stated in terms of its designation. (Note, however, that if a government wants to continue to pursue social and other non-economic objectives, it can still do so through the designation.)   Sub-paragraph (d) would also clarify that outside the terms of a monopoly's [d) Except to comply with any terms of its designation that are not inconsistent with subparagraph (a) or (b), acts solely in accordance with commercial considerations in its purchase or sale of the monopoly good or service in the relevant market, including with regard to price, quality, availability, marketability, transportation and other terms and conditions of purchase or sale.]

[Nothing in Article A shall be construed to prevent a monopoly from charging different prices in different geographic markets, where such differences are based on normal commercial considerations, such as taking account of supply and demand conditions in those markets.[90]

Article A, paragraphs 3(c) and 3(d) differences in pricing between classes of customers, between affiliated and non-affiliated firms, and cross-subsidisation are not in themselves inconsistent with this provision; rather, they are subject to this subparagraph when they are used as instruments of anti-competitive behaviour by the monopoly firm].[91]

4.   Each Contracting Party is allowed to lodge a reservation to the Agreement concerning an activity previously monopolised at the moment of the elimination of the monopoly.][92]

5.   Each Contracting Party shall notify[93] to the Parties Group any existing designated monopoly within [60][94] days after the entry into force of the Agreement, any newly designated

---

designation, a monopoly should act in accordance with commercial considerations just like any other enterprise (i.e. that it not use its monopoly power to influence the market). This is, in the view of this delegation, particularly important given the potential power of monopolies over markets in the context of accession. Finally, the proposed language in the two notes would make it clear that charging different prices to different customers, for example, might be justified on the basis of commercial considerations. Consideration could be given to a definition of "commercial considerations" along the lines of the accepted wording in GATT Article XVII.

Many delegations remain sceptical, however, about the feasibility and desirability of requiring monopolies to act in accordance with "commercial considerations".

[90] Delegations discussed whether this paragraph should be maintained as an interpretative note, particularly in case subparagraph (d) is deleted. One delegation considers that this clarification has a bearing on all the provisions of paragraph 3, particularly subparagraph 3(a). Another delegation is of the view that the only relevant link with other subparagraphs, with the exception of subparagraph d), is to subparagraph (a). In this context, subparagraph (d) is not necessary because of the general understanding that the non-discrimination principle in subparagraph (a) is limited to "like circumstances" thereby allowing for differentiation on the basis of commercial considerations. While other delegations did not exclude a possible link to other subparagraphs, for example subparagraph (b), they support its deletion.

[91] A large majority are of the view that the clarification intended by this paragraph is not necessary, especially if subparagraph d) is deleted. One delegation considers that this explanatory paragraph is also relevant to subparagraph 3(c).

[92] Proposal by one delegation. Some delegations are opposed to the principle of lodging country exceptions after into force of the MAI. Another delegation proposes that such reservations be made the subject of scrutiny by the "Parties Group" to ensure that they do not negatively affect the level of liberalisation under the MAI.

[93] One delegation suggests that the concept of prior notification found in Article VIII.4 of the GATS should also be examined and that the Parties Group should have a role in examining all notifications resulting from this article.

[94] It is suggested that the period of three months, which is the notification period for monopolies under paragraph VIII.4 of the GATS, could be an alternative. The length of the notification period could also be decided in light of other notification requirements that might arise under the Agreement. One delegation points out to the difficulty it would have in notifying the very large number of monopolies designated by subnational authorities. It is agreed

monopoly within [60] days after its creation, and any elimination of a designated monopoly [and related new reservation to the Agreement] [95] within [60] days after its elimination.

[6.   Neither investors of another Contracting Party nor their investments may have recourse to investor-state arbitration for any matter arising out of paragraph 3 of this Article.][96]

[B.   Article on [state enterprises][entities with which a Government has a specific relationship]

i)   Zero option. [97]

ii)   *Additional provisions*

a. *Proposal by two delegations*[98]

[1.   Each Contracting Party shall ensure that any state enterprise that it maintains or establishes accords non-discriminatory treatment in the sale, in the Contracting Party's territory, of its goods or services to investors of another Contracting Party and their investments.

2.   Neither investors of another Contracting Party nor their investments may have recourse to investor-state arbitration for any matter arising out of paragraph 2 of this Article.[99]]

---

that a solution needs to be found to the practical problem that the Contracting Parties may encounter with respect to the designation of every single monopoly designated at a subnational level authority. It is suggested that the alternative approach found in the Energy Charter to notify a summary of the types of monopolies under the jurisdiction of subnational levels of government could be considered. One delegation does not agree that this paragraph applies with respect to subnational governments.

[95] The issue of notification of monopolies is also linked to the question dealt with under paragraph 4 of this Article.

[96] Three delegations point to the novelty and complexity of the proposed provisions on monopolies, which argue in favour of limiting the dispute settlement procedures to state-to-state disputes. They also believe that most governments do not even allow private "anti-trust" actions in their own courts by their citizens; thus it would be a leap to suggest that there be privately-initiated scrutiny of monopolies' anti-competitive actions pursuant to 3(c). These delegations consider that state-to-state dispute settlement should provide a useful procedural compromise. Many delegations consider, however, this paragraph should be deleted as they believe that Contracting Parties should only sign up to commitments that they would be prepared to defend against individual investors.

[97]A large majority of delegations support this option, particularly since the anti-circumvention clause in Section VIII is intended to cover all enterprises, *i.e.* both state and private enterprises, to which authority has been granted .

A number of delegations underline the legal and practical difficulties that governments would encounter in ensuring the conformity of the behaviour of state enterprises and all their affiliates with the obligations of additional provisions, such as those proposed by two delegations.

[98] Two delegations believe that the need for such provisions is predicated by the fact that state enterprises are different from private enterprises because of the links with governmental authorities. They felt that the term "state enterprise" could be replaced by "an enterprise that it owns or controls".

One delegations points out that under existing legislation in their country, the state as a shareholder has no special privilege in comparison with any other shareholder. This would require legislative action.

[99] Some delegations point out that this paragraph would be needed whichever alternative is chosen. Other delegations consider that any additional disciplines that might be adopted would need to be subject to both state-to-state and investor-to-state dispute settlement. One delegation would like this paragraph to apply to both paragraph 1 and the article on Entities with Delegated Governmental Authority.

b. *Proposal by one delegation* [100]

[1.   Each Contracting Party shall ensure that any entity that a national or a subnational government owns or controls through ownership interest or which a national or subnational governments authority has a relationship with through any specific legislative, regulatory or administrative act, any contracts, or any practices related to some of its activities acts in a manner that is not inconsistent with the Contracting Party's obligations under this Agreement in connection with these activities.]]

C.   Definitions Related to Articles on Monopolies [and State Enterprises]

1.   "Delegation" means a legislative grant, and a government order, directive or other act transferring to the monopoly or state enterprise, or authorising the exercise by the monopoly or state enterprise of, governmental authority.

2.   "Designate" means to establish or authorise, or to expand the scope of a monopoly. [101]

3.   "Monopoly" means any person or entity designated by a [national [or subnational] [102] government authority] [Contracting Party] as the sole supplier or buyer of a good or service in a relevant market in the territory of a Contracting Party . It does not include a person or entity that has an exclusive intellectual property right solely by reason of such right or the exercise of such right [103] [104].

---

[100] This proposal is offered as a compromise by one delegation which favours, nevertheless, Option (a) (*i.e.* no additional provisions) as its first option. It is meant to cover all possible avenues for exercising influence other than government ownership (such as through the granting of contracts to private enterprises). This proposal did not receive broad support.

[101] One delegation maintains a scrutiny reserve on this paragraph which is also related to the coverage of the chapeau of paragraph 3 of the article on monopolies.

[102] A large majority of delegations consider that, in substance, the MAI disciplines on monopolies should apply to all levels of governments. This could be achieved in a number of ways. The preferred option by most delegations holding this view is the second bracketed text "Contracting Party". This would present the advantage of ensuring consistency with the coverage of this term across the Agreement. Other delegations remain of the opinion, however, that the most secure way to capture all designated monopolies would be to have a specific reference to subnational authorities in the definition. One delegation suggests the alternative wording of "the competent authority of a Contracting Party"; this language is considered to be a promising compromise for delegations supporting the broadest definition of monopolies and should be discussed further. One delegation could accept the deletion of the reference to "national or subnational government" on the understanding that a reference would be made in paragraph 3 in Section A that it does not apply to subnational monopolies. Another delegation favours a definition limited to monopolies designated by national governments and suggests the deletion of the reference to "subnational" authorities".

[103] There is agreement that the definition of monopolies should explicitly exclude exclusive rights derived agreed by intellectual property rights. The present wording takes into account drafting changes in the Intellectual Property Experts Group. These experts would also like to add at the end of the second sentence the following bracketed text. Such an addition would read "[nor does it include an entity charged with the collective management of intellectual property rights]". This phrase would exclude royalty collection agencies (which sometimes have a legal monopoly).

Some delegations reserve their position pending the outcome, *inter alia*, of the discussion on the relationship between monopolies and concessions, authorisations, etc.

4.   "Relevant market" means the geographic and product market for a good or service in the territory of the Contracting Party.[105]

---

[104] Delegations agree to delete the bracketed text at the end of the second sentence : "[nor does it include a person or entity that has an exclusive right such as concession, license, authorisation or permit.].   France agreement's is subject to a satisfactory solution to the drafting of paragraph 2 of draft article on monopolies based on the various alternatives outlined in footnote 59. It is also based on the understanding, that France would like to see recorded as a new sentence at the end of the monopoly definition that "this definition encompasses a person or entity which has been granted exclusive rights such as concessions, licenses, authorisations or permits. This understanding was not agreed, at least as written.   One delegation mentioned the usefulness of distinguishing between the granting of exclusive rights for the access to a resource (mineral resource, the use of the radioelectric spectrum) from those exclusive rights given for the marketing of a good in its relevant market (such as the right to sell gasoline). In this delegation's view, the exclusivity in the first case does not necessarily give monopoly rights (there could be more than one transmitter of telephone signals using different parts of the readioelectric spectrum or several exploiters of mineral resources using different mine sites°. In the second case, however, an exclusive right to commercialise a good in the relevant market constitutes a monopoly because this right is given expressly to one person or entity in a given market).

There is a broad consensus that, in conformity with item (vii) of the MAI definition of "investment", any rights conferred pursuant to law or contract such as concessions, licenses, authorisations, and permits are to be covered fully by the obligations of the MAI. Several delegations also share the view that any person or entity which acquires monopoly rights as a result of the implementation of such law or contract should also fulfil the obligations of paragraph 3 of the Monopoly article in the exercise of such rights. These delegations disagree , however, on how or whether to translate these understandings into text.

Some delegations are opposed to the inclusion of concessions into the monopoly definition; they consider that these are two different legal concepts which should be treated separately under the MAI. Accordingly, one delegation considers that the bracketed text at the end of the second sentence of the definition of monopoly "nor does it include a person or entity that has an exclusive right such as concession, license, authorisation or permit" should be maintained. One delegation also considers that monopolies and concessions are different legal entities. However, the exclusion of concessions from this definition would imply too much of a carve-out for the MAI. This is the reasoning behind the various attempts made by this delegation (footnote 54) to ensure the highest level of obligations possible in these two areas. Ideally, in this delegation's view, the problem of the interface between monopolies and concessions should be solved in the definition itself; this could be done adopting the legal approach embodied in articles 90-91 of the EC Treaty which covers both exclusive rights (i.e. monopolies) and special rights.

Delegations are invited to reflect further on these issues.

[105]   Some delegations propose the inclusion of the word "commercial" before "goods and services" to clarify, in particular, that the "relevant markets" for monopolies would not include government services such as the delivery of passports or driving licenses. A majority of delegations also recognises that the inclusion of the terms "in the territory of the Contracting Party" at the end of the paragraph presents the advantage of giving greater precision to the concept of "relevant market", also used in paragraphs 3(a) and 3(b) of article A on monopolies. The inclusion of these terms would also do away with the need for making a similar reference in paragraph 3 on the definition of "Monopoly".

One delegation is of the view that the proposed definition needs to be improved for greater precision and clarity. Another delegation draws the attention to the fact that the concept of "relevant market" has been discussed in the OECD Competition Policy Committee and that the result of this work should be taken into account.

One delegation proposes to add the following sentences after "Contracting Party": "A product market for a good or a service covers that good or service and its close substitutes. A product or service is a close substitute of another product or service when a small but significant increase in the price of the other product or service, all other prices remaining equal, leads to a significant increase in the demand for the first product or service." This delegation argues that this definition will be useful to narrow down the definition of monopoly and will exclude from it those firms that although have been granted exclusive rights compete in the market against other firms producing close substitutes. Other delegations point out that the notion of close substitutes is normally included in national competition policies and consider the addition by this delegation unnecessary.

5.   "Non-discriminatory treatment" means the better of national treatment and most favoured nation treatment, as set out in the relevant provisions of this Agreement.[106]

[6.   "State enterprises" means, [subject to Annex ....,] an enterprise owned, or controlled through ownership interest, by a Contracting Party.][107]

[D.   Article on Concessions[108] [109]
Transparency

The procedure for granting a concession[110] must envisage, at least, one publication in a journal of official notices.   The notice must contain all the relevant information about the purpose and nature of the activity subject to concession, its conditions and deadline.   The publication must be made sufficiently in advance in order to enable all interested persons to submit applications or additional relevant information.   The reasons for the rejection of an application will be made known to the applicant upon request.]

---

[106]   Three delegations question the need for this definition.

[107]   A number of delegations question the need for a definition of state enterprises.

[108]   This draft article reproduces a compromise proposal by one delegation after it became clear that the revised proposal by another delegation found in section VI.D of the special topics report did not attract sufficient support to serve as a basis for discussing specific transparency provisions on concessions. This proposal is intended to establish transparency requisites when granting a concession. In no case it intends to establish an obligation for the Contracting Parties in relation to the type of procedure to followed when granting a concession. Accordingly, it covers the possibility of granting concessions through tender as well as non-tender procedures. Some delegations feel that an article along these lines could be useful when the government takes the initiative of announcing that an activity is open to an application for a concession.

Several delegations continue to question the need for an additional article to the general Transparency article of the MAI. Some of these delegations note that the procedures for the award of concessions are defined by their domestic legislations. Some delegations note that their domestic legal regime does not provide for a tendering process for the granting of concessions. A few delegations remain opposed to the inclusion of any article on concessions, whatever its form or content . One delegation stresses the link between disciplines on concessions and disciplines on monopolies (see footnotes 54 and 80).

Some delegations see some parallelism between a Transparency article for concessions and the Transparency article envisaged for Privatisation in section V of the report. The Chairman invites delegations sharing this view to explore how this Privatisation Transparency article could be modified or adapted for concessions.

[109]   One delegation provided a background note on natural resources and concessions in the context of the MAI.

[110]   One delegation would prefer the phrase "concession contract" instead of the word "concession".

[*Definition*[111]

1.   A concession is any delegation, direct or indirect, which entails a transferring of operation of activities, carried out by a government authority, national or subnational, or any public or para-public authority[, to a distinct and independent legal entity].

2.   The delegation shall be realised either by any laws, regulations, administrative rulings or established policies, or by any private or public contract. The aim of the delegation is to entrust to a distinct [and independent] legal body with the operation of public services, including the operation of networks or infrastructures, or the exploitation of natural resources[112] and if needed with the construction of all or part of networks or infrastructures.

3.   [If necessary: The legal act of delegation includes the modes of payment to the investor. These modes of payment can consist of any price paid by consumers, any royalty, tax licence, subsidy or contribution from the delegatory authority, or any combination of the modes]].

[VII.   ARTICLE ON THE GRANTING OF AUTHORISATIONS FOR THE PROSPECTION, EXPLOITATION AND PRODUCTION OF MINERALS, INCLUDING HYDROCARBONS[113] [114]

---

[111]   This definition reproduces a draft proposal by one delegation, supported by another delegation (provided that concessions are explicitly excluded from the definition of monopoly -- see footnote 80), as amended by this delegation in January 1998 (the changes are bracketed in paragraphs 1 and 2). This draft definition has never been discussed at length by delegations. It is recognised that the need for it would arise only if the MAI were to include special transparency provisions on concessions. It is recognised that the elaboration of a definition for concessions could be a rather difficult task given the different coverage of this concept in national legislations.

[112]   One delegation proposes the deletion of the reference to natural resources

[113]   Proposal by one delegation. This delegation also proposes to add to paragraph (vii) of the current definition of "investment" in the MAI, the following language with respect to mineral resources, including hydrocarbons resources:

> " -- Rights conferred pursuant to law or contract regarding property ownership over mineral resources, including hydrocarbon resources;

> -- rights conferred pursuant to any law, regulation, administrative or contractual provision or instrument issued thereunder by which the competent authorities of a Contracting Party entitle an investor or a group of investors to exercise, on its own behalf and at its own risk, the exclusive right to prospect for or explore for or produce minerals, including hydrocarbons, in a geographical area."

[114]   There is general agreement that the MAI obligations (NT, MFN, Performance Requirements...) should apply fully to the granting of authorisations for the prospection, exploitation and production of minerals, including hydrocarbons . This is also valid for any rights granted in connection with the prospection, exploitation and production of any other natural resources. Views differ, however, as to whether additional language, along the lines that proposed by one delegation or another formulation, need to be incorporated into the MAI to confirm this understanding.

Some delegations are prepared to work on the basis of the text provided some amendments are made to it. One delegation suggests replacing the word " authorisation" by the word "concessions" which would corresponds more accurately to this delegation's legal situation as well to that of other countries. Some delegations consider that the words "To the extent that the measures are consistent with the Agreement" would convey greater certainty as to the consistency of the proposed article with other MAI provisions that the words "Consistent with the present Agreement," appearing at the beginning of paragraph 2. Some delegations wonder if the reference to state participation in sup-paragraph 2(c) is all that necessary; some other delegations consider, that other conditions or requirements may need to be mentioned. Several delegations are of the view that paragraph 3 could create confusion

"(1)   For the purpose of the present Article, "authorisation" means any law, regulation, administrative or contractual provision or instrument issued thereunder by which the competent authorities of a Contracting Party entitle any investor or a group of investors to exercise, on its own behalf and on its own risk, the exclusive right to prospect or explore for or produce minerals, including hydrocarbons, in a geographical area.

(2)   Consistent with the present Agreement, the Contracting Parties may establish:

(a)   procedures to be followed for the granting of authorisations according to which all interested investors may submit applications pursuant to this article[115];

(b)   criteria on the basis of which authorisations are granted;

(c)   conditions and requirements, including requirement of state participation, concerning the exercise or termination of the activities of prospecting, exploring for and producing minerals, including hydrocarbons, whether contained in the authorisation or to be accepted prior to the grant of the authorisation.

(3)   The Contracting Parties shall apply such procedures, criteria, conditions and requirements as referred to in paragraph (2) above in a transparent and objective manner and in a way which ensures that there is no discrimination on grounds of nationality between investors as regards access to and exercise of the activities of prospecting, exploring for and producing minerals, including hydrocarbons.]

---

as the applicability of the National Treatment/MFN obligations and support its deletion. In their view, the operative part of the article should be limited to the paragraph 2. Other delegations see value in referring specifically to the these obligations in the paragraph to avoid potential problems of interpretation of the MAI obligations to the granting of authorisations, concessions, etc. in the future. One delegation suggests the addition of the words " when granting the authorisation s" at the end of paragraph 3.

Drawing on the approach elaborated under the draft privatisation article, some delegations propose a two - pronged alternative solution which would a) recognise the sovereign rights of the State over the country's natural resources while b) confirming the full applicability of the MAI obligations at the time of the granting to MAI investors and their investments of any specific right under a concession, license, authorisation or permit concerning the prospection, exploitation or production of all natural resources, including hydrocarbons or minerals.

[115]   One delegation proposes to delete the last part of the sentence "according to which all interested investors may submit applications pursuant to this article" since the wording of this phrase implies that when a Contracting Party has procedures for the granting of authorisation, these procedures must involve a tender process.

ENTITIES WITH DELEGATED GOVERNMENTAL AUTHORITY[116]

Each Contracting Party shall ensure that any entity to which it has delegated a regulatory, administrative or other governmental authority acts in a manner that is not inconsistent with the Contracting Party's obligations under this Agreement wherever such entity exercises that delegated authority.

INVESTMENT INCENTIVES

Provisions

Alternative 1

Several delegations believe that no additional text is necessary. They consider that the current draft articles in the MAI are sufficient to cover investment incentives at this time.

Alternative 2

Many delegations, however, would favour specific provisions on incentives in the MAI although they hold different views as to their nature and scope. Some proposed a built-in agenda for future work. Discussion of possible provisions focused on the following draft article which is regarded as a compromise text by those who would still prefer more far-reaching disciplines.

Article [117]

1.   The Contracting Parties confirm that Article XX (on NT and MFN) and Article XX (Transparency) applies to [the granting of][118] investment incentives. [119]

2.   [The Contracting Parties acknowledge that[, in certain circumstances,] even if applied on a non-discriminatory basis, investment incentives may have distorting effects on the flow of capital

---

[116] This article covers <u>all</u> entities, including monopolies and state enterprises, with respect to the exercise of any delegated regulatory, administrative or other governmental authority. This provision renders the need for a provision on this subject under the Monopolies article unnecessary. Paragraph 3(a) in the special topics report could accordingly be deleted. One delegation can only consider this provision if its concern relating to the chapeau of the Monopoly Article (see footnote 59) could be adequately covered and, secondly, points out that the Vienna Convention of the Law of Treaties may, in the view of this delegation, make this provision redundant.

Several delegations consider it essential that the proposed anti-circumvention clause apply to monopolies designated by subnational authorities. It is recognised, however, that this matter is linked to the general treatment of subnational entities under the MAI.

[117] The Group proceeded on the basis of report of EG2 with respect to the treatment of tax incentives.

[118] Some delegations favour the deletion of "the granting of".

[119] While it is agreed that investment incentives should be subject to NT and MFN obligations, there are different views on the desirability of making this explicit. Consequently, some delegations consider this paragraph to be unnecessary. One delegation maintains a pre-scrutiny reservation on the text of this draft article. The dispute settlement mechanism would, in particular, apply to this article. One delegation raises the possibility of taking reservations with regard to NT.

and investment decisions.[120] [Any Contracting Party which considers that its investors or their investments are adversely affected by an investment incentive adopted by another Contracting Party and having a distorting effect, may request consultations with that Contracting Party.] [The former Contracting Party may also bring the incentive before the Parties Group for its consideration.]] [121] [122]

3.[123] [In order to further avoid and minimise such distorting effects and to avoid undue competition between Contracting Parties in order to attract or retain investments, the Contracting Parties [shall] enter into negotiations with a view to establishing additional MAI disciplines [within three years] after the signature of this Agreement.[124] These negotiations shall recognise the role of investment incentives with regard to the aims of policies, such as regional, structural, social, environmental or R&D policies of the Contracting Parties, and other work of a similar nature undertaken in other fora. These negotiations shall, in particular, address the issues of positive discrimination,[125] [transparency[126]], standstill and rollback[127].]

4. [For the purpose of this Article, an "investment incentive" means:

The grant of a specific advantage arising from public expenditure [a financial contribution] in connection with the establishment, acquisition, expansion, management, operation or conduct of an investment of a Contracting Party or a non-Contracting Party in its territory].

---

[120] Several delegations point out that not all investment incentives are bad -- the problem arises in drawing a line between good and bad incentives. It is suggested that the distorting effects of investment incentives on investment decisions and capital flows should be balanced against their possible benefits in achieving legitimate social objectives. Other delegations note that these concerns were addressed in paragraph 3 of the draft article.

[121] Some Delegations remain unconvinced by the need for special consultation procedures for non-discriminatory investment incentives as defined in paragraph 2, although final judgement would need to await the decisions taken on the coverage of the MAI. The presumption is that, as with other agreements, consultations would be the first procedural step of the dispute settlement mechanism of the MAI. It should be possible to revisit the adequacy of the provisions on dispute settlement and the role of the Parties Group when their configuration is better known. One delegation questions whether the dispute settlement mechanism of the MAI could apply to investment distorting investment incentives or to investment incentives granted illegally. These questions would also deserve further attention. Some delegations question the role of the parties group in any consultation process.

[122] One delegation suggests the first sentence of paragraph 3 could be added to paragraph 4, and the rest of paragraph 3 deleted.

[123] The form and placement of this text would have to be decided.

[124] Some delegations feel that the MAI should include additional disciplines on investment incentives from the time it enters into force. Another delegation cautions that additional disciplines could have far-reaching implications for other multilateral agreements as well as for national tax laws and regulatory regimes.

[125] Some delegations express the view that positive discrimination should be prohibited and this should be placed in the text.

[126] One delegation considers the transparency Article of the MAI would already be sufficient.

[127] Some delegations consider it very difficult to recommend future negotiations without agreement on their nature and scope.

RECOGNITION ARRANGEMENTS [128]

AUTHORISATION PROCEDURES [129]

MEMBERSHIP OF SELF-REGULATORY BODIES [130]

INTELLECTUAL PROPERTY

Intellectual property issues are being examined by intellectual property experts. The most recent status of discussions is reproduced here.

Transfers[131]

Agreed: text on collective management charges should be added to the first sentence in paragraph 2 of the Commentary on Transfers after "purposes": ", or any authorised deduction by an entity charged with collective management of intellectual property rights."

Not agreed: whether the modified paragraph should remain in the Commentary or be placed in the text of the Agreement.

Monopolies[132]

Agreed: the definition of "monopoly" should be amended to refine the definition's treatment of intellectual property rights:

"Monopoly" means any person or entity designated by a [national [or subnational] government authority] [Contracting Party] as the sole supplier or buyer of a good or service in a relevant market in the territory of a Contracting Party, but does not include a person or entity that has an exclusive intellectual property right, concession, licence authorisation or permit solely by reason of such right or exercise of such right [nor does it include an entity charged with the collective management of intellectual property rights].

Not agreed: as indicated by the final bracketed phrase, whether entities charged with collective management of IPRs should also be excluded from the definition.

---

[128] See Commentary.

[129] See Commentary.

[130] See Commentary.

[131] See Section IV, below.

[132] See Section III, above.

Performance Requirements[133]

Agreed: paragraph 1(f) in the Article on Performance Requirements requires explicit reference to the transfer of IPRs. Not agreed:

(a)   whether the current wording of paragraph 1(f) adequately covers future IPRs and moral rights; and

(b)   whether paragraphs 1(b) and (c) of the Article on Performance Requirements have an impact on IPRs.

Expropriation[134]

Agreed: text is needed to ensure that certain IP management and legal provisions do not constitute expropriation.

Not agreed: flowing from proposed text:

"The creation, limitation, revocation, annulment, statutory licensing, compulsory licensing and compulsory collective management of IPRs, the withholding of authorised deductions by an entity charged with the collective management of IPRs, and the sharing of remuneration between different holders of IPRs are not expropriation within the terms of this agreement, to the extent that they are not inconsistent with specialised IPR conventions."

(a)   whether there should be a specific IP text or reliance on a general text clarifying that expropriation does not include normal government regulatory activity;

(b)   whether and how the statement should be qualified;

(c)   whether that list of actions should be exhaustive or illustrative;

(d)   whether the current wording adequately covers future rights;

(e)   whether the question of consistency with IPR agreements should be worded positively;

(f)   whether a specific IP text should be in the text of the Agreement, in an interpretative footnote or in the Commentary; and

(g)   whether the word "creation" adequately covers the intended concept.

---

[133]   See Section III, above.

[134]   See Section IV, below.

National Treatment and MFN Treatment[135] and General Treatment[136]

Agreed: MAI obligations should not extend NT/MFN obligations in existing IP agreements.

Not agreed:

(a)   whether there should be a NT/MFN exception through a link to existing IP agreements;

(b)   whether there should be a NT/MFN exception to MAI obligations for IPRs;

(c)   whether the eventual solution should also be applied to the General Treatment articles; and

(d)   the applicability of the MAI obligations with respect to future IPRs.

Definitions of "Investment" and "Investor"[137]

Agreed: there needs to be clarification of the definition of "investment". The required clarification is tied to the resolution of the eventual substantial MAI obligations for IPRs.

Not agreed:

(a)   whether the definition of "investment" should be limited to those IPRs included in the TRIPS Agreement;

(b)   whether it should exclude copyrights and related rights;

(c)   whether it should include future IPRs;

(d)   whether it should include only the "economic aspects" of IPRs;

(e)   whether it should include only those rights provided domestically; and

(f)   what implications the definition of "investor" has for an IP "rightsholder".

Dispute Settlement[138]

Agreed: IP experts wish to limit forum shopping and conflicting jurisprudence with the WTO.

---

[135] See Section III, above

[136] See Section IV, below.

[137] See Section II, above.

[138] See Section V, below.

Not agreed:

(a) how to achieve these goals;

(b) the desirability of applying investor-state dispute settlement to IPRs; and

(c) whether the existing MFN obligations in the TRIPS Agreement create the risk of "free-riders".

Information Transfers and Data Processing[139]

Agreed: there are concerns that the text of the generalisation of financial services (see Information Transfer and Data Processing, page 57) has implications for IPRs, and may have to be amended or deleted to take these concerns into account.

Exhaustion of Rights

Not agreed: whether there needs to be any language on this issue to ensure that the MAI does not create new obligations in this area.

PUBLIC DEBT [140]

CORPORATE PRACTICES [141]

TECHNOLOGY R&D [142]

NOT LOWERING STANDARDS (LABOUR AND ENVIRONMENT)[143] [144] [145]

---

[139] See Section IV, below.

[140] See Commentary.

[141] The Chairman concluded that there is full agreement that government-imposed discriminatory practices would be covered by the MAI. In view of the views expressed by a clear majority of delegations, the MAI should not contain disciplines on non-government imposed discriminatory corporate practices. However, Contracting Parties to the MAI should follow future developments in this area and could take up the matter again if the need arises.

[142] See Commentary.

[143] Three delegations continue to oppose any reference to a "not lowering standards" article on labour. One delegation thinks the issue of "not lowering standards" in the environmental area would be more appropriately dealt with in the context of a general article on investment incentives.

[144] One delegation anticipates presenting proposed text based on its *Draft Position Paper on "Labour and the Environment" (Regarding "not lowering standards")* presented to the High Level Meeting on 16 February 1998.

[145] One delegation suggests that any alternative referring to the term "domestic labour standards" should be accompanied by a definition of that term so as to ensure a common understanding of its meaning within the agreement.

Alternative 1

[The Parties recognise that it is inappropriate to encourage investment by lowering [domestic] health, safety or environmental [standards] [measures][146] or relaxing [domestic] [core][147] labour standards.[148] Accordingly, a Party should not waive or otherwise derogate from, or offer to waive or otherwise derogate from, such [standards] [measures] as an encouragement for the establishment, acquisition, expansion or retention in its territory of an investment of an investor. If a Party considers that another Party has offered such an encouragement, it may request consultations with the other Party and the two Parties shall consult with a view to avoiding any such encouragement.]

Alternative 2

[A Contracting Party [shall] [should][149] not waive or otherwise derogate from, or offer to waive or otherwise derogate from [domestic] health, safety or environmental [measures] [standards] or [domestic] [core] labour standards as an encouragement for the establishment, acquisition, expansion or retention of an investment of an investor.]

Alternative 3[150]

[1.   The Parties recognise that it is inappropriate to encourage investment by lowering domestic health, safety or environmental measures or relaxing international core labour standards.

2.   A Contracting Party [shall] [should] accord to investors of another Contracting Party and their investments treatment no more favourable than it accords its own investors by waving or otherwise derogating from, or offering to waive or otherwise derogate from domestic health, safety, environmental or labour measures, with respect to the establishment, acquisition,

---

[146] If "measure" is preferred, then the word "lowering" should be replaced by "relaxing". In either case, the term selected should be defined. For reference purposes, delegations mentioned the definition of "measure" in NAFTA or to be found in the Transparency Article of the and the definition of "standard" in NAFTA and in the WTO Agreement on Technical Barriers to Trade.

[147] Delegations note that no universally accepted definitions existed for "core" or "domestic" standards. Most delegations prefer "domestic" which was recognised to be wider in scope.

[148] A major difference of view as between Alternative 1 and Alternative 2 concerns the first sentence of Alternative 1. This sentence is part of a difference of approach as to whether the provision should refer to respect for universal standards or only to the relaxation of domestic standards. Views differ on whether this sentence is useful or necessary.

[149] If "should" were preferred, it might be desirable to add the last sentence of Alternative 1. Those preferring "should" argued that use of the word "shall" would prevent the authorities offering necessary waivers under domestic law, for example, to help resolve a specific case of damage to the environment and might prevent resolution of particular cases through consultations and persuasion. They also express concern that "shall" might expose the authorities to dispute settlement challenge. One delegation expresses concern over the use of the broader phrase "domestic labour" standards with recourse to dispute settlement in that it could create disputes under the MAI over changes in programmes relating to minimum wages or retirement qualifications; this delegation questions if this is what is intended by this provision. Those preferring "shall" argued that the purpose of this Article is to prohibit a waiver or derogation only if used as an encouragement to an investment.

[150] Proposal of one delegation.

expansion, operation, management, maintenance, use, enjoyment and sale or other disposition of an investment.

3.   A Contracting Party [shall] [should] not take any measure which derogates from, or offer to derogate from, international health, safety or environmental laws or international core labour standards as an encouragement for investment on its territory.]

Alternative 4 (Environment Only)[151]

[1.   The Parties recognise that it is inappropriate to encourage investment by relaxing health, safety or environmental measures.

2.   Accordingly, a Contracting Party shall accord to investors of another Contracting Party and their investments treatment no more favourable than it accords to its own investors and their investments by waving or otherwise derogating from, or offering to waive or otherwise derogate from health, safety environmental measures, with respect to the establishment, acquisition, expansion, operation, management, maintenance, use, enjoyment and sale or other disposition of investments.

3.   In addition, a Contracting Party should not encourage investment by lowering its health, safety and environmental standards in general. If a Party considers that another Party has offered such an encouragement, it may request consultations with the other Party and the two Parties shall consult with a view to avoiding any such encouragement.]

PROPOSED "ADDITIONAL CLAUSE" ON LABOUR AND ENVIRONMENT [152]

---

[151] Proposal of one delegation.

[152] One delegation proposes to delete paragraph 4 of the existing text on performance requirements and add a general exception article:

   Subject to the requirement that such measures are not applied in a manner which would constitute a means of arbitrary or unjustifiable discrimination or a disguised restriction on investment, nothing in this agreement shall be construed to prevent the adoption, maintaining or enforcement by any Contracting party of measures:

   (a) necessary to protect human, animal or plant life or health

   (b) relating to the conservation of living or non-living exhaustible natural resources.

   One delegation proposes as a general article the text of NAFTA Article 1114(1) with a second paragraph to address investment outflows:

   Nothing in this agreement shall be construed to prevent a Contracting Party from adopting, maintaining or enforcing any measure otherwise consistent with this Agreement that it considers appropriate to ensure that investment activity in its territory is undertaken in a manner sensitive to environmental concerns.

   Likewise, no Contracting party shall adopt, maintain or enforce any environmental measure in a manner which would constitute a disguised restriction for investment outflows from that Contracting Party to another Contracting party, or for investment among Contracting parties.

   The "Package of Additional Environmental Proposals" presented to the Negotiating Group on 14 January 1998 also proposes the language of NAFTA Article 1114(1).

IV. INVESTMENT PROTECTION

1. GENERAL TREATMENT [153]

1.1.   Each Contracting Party shall accord to investments in its territory of investors of another Contracting Party fair and equitable treatment and full and constant protection and security. In no case shall a Contracting Party accord treatment less favourable than that required by international law.

1.2.   A Contracting Party shall not impair by [unreasonable or discriminatory] [unreasonable and discriminatory] measures the operation, management, maintenance, use, enjoyment or disposal of investments in its territory of investors of another Contracting Party.

2. EXPROPRIATION AND COMPENSATION

2.1.   A Contracting Party shall not expropriate or nationalise directly or indirectly an investment in its territory of an investor of another Contracting Party or take any measure or measures having equivalent effect (hereinafter referred to as "expropriation") except:

  a)   for a purpose which is in the public interest,

  b)   on a non-discriminatory basis,

  c)   in accordance with due process of law, and

  d)   accompanied by payment of prompt, adequate and effective compensation in accordance with Articles 2.2 to 2.5 below.

2.2.   Compensation shall be paid without delay.

2.3.   Compensation shall be equivalent to the fair market value of the expropriated investment immediately before the expropriation occurred. The fair market value shall not reflect any change in value occurring because the expropriation had become publicly known earlier.

2.4.   Compensation shall be fully realisable and freely transferable.

2.5.   [Compensation shall include interest at a commercial rate established on a market basis for the currency of payment from the date of expropriation until the date of actual payment.][154]

---

[153]   One delegation proposes to delete Article 1.2 and revise Article 1.1 as follows:

"Each Contracting Party shall accord to investments in its territory of investors of another Contracting Party fair and equitable treatment and full and constant protection and security. Such treatment shall also apply to the operation, management, maintenance, use, enjoyment or disposal of such investments. In no such case shall a Contracting Party accord treatment less favourable than that required by international law."

[154]   DG3 has identified four options for calculating compensation which are set out in the commentary. The Negotiating Group Chairman has noted that a large majority are in favour of having no explicit provision in the

2.6.   Due process of law includes, in particular, the right of an investor of a Contracting Party which claims to be affected by expropriation by another Contracting Party to prompt review of its case, including the valuation of its investment and the payment of compensation in accordance with the provisions of this article, by a judicial authority or another competent and independent authority of the latter Contracting Party.

3.   *PROTECTION FROM STRIFE*

3.1.   An investor of a Contracting Party which has suffered losses relating to its investment in the territory of another Contracting Party due to war or to other armed conflict, state of emergency, revolution, insurrection, civil disturbance, or any other similar event in the territory of the latter Contracting Party, shall be accorded by the latter Contracting Party, as regards restitution, indemnification, compensation or any other settlement, treatment no less favourable than that which it accords to its own investors or to investors of any third State, whichever is most favourable to the investor.

3.2.   Notwithstanding Article 3.1, an investor of a Contracting Party which, in any of the situations referred to in that paragraph, suffers a loss in the territory of another Contracting Party resulting from

(a)   requisitioning of its investment or part thereof by the latter's forces or authorities, or

(b)   destruction of its investment or part thereof by the latter's forces or authorities, which was not required by the necessity of the situation,

shall be accorded by the latter Contracting Party restitution or compensation which in either case shall be prompt, adequate and effective and, with respect to compensation, shall be in accordance with Articles 2.1 to 2.5.

4.   *TRANSFERS*

4.1.   Each Contracting Party shall ensure that all payments relating to an investment in its territory of an investor of another Contracting Party may be freely transferred into and out of its territory without delay. Such transfers shall include, in particular, though not exclusively :

a)   the initial capital and additional amounts to maintain or increase an investment ;

b)   returns;155

c)   payments made under a contract including a loan agreement;

MAI addressing this issue. However, to respond to the concerns of some countries that this approach might lead to uncertainty, the MAI could contain an interpretative note providing that in the case of undue delay in the payment of compensation on the part of a Contracting Party, any exchange rate loss arising from this delay should be borne by the host country.

[155]   As defined in the Article on definitions.

---

d)   proceeds from the sale or liquidation of all or any part of an investment ;

e)   payments of compensation under Articles 2 and 3;

f)   payments arising out of the settlement of a dispute;

g)   earnings and other remuneration of personnel engaged from abroad in connection with an investment.

4.2.   Each Contracting Party shall further ensure that such transfers may be made in a freely convertible[156] currency. [Freely convertible currency means a currency which is widely traded in international foreign exchange markets and widely used in international transactions.] or [Freely convertible currency means a currency which is, in fact, widely used to make payments for international transactions and is widely traded in the principal exchange markets].

4.3.   Each Contracting Party shall also further ensure that such transfers may be made at the market rate of exchange prevailing on the date of transfer.

[4.4.   In the absence of a market for foreign exchange, the rate to be used shall be the most recent exchange rate for conversion of currencies into Special Drawing Rights.]

4.5.   Notwithstanding Article 4.1(b) above, a Contracting Party may restrict the transfer of a return in kind in circumstances where the Contracting Party is permitted under the GATT 1994 to restrict or prohibit the exportation or the sale for export of the product constituting the return in kind. Nevertheless, a Contracting Party shall ensure that transfers of returns in kind may be effected as authorised or specified in an investment agreement, investment authorisation, or other written agreement between the Contracting Party and an investor or investment of another Contracting Party.[157]

4.6.[158]   Notwithstanding paragraphs 1 to 5 of this Article, a Contracting Party may delay or prevent a transfer through the equitable, non-discriminatory and good faith application of measures:

(a)   to protect the rights of creditors,

(b)   relating to or ensuring compliance with laws and regulations

(i)   on the issuing, trading and dealing in securities, futures and derivatives,

(ii)   concerning reports or records of transfers, or

---

[156] The agreement of one delegation in Article 4.2 on the deletion of "usable" and acceptance of the word "convertible" supposes agreement on its definition and on Article 4.6.

[157] One delegation has difficulties with the obligations referred to in the second sentence.

[158] This version of paragraph 4.6 was refined by DG3 taking account of earlier proposals by financial experts.

(c)   in connection with criminal offences and orders or judgements in administrative and adjudicatory proceedings;

provided that such measures and their application shall not be used as a means of avoiding the Contracting Party's commitments or obligations under the Agreement.[159]

5.   *INFORMATION TRANSFER AND DATA PROCESSING* [160]

1.   No Contracting Party shall take measures that prevent transfers of information or the processing of information outside the territory of a Contracting Party, including transfers of data by electronic means, where such transfer of information or processing of information is:

a)   necessary for the conduct of the ordinary business of an enterprise located in a Contracting Party that is the investment of an investor of another Contracting Party; or

b)   in connection with the purchase or sale by an enterprise located in a Contracting Party that is the investment of an investor of another Contracting Party of:

i)   data processing services; or

ii)   information, including information provided to or by third parties.

2.   Nothing in paragraph 1:

a)   affects the enterprise's obligation to comply with any record keeping and reporting requirements; or

b)   restricts the right of a Contracting Party to protect privacy, including the protection of personal data, intellectual and industrial property, and the confidentiality of individual records and accounts, so long as such right is not used to circumvent the provisions of the Agreement.

6.   *SUBROGATION*

If a Contracting Party or its designated agency makes a payment under an indemnity, guarantee or contract of insurance[161] given in respect of an investment of an investor in the

---

[159] Some DG3 delegations consider that if the footer were to be deleted and included in a MAI general anti-abuse clause, the need to re-introduce a more specific footer, such as the one proposed by one delegation, "provided that such measures and their application shall not unreasonably impair the free and undelayed transfer ensured by this Agreement", may have to be considered.

[160] DG3 recommends adoption of this generalised text after taking account of the text earlier by financial experts.

[161] Two delegations cannot agree to deletion of the words "non-commercial risks" at this stage.

territory of another Contracting Party, the latter Contracting Party shall recognise the assignment of any right or claim of such investor to the former Contracting Party or its designated agency and the right of the former Contracting Party or its designated agency to exercise by virtue of subrogation any such right and claim to the same extent as its predecessor in title.[162]

7.   *PROTECTING EXISTING INVESTMENTS*

[This Agreement shall apply to investments made prior to its entry into force for the Contracting Parties concerned [consistent with the legislation of the Contracting Party in whose territory it was made] as well as investments made thereafter. This Agreement shall not apply to claims arising out of events which occurred, or to claims which had been settled, prior to its entry into force.] or [This Agreement shall apply to investments existing at the time of entry into force as well as to those established or acquired thereafter.]

V.   DISPUTE SETTLEMENT [163]

STATE-STATE PROCEDURES

A.   *GENERAL PROVISIONS*

1.   The rules and procedures set out in Articles A-C shall apply to the avoidance of conflicts and the resolution of disputes between Contracting Parties regarding the interpretation or application of the Agreement unless the disputing parties agree to apply other rules or procedures. However, the disputing parties may not depart from any obligation regarding notification of the Parties Group and the right of Parties to present views, under Article B, paragraphs 1.a and 4.c, and Article C, paragraphs 1.a, 4, and 6.e.

2.   Contracting Parties and other participants in proceedings shall protect any confidential or proprietary information which may be revealed in the course of proceedings under Articles B and C and which is designated as such by the Party providing the information. Contracting Parties and other participants in the proceedings may not reveal such information without written authorisation from the Party which provided it.

3.   [EC or Contracting Party REIO text being developed for possible inclusion]

---

[162] One delegation has difficulties with the obligations in this paragraph.

[163] Note: It is understood that for a number of delegations further work is needed on dispute settlement. In particular, different options remain in the field of multilateral consultations and scope of dispute settlement. The present text has been prepared by the Chairman of the Expert Group on Dispute Settlement on the basis of the discussions in the Group. It is under consideration by the Negotiating Group.

B.   *CONSULTATION, CONCILIATION AND MEDIATION*

1.   Consultations

a.   One or more Contracting Parties may request any other Contracting Party to enter into consultations regarding any dispute between them about the interpretation or application of the Agreement. The request shall be submitted in writing and shall provide sufficient information to understand the basis for the request, including identification of any actions at issue. The requested Party shall enter into consultations within thirty days of receipt of the request. The requesting Contracting Party shall provide the Parties Group with a copy of the request for consultation, at the time it submits the request to the other Contracting Party.

b. A Contracting Party may not initiate arbitration against another Contracting Party under Article C of this Agreement unless the former Contracting Party has requested consultation and has afforded that other Contracting Party a consultation period of no less than 60 days after the date of the receipt of the request.

2.   Multilateral Consultations

a.   In the event that consultations under paragraph 1 of this Article have failed to resolve the dispute within 60 days after the date of receipt of the request for those consultations, the Contracting Parties in dispute may, by agreement, request the Parties Group to consider the matter.

b.   Such request shall be submitted in writing and shall give the reason for it, including identification of any actions at issue, and shall indicate the legal basis for the complaint.

c.   The Parties Group may make recommendations to the Contracting Parties in dispute. The Parties Group shall conclude its deliberations within 60 days after the date of receipt of the request

3.   Mediation or Conciliation

If the Parties are unable to reach a mutually satisfactory resolution of a matter through consultations, they may have recourse to good offices or to mediation or conciliation under such rules and procedures as they may agree.

4.   Confidentiality of Proceedings, Notification of Results

a.   Proceedings involving consultations, mediation or conciliation shall be confidential.

b.   No Contracting Party may, in any binding legal proceedings, invoke or rely upon any statement made or position taken by another Contracting Party in consultations, conciliation or mediation proceedings initiated under this Agreement, with the exception of factual representations.

c. The Parties to consultations, mediation, or conciliation under this Agreement shall inform the Parties Group of any mutually agreed solution.

C. *ARBITRATION*

1. Scope and Initiation of Proceedings

a. Any dispute between Contracting Parties as to whether one of them has acted in contravention of this Agreement shall, at the request of any Contracting Party that is a party to the dispute and has complied with the consultations requirements of Article B, be submitted to an arbitral tribunal for decision. A request, identifying the matters in dispute, shall be delivered to the other Party through diplomatic channels, unless that Contracting Party has designated another channel for receipt of notification and so notified the Depositary, and a copy of the request shall be delivered to the Parties Group.

b. A Contracting Party may not initiate proceedings under this Article for a dispute which its investor has submitted, or consented to submit, to arbitration under Article D, unless the other Contracting Party has failed to abide by and comply with the award rendered in that dispute or those proceedings have terminated without resolution by an arbitral tribunal of the investor's claim.

c. If a dispute arises between Contracting Parties as to whether one of them has acted in contravention of a substantially similar obligation of that Contracting Party under this Agreement and another agreement to which both are party, the complaining Contracting Party may submit it for decision under the agreement of its choice. In doing so, it waives its right to submit the matter for decision under the agreement not chosen.

2. Formation of the Tribunal

a. Within 30 days after receipt of a request for arbitration, the Parties to the dispute shall appoint by agreement three members of the tribunal and designate one of them as Chairman. Except for compelling reasons, the members shall be persons proposed by the Secretary General ICSID. At the option of either party or, where there is more than one Party on the same side of the dispute, either side, two additional members may be appointed, one by each party or side.

b. If the necessary appointments have not been made within the periods specified in subparagraph a, above, either Party or side to the dispute may, in the absence of any other agreement, invite the Secretary General of the Centre for the Settlement of Investment Disputes to make the necessary appointments. The Secretary-General shall do so, to the extent feasible, in consultations with the Parties to the dispute and within thirty days after receipt of the request.

c. Parties and the Secretary-General should consider appointment to the tribunal of members of the roster maintained pursuant to subparagraph f, below. If arbitration of a dispute is considered by either Contracting Party to the dispute or the Secretary-General to require special expertise on the tribunal, rather than solely through expert advice under the rules governing the arbitration, the appointment of individuals possessing expertise not found on the roster should be considered.

d. Members of a particular arbitral tribunal shall be independent and impartial.

e. Any vacancies which may arise in a tribunal shall be filled by the procedure by which the original appointment had been made.

f. The Parties Group shall maintain a roster of highly qualified individuals willing and able to serve on arbitral tribunals under this Agreement. Each Contracting Party may nominate up to four persons who shall be included as members of the roster. Nominations are valid for five year terms. At the end of a term, the Contracting Party which nominated a member may renew the nomination or nominate a new member of the roster. A member shall withdraw from the roster if no longer willing or able to serve and the Contracting Party which nominated that member may nominate another member for a full term.

3. Consolidation

a. Contracting Parties in dispute with the same Contracting Party over the same matter should act together as far as practicable for purposes of dispute settlement under this Article. Where more than one Contracting Party requests the submission to an arbitral tribunal of a dispute with the same Contracting Party relating to the same question, a single arbitral tribunal should be established to consider such disputes whenever feasible.

b. To the extent feasible, if more than one arbitral tribunal is formed, the same persons shall be appointed as members of both and the timetables of the proceedings shall be harmonised.

4. Third Parties

Any Contracting Party wishing to do so shall be given an opportunity to present its views orally or in writing to the arbitral tribunal on the issues of a legal nature in dispute. Such a Contracting Party shall be given access to the documents of the proceedings, other than confidential or proprietary information designated under Article A, paragraph 2. The tribunal shall establish the deadlines for such submissions in light of the schedule of the proceedings and shall notify such deadlines, at least thirty days in advance thereof, to the Parties Group.

5. Scientific and Technical Expertise

a. On request of a disputing Contracting Party or, unless the disputing Contracting Parties disapprove, on its own initiative, the tribunal may request a written report of a scientific or technical review board, or expert, on any factual issue concerning environmental, health, safety or other scientific or technical matters raised by a disputing Contracting Party in a proceeding, subject to such terms and conditions as such Parties may agree.

b. The board, or expert, shall be selected by the tribunal from among highly qualified, independent experts in the scientific or technical matters, after consultations with the disputing Parties and the scientific or technical bodies identified by those Parties.

c. The disputing Contracting Parties shall be provided:

    i. advance notice of, and an opportunity to provide comments to the tribunal on the proposed factual issues to be referred to the board, or expert; and

    ii. a copy of the board's, or expert's, report and an opportunity to provide comments on the report to the tribunal.

d. The tribunal shall take the report and any comments by the disputing Contracting Parties on the report into account in the preparation of its award.

6. Proceedings and Awards

a. The tribunal shall decide disputes in accordance with this Agreement, interpreted and applied in accordance with the applicable rules of international law.

b. The tribunal may, at the request of a Party, recommend provisional measures which either Party should take to avoid serious prejudice to the other pending its final award.

c. The tribunal, in its award, shall set out its findings of law and fact, together with the reasons therefore, and may, at the request of a Party, award the following forms of relief:

    i. a declaration that an action of a Party is in contravention of its obligations under this Agreement;

    ii. a recommendation that a Party bring its actions into conformity with its obligations under the Agreement;

    iii. pecuniary compensation for any loss or damage to the requesting Party's investor or its investment; and

iv.   any other form of relief to which the Party against whom the award is made consents, including restitution in kind to an investor.

d.   The tribunal shall draft its award consistently with the requirement of confidentiality set out in Article A, paragraph 2. It shall issue its award in provisional form to the Parties to the dispute on a confidential basis, as a general rule within 180 days after the date of formation of the tribunal. The parties to the dispute may, within 30 days thereafter, submit written comment upon any portion of it. The tribunal shall consider such submissions, may solicit additional written comments of the parties, and shall issue its final award within 15 days after closure of the comment period.

e.   The tribunal shall promptly transmit a copy of its final award to the Parties Group, which shall make it publicly available.

f.   Tribunal awards shall be final and binding between the parties to the dispute, subject to paragraph 7 below.

g.   Each party shall pay the cost of its representation in the proceedings. The costs of the tribunal shall be paid for equally by the Parties unless the tribunal directs that they be shared differently. Fees and expenses payable to tribunal members will be subject to schedules established by the Parties Group and in force at the time of the constitution of the tribunal.

7.   Nullification

a.   Either party to the dispute may request the annulment of an award, in whole or in part, on one or more of the following grounds, that:

i.   the Tribunal was not properly constituted;

ii.   the Tribunal has manifestly exceeded its powers;

iii.   there was corruption on the part of a member of the Tribunal or on the part of a person providing decisive expertise or evidence;

iv.   there has been a serious departure from a fundamental rule of procedure; or

v.   he award has failed to state the reasons on which it is based.

b.   The request shall be submitted for decision by a tribunal which shall be constituted and operate under the rules applicable to a dispute submitted under paragraph 1 of this article .

c.   Such a request must be submitted within 120 days after the date on which the award was rendered or after the discovery of the facts relevant to nullification on the grounds of corruption, whichever is later and, in any event, within five years after the date on which the award was rendered.

d. The tribunal may nullify the award in whole or in part. If the award is nullified, the fact of nullification shall be communicated to the Parties Group. In such a case, the dispute may be submitted for decision to a new tribunal constituted under this Article or to any other available forum, notwithstanding the Contracting Parties waiver under paragraph 1.c. of this article.

8. Default Rules

The PCA Optional Rules for Arbitrating Disputes between Two States shall apply to supplement provisions of these Articles. The Parties Group may adopt supplemental provisions to ensure the smooth functioning of these rules, in particular to clarify the inter-relationship between these rules and the PCA Optional Rules.

9. Response to Non-compliance[164]

a. If a Contracting Party fails within a reasonable period of time to comply with its obligations as determined in the award, such Contracting Party shall, at the request of any Contracting Party in whose favour the award was rendered, enter into consultations with a view to reaching a mutually acceptable solution. If no satisfactory solution has been agreed within thirty days after the date of the request for consultations, any Contracting Party in whose favour the award was rendered, shall notify the other Contracting Party and the Parties Group if it intends to [take measures in response][suspend the application to the other Contracting Party of obligations under this agreement].

b. The effect of any such [responsive measures][suspension] must be proportionate to the effect of the other Party's non-compliance.[165] Such measures may not include suspension of the application of Article[s _ (General Treatment) and] _ (Expropriation) [and should not include denial of other protections to established investment].

c. At the request of any Party to the award upon conclusion of the thirty day period for consultation, the Parties Group shall consider the matter. [Until twenty days after the receipt by the Parties Group Secretariat of the request, responsive measures shall not be taken.] The Parties Group may:

    i. make recommendations, by consensus minus the disputing Contracting Parties;

---

[164] Note: The text in paragraph 9 has been circulated separately. The Commentary indicates the general state of development on this issue in informal consultations at expert level.

[165] As variant of this approach, one delegation suggests utilizing language based on the WTO agreements:

"The level of the suspension of benefits ... shall be equivalent to the level of the nullification or impairment of benefits, which the aggrieved Party reasonably expected to accrue to it, resulting from the non-compliance."

ii.   suspend the non-complying Party's right to participate in decisions of the Parties Group, by consensus minus the non-complying Contracting Party; and

iii.   [by consensus minus the Contracting Party which had intended to take responsive measures, decide that some or all of the responsive measures shall not be taken. The Contracting Party shall comply with that decision.]

d.   Any dispute concerning the alleged failure of a Contracting Party to comply with its obligations as determined in an award or the lawfulness of any responsive measures shall, at the request of any Contracting Party that is party to the dispute, be submitted for decision to the arbitral tribunal which rendered the award or, if the original tribunal is unavailable, to a single member or three member arbitral tribunal designated by the Secretary-General. The request shall be submitted in the same fashion, and the proceedings carried out in accordance with the same rules as are applicable to a request made under paragraph 1.a of this Article, with such modifications as the tribunal deems appropriate, and the final award shall be issued no later than 60 days after the date of the request, in case of the original tribunal, or after the date of its formation, in the case of a new tribunal. [No responsive measures may be taken from the time of submission of a dispute unless authorised by the tribunal as an interim measure or found lawful.]

INVESTOR-STATE PROCEDURES

D.   *DISPUTES BETWEEN AN INVESTOR AND A CONTRACTING PARTY*

1.   Scope and Standing

a.   This article applies to disputes between a Contracting Party and an investor of another Contracting Party concerning an alleged breach of an obligation of the former under this Agreement which causes loss or damage to the investor or its investment.

b.   An investor of another Contracting Party may also submit to arbitration under this article any investment dispute concerning any obligation which the Contracting Party has entered into with regard to a specific investment of the investor through:

i.   An investment authorisation granted by its competent authorities specifically to the investor or investment,

ii.   a written agreement granting rights with respect to [categories of subject matters]

on which the investor has relied in establishing acquiring, or significantly expanding an investment.

2.   Means of Settlement

Such a dispute should, if possible, be settled by negotiation or consultation. If it is not so settled, the investor may choose to submit it for resolution:

a.   to any competent courts or administrative tribunals of the Contracting Party to the dispute;

b.   in accordance with any dispute settlement procedure agreed upon prior to the dispute arising; or

c.   by arbitration in accordance with this Article under:

i.   the Convention on the Settlement of Investment Disputes between States and Nationals of other States (the "ICSID Convention"), if the ICSID Convention is available;

ii.   the Additional Facility Rules of the Centre for Settlement of Investment Disputes ("ICSID Additional Facility"), if the ICSID Additional Facility is available;

iii.   the Arbitration Rules of the United Nations Commission on International Trade Law ("UNCITRAL"); or

iv.   the Rules of Arbitration of the International Chamber of Commerce ("ICC").

3. Contracting Party Consent

a.   Subject only to paragraph 3.b, each Contracting Party hereby gives its unconditional consent to the submission of a dispute to international arbitration in accordance with the provisions of this Article.

b.   A Contracting Party may, by notifying the Depositary upon deposit of its instrument of ratification or accession, provide that its consent given under paragraph 3.a only applies on the condition that the investor and the investment waive in writing the right to initiate any other dispute settlement procedure with respect to the same dispute and withdraw from any such procedure in progress before its conclusion. A Contracting Party may, at any time, reduce the scope of that limitation by notifying the Depositary.

4.   Time periods and notification

An investor may submit a dispute for resolution pursuant to paragraph 2.c of this Article after sixty days following the date on which notice of intent to do so was received by the Contracting Party in dispute, but no later than five years from the date the investor first acquired or should have acquired knowledge of the events which gave rise to the dispute. Notice of intent, a copy of which shall be delivered to the Parties Group, shall specify:

a.   the name and address of the disputing investor;

b.   the name and address, if any, of the investment;

c.   the provisions of this Agreement alleged to have been breached and any other relevant provisions;

d.   the issues and the factual basis for the claim; and

e.   the relief sought, including the approximate amount of any damages claimed.

5.   Written Agreement of the Parties

The consent given by a Contracting Party in subparagraph 3.a, together with either the written submission of the dispute to resolution by the investor pursuant to subparagraph 2.c or the investor's advance written consent to such submission, shall constitute the written consent and the written agreement of the parties to the dispute to its submission for settlement for the purposes of Chapter II of the ICSID Convention, the ICSID Additional Facility Rules, Article 1 of the UNCITRAL Arbitration Rules, the Rules of Arbitration of the ICC, and Article II of the United Nations Convention on the Recognition and Enforcement of Foreign Arbitral Awards (the "New York Convention"). Neither party may withdraw its consent unilaterally, except as provided in paragraph 9.e of this Article.

6.   [EC or Contracting Party REIO text being developed, for possible inclusion]

7.   Appointments to Arbitral Tribunals

a.   Unless the parties to the dispute otherwise agree, the tribunal shall comprise three arbitrators, one appointed by each of the disputing parties and the third, who shall be the presiding arbitrator, appointed by agreement of the disputing parties.

b.   If a tribunal has not been constituted within 90 days after the date that a claim is submitted to arbitration, the arbitrator or arbitrators not yet appointed shall, on the request of either disputing party, be appointed by the appointing authority. For arbitration under paragraph 2, subparagraphs c.i, c.ii and c.iii, and paragraph 9, the appointing authority shall be the Secretary-General of ICSID. For arbitration under paragraph 2, subparagraph c.iv, the appointing authority shall be the International Court of Arbitration of the ICC.

c.   The parties to a dispute submitted to arbitration under this article and the appointing authority should consider the appointment of:

i.   members of the roster maintained by the Contracting Parties pursuant to Article C, paragraph 2.f; and

ii.   individuals possessing expertise not found on the roster, if arbitration of a dispute requires special expertise on the Tribunal, rather than solely through expert advice under the rules governing the arbitration.

d.   The appointing authority shall, as far as possible, carry out its function in consultation with the parties to the dispute.

e.   In order to facilitate the appointment of arbitrators of the parties' nationality on three member ICSID tribunals under Article 39 of the ICSID Convention and Article 7 of Schedule C of the ICSID Additional Facility Rules, and without prejudice to each party's right independently to select an individual for appointment as arbitrator or to object to an arbitrator on grounds other than nationality:

   i.   the disputing Contracting Party agrees to the appointment of each individual member of a tribunal under paragraph 2.c.i or ii of this Article; and

   ii.   a disputing investor may initiate or continue a proceeding under paragraph 2.c.i or ii only on condition that the investor agrees in writing to the appointment of each individual member of the tribunal.

8.   Standing of the Investment

An enterprise constituted or organised under the law of a Contracting Party but which, from the time of the events giving rise to the dispute until its submission for resolution under paragraph 2.c, was an investment of an investor of another Contracting Party, shall, for purposes of disputes concerning that investment, be considered "an investor of another Contracting Party" under this article and "a national of another Contracting State" for purposes of Article 25(2)(b) of the ICSID Convention regarding a dispute not submitted for resolution by the investor which owns or controls it.

9.   Consolidation of Multiple Proceedings

a.   In the event that two or more disputes submitted to arbitration with a Contracting Party under paragraph 2.c have a question of law or fact in common, the Contracting Party may submit to a separate arbitral tribunal, established under this paragraph, a request for the consolidated consideration of all or part of them. The request shall stipulate:

   i.   the names and addresses of the parties to the proceedings sought to be consolidated,

   ii.   the scope of the consolidation sought, and

   iii. the grounds for the request.

The Contracting Party shall deliver the request to each investor party to the proceedings sought to be consolidated and a copy of the request to the Parties Group.

b.	The request for consolidated consideration shall be submitted to arbitration under the rules chosen by agreement of the investor parties from the list contained in paragraph 2.c. The investor parties shall act as one side for the purpose of the formation of the tribunal.

c.	If the investor parties have not agreed upon a means of arbitration and the nomination of an arbitrator within 30 days after the date of receipt of the request for consolidated consideration by the last investor to receive it:

　　i.	the request shall be submitted to arbitration in accordance with this article under the UNCITRAL rules, and

　　ii.	the appointing authority shall appoint the entire arbitral tribunal, in accordance with paragraph 7.

d.	The arbitral tribunal shall assume jurisdiction over all or part of the disputes and the other arbitral proceedings shall be stayed or adjourned, as appropriate if, after considering the views of the parties, it decides that to do so would best serve the interest of fair and efficient resolution of the disputes and that the disputes fall within the scope of this paragraph.

e.	An investor may withdraw the dispute from arbitration under this paragraph 9 and such dispute may not be resubmitted to arbitration under paragraph 2.c. If it does so no later than 15 days after receipt of notice of consolidation, its earlier submission of the dispute to that arbitration shall be without prejudice to the investor's recourse to dispute settlement other than under paragraph 2.c.

f.	At the request of the Contracting Party, the arbitral tribunal established under this paragraph may decide, on the same basis and with the same effect as under paragraph 9.d, whether to assume jurisdiction over all or part of a dispute falling with the scope of paragraph 9.a which is submitted to arbitration after the initiation of consolidation proceedings.

## 10.	Preliminary Objections

a.	Any objection to the jurisdiction of the tribunal or to the admissibility of the application shall be raised no later than in the statement of defence.

b.	Upon receipt of such an objection, the tribunal may suspend the proceedings on the merits.

c.	After hearing the parties, the tribunal should give its decision, by which it shall either uphold the objection or reject it, within 60 days after the date on which the objection was made.

11.   Indemnification

A Contracting Party shall not assert as a defence, counter-claim, right of set-off or for any other reason, that indemnification or other compensation for all or part of the alleged damages has been received or will be received pursuant to an indemnity, guarantee or insurance contract.[166]

12.   Third Party Rights

The arbitral tribunal shall notify the Parties Group of its formation. Taking into account the views of the parties, it may give to any Contracting Party requesting it an opportunity to submit written views on the legal issues in dispute, provided that the proceedings are not unduly delayed thereby. Any Contracting Party requesting it within thirty days after receipt by the Parties Group of the notification of the tribunal's formation shall be given an opportunity to present its views on issues in dispute in which it has a legal interest.

13.   Scientific and Technical Expertise

a.   On request of a disputing Contracting Party or, unless the disputing Contracting Parties disapprove, on its own initiative, the tribunal may request a written report of a scientific or technical review board, or expert, on any factual issue concerning environmental, health, safety or other scientific or technical matters raised by a disputing Contracting Party in a proceeding, subject to such terms and conditions as such Parties may agree.

b.   The board, or expert, shall be selected by the tribunal from among highly qualified, independent experts in the scientific or technical matters, after consultations with the disputing Parties and the scientific or technical bodies identified by those Parties.

c.   The disputing Contracting Parties shall be provided:

i.   advance notice of, and an opportunity to provide comments to the tribunal on, the proposed factual issues to be referred to the board, or expert; and

ii.   a copy of the board's, or expert's, report and an opportunity to provide comments on the report to the tribunal.

d.   The tribunal shall take the report and any comments by the disputing Contracting Parties on the report into account in the preparation of its award.

14.   Applicable law

a.   Issues in dispute under paragraph 1.a. of this article shall be decided in accordance with this Agreement, interpreted and applied in accordance with the applicable rules of international law.

---

[166] This subparagraph does not bar as a defence, counter-claim, right of set-off or for any other reason, that the Contracting Party has already paid indemnification or other compensation to the subrogee or assignee of the investor's rights in the matter.

b.   Issues in dispute under paragraph 1.b. of this article shall be decided in accordance with such rules of law as may be agreed by the parties to the dispute. In the absence of such agreement, such issues shall be decided in accordance with the law of the Contracting Party to the dispute (including its rules on the conflict of laws), the law governing the authorisation or agreement and such rules of international law as may be applicable.

15.   Interim measures of relief

a.   An arbitral tribunal established under this Article may recommend an interim measure of protection to preserve the rights of a disputing Contracting Party or to ensure that the Tribunal's jurisdiction is made fully effective.

b.   The seeking of interim relief not involving the payment of damages, from judicial or administrative tribunals, by a party to a dispute submitted to arbitration under this article, for the preservation of its rights and interests pending resolution of the dispute, is not deemed a submission of the dispute for resolution for purposes of a Contracting Party's limitation of consent under paragraph 3.b, and is permissible in arbitration under any of the provisions of paragraph 2.c.

16.   Final awards

a.   The arbitral tribunal, in its award shall set out its findings of law and fact, together with the reasons therefor and may, at the request of a Party, provide the following forms of relief:

    i.   a declaration that the Contracting Party has failed to comply with its obligations under this Agreement;

    ii.   pecuniary compensation, which shall include interest from the time the loss or damage was incurred until time of payment;

    iii.   restitution in kind in appropriate cases, provided that the Contracting Party may pay pecuniary compensation in lieu thereof where restitution is not practicable; and

    iv.   with the Agreement of the parties to the dispute, any other form of relief.

b.   In appropriate cases where the loss or damage was incurred by an investment which remains a going concern, the tribunal may direct that the compensation or restitution be made to the investment.

c.   An arbitration award shall be final and binding between the parties to the dispute and shall be carried out without delay by the party against whom it is issued, subject to its post-award rights under the arbitral systems utilised.

d.   The award shall be drafted consistently with the requirements of paragraph 17 and shall be a publicly available document. A copy of the award shall be delivered to the Parties Group by the Secretary-General of ICSID, for an award under the

ICSID Convention or the Rules of the ICSID Additional Facility; by the Secretary-General of the ICC International Court of Arbitration, for an award under its rules; and by the tribunal, for an award under the UNCITRAL rules.

17. Confidential and Proprietary Information

Parties and other participants in proceedings shall protect any confidential or proprietary information which may be revealed in the course of the proceedings and which is designated as such by the party providing the information. They shall not reveal such information without written authorisation from the party which provided it.

18. Place of Arbitration and Enforceability

Any arbitration under this article shall be held in a state that is party to the New York Convention. Claims submitted to arbitration under this article shall be considered to arise out of a commercial relationship or transaction for purposes of Article 1 of that Convention. Each Contracting Party shall provide for the enforcement of the pecuniary obligations imposed by an award rendered pursuant to this Article D.

19. Tribunal member fees

Fees and expenses payable to a member of an arbitral tribunal established under these Articles will be subject to schedules established by the Parties Group and in force at the time of the constitution of the tribunal.

20. Supplemental Provisions

The Parties Group may adopt supplemental provisions to ensure the smooth functioning of these rules, in particular to clarify the inter-relationship between these rules and the rules of arbitration available under paragraph 2.c of this article D.

VI. EXCEPTIONS AND SAFEGUARDS

GENERAL EXCEPTIONS [167]

1.   This Article shall not apply to Article IV, 2 and 3 (Expropriation and compensation and protection from strife).

2.   Nothing in this Agreement shall be construed:

a.   to prevent any Contracting Party from taking any action which it considers necessary for the protection of its essential security interests:

(i)   taken in time of war, or armed conflict, or other emergency in international relations;

---

[167]   This text was proposed for discussion by the Chairman. It is under consideration by the Negotiating Group.

(ii) relating to the implementation of national policies or international agreements respecting the non-proliferation of weapons of mass destruction;

(iii) relating to the production of arms and ammunition;

b. to require any Contracting Party to furnish or allow access to any information the disclosure of which it considers contrary to its essential security interests;

c. to prevent any Contracting Party from taking any action in pursuance of its obligations under the United Nations Charter for the maintenance of international peace and security.

3. Subject to the requirement that such measures are not applied in a manner which would constitute a means of arbitrary or unjustifiable discrimination between Contracting Parties, or a disguised investment restriction, nothing in this Agreement shall be construed to prevent any Contracting Party from taking any measure necessary for the maintenance of public order.[168]

4. Actions or measures taken pursuant to this Article shall be notified to the Parties Group.

5. If a Contracting Party (the "requesting Party") has reason to believe that actions or measures taken by another Contracting Party (the "other Party") under this article have been taken solely for economic reasons, or that such actions or measures are not in proportion to the interest being protected, it may request consultations with that other Party in accordance with Article V, B.1 (State-State Consultation Procedures). That other Party shall provide information to the requesting Party regarding the actions or measures taken and the reasons therefor.

TRANSACTIONS IN PURSUIT OF MONETARY AND EXCHANGE RATE POLICIES[169]

1. Articles XX (National Treatment), YY (Most Favoured Nation Treatment) and ZZ (Transparency) do not apply to transactions carried out in pursuit of monetary or exchange rate policies by a central bank or monetary authority of a Contracting Party.

2. Where such transactions do not conform with Articles XX (National Treatment), YY (Most Favoured Nation Treatment) and ZZ (Transparency), they shall not be used as a means of avoiding the Contracting Party's commitments or obligations under the Agreement.

---

[168] The public order exception may be invoked only where a genuine and sufficiently serious threat is posed to one of the fundamental interests of society.

[169] While one delegation questions the need for any specific provisions carving out transactions by a central bank or monetary authority in pursuit of monetary and exchange rate policies, most delegations can support adoption of this text.

TEMPORARY SAFEGUARD

1.   A Contracting Party may adopt or maintain measures inconsistent with its obligations under:

- Article xx (Transfers);

- Article yy, paragraph 1.1 (National Treatment) relating to cross-border capital transactions[170]

  (a)   in the event of serious balance-of-payments and external financial difficulties or threat thereof; or

  (b)   where, in exceptional circumstances, movements of capital cause, or threaten to cause, serious difficulties for macroeconomic management, in particular monetary and exchange rate policies[171].

2.   Measures referred to in paragraph 1:

  (a)   shall be consistent with the Articles of Agreement of the International Monetary Fund;

  (b)   shall not exceed those necessary to deal with the circumstances described in paragraph 1[172];

  (c)   shall be temporary and shall be eliminated as soon as conditions permit.

3.   (a)   Measures referred to in paragraph 1 shall be promptly notified to the Parties Group and to the International Monetary Fund, including any changes in such measures.

  (b)   Measures referred to in paragraph 1 and any changes therein shall be subject to review and approval or disapproval within six months of their adoption and every six months thereafter until their elimination.

  (c)   These reviews shall address the compliance of any measure with paragraph 2, in particular the elimination of measures in accordance with paragraph 2 (c).

---

[170] It is understood that such measures may not discriminate between resident entities owned or controlled by investors of other Contracting Parties and resident entities controlled by local investors. Some delegations question whether this bullet is necessary, but would like to consider the IMF arguments in this respect. See Commentary.

[171] Several delegations feel that the reference to "macroeconomic management" is too broad. They could accept paragraph 1 (b) if "macroeconomic management, in particular monetary and exchange rate policies" were replaced with "the operation of monetary or exchange rate policies". Some delegations question whether paragraph 1 (b) was necessary. On the other hand, other delegations would have preferred a provision in which restrictions could be taken in cases of serious difficulties for "the operation of <u>economic</u>, monetary or exchange rate policies".

[172] One delegation suggests adding: "and shall provide for the least disruptive effect to the functioning of the Agreement". Reference is also made in this context to the language in paragraph 2. (c) of Article XII of the GATS: "shall avoid unnecessary damage to the commercial, economic and financial interest of any other Member".

4.   Measures referred to in paragraph 1 and any changes therein that are approved by the International Monetary Fund in the exercise of its jurisdiction shall be considered as consistent with this Article.

5.   With regard to measures referred to in paragraph 1, and any changes therein, not falling within paragraph 4:

(a)   The Parties Group shall consider the implications of the measures adopted under this Article for the obligations of the Contracting Party concerned under this Agreement.

(b)   The Parties Group shall request an assessment by the International Monetary Fund of the conditions mentioned under paragraph 1 and of the consistency of any measures with paragraph 2. Any such assessment by the International Monetary Fund shall be accepted by the Parties Group.

(c)   Unless the International Monetary Fund determines that the measure is either consistent or inconsistent with the provisions of this Article, the Parties Group may either approve or disapprove the measure. The Parties Group shall establish procedures for this purpose.

6.   The Contracting Parties shall seek agreement with the International Monetary Fund regarding the role of the International Monetary Fund in the review procedures established under this Article.

7.   Measures referred to in paragraph 1 and any changes therein that are approved by the International Monetary Fund in the exercise of its jurisdiction or determined to be consistent with this Article by the International Monetary Fund or the Parties Group cannot be subject to dispute settlement[173].

Additional Article

If a dispute arises under this Article or under Article ..... (obligations under the Articles of Agreement of the Fund), a Dispute Settlement Panel shall request an assessment by the International Monetary Fund of the consistency of the measures with its Articles of Agreement, of the conditions mentioned under paragraph 1 and of the consistency of any measures as applied with paragraph 2. Any such assessment by the International Monetary Fund shall be accepted by the Panel.[174]

---

[173]   The dispute settlement provisions would apply if the measure as actually applied differed from that approved or determined to be consistent with this Article.

[174]   Text proposed by the IMF and supported by most delegations. Placement of this proposed text in the Agreement may need to be considered further. Four delegations oppose the proposal that assessments by the IMF shall be accepted by the Panel and expressed concern that, as drafted, this text leaves no room for the Panel to assess compliance with the MAI Safeguard provision.

VII.   FINANCIAL SERVICES [175, 176] [177]

PRUDENTIAL MEASURES

1.   Notwithstanding any other provisions of the Agreement, a Contracting Party shall not be prevented from taking prudential measures with respect to financial services, including measures for the protection of investors, depositors, policy holders or persons to whom a fiduciary duty is owed by an enterprise providing financial services, or to ensure the integrity and stability of its financial system.

2.   Where such measures do not conform with the provisions of the Agreement, they shall not be used as a means of avoiding the Contracting Party's commitments or obligations under the Agreement.

RECOGNITION ARRANGEMENTS

1.   A Contracting Party may recognise prudential measures of any other Contracting Party or non-Contracting Party in determining how the Contracting Party's measures relating to financial services shall be applied. Such recognition, which may be achieved through harmonisation or otherwise, may be based on an agreement or arrangement with the other Contracting Party or non-Contracting Party concerned or may be accorded autonomously.

2.   A Contracting Party that is a party to such an agreement or arrangement referred to in paragraph 1, whether future or existing, shall afford adequate opportunity for other interested Contracting Parties to negotiate their accession to such agreements or arrangements, or to negotiate comparable ones with it, under circumstances in which there would be equivalent regulation, oversight, implementation of such regulation, and, if appropriate, procedures concerning the sharing of information between the parties to the agreement or arrangement. Where a Contracting Party accords recognition autonomously, it shall afford adequate opportunity for any other Contracting Party to demonstrate that such circumstances exist.

---

[175] EG5 has agreed that the financial services sector, which is highly regulated for prudential reasons, is unique in some respects and to some extent calls for specific treatment. However, a number of delegations consider that the general provisions of the MAI are sufficient to meet the needs of the financial services sector in a number of potential areas.

[176] The Negotiating Group has discussed financial services issues at its April 1997 and January 1998 meetings. The proposed text on prudential measures and the definition of financial services were agreed. Proposed texts on payments and clearing systems/lender of last resort and dispute settlement have not yet been discussed by the Negotiating Group. Placement of financial services texts is to be decided. See also Commentary.

[177] With the exception of a few delegations who are hesitant, DG3 recommends the adoption of an Interpretative Note stating that "the inclusion of text specific to financial services shall be without prejudice to the interpretation of the obligations of the MAI with respect to other sectors".

AUTHORISATION PROCEDURES

1.   Each Contracting Party's regulatory authorities shall make available to interested persons their requirements for completing applications relating to an investment in, or the operations of, a financial services enterprise.

2.   On the request of an applicant, the regulatory authority shall inform the applicant of the status of its application. If such authority requires additional information from the applicant, it shall notify the applicant without undue delay.

3.   A regulatory authority shall make an administrative decision on a completed application of an investor in a financial services enterprise or a financial services enterprise that is an investment of an investor of another Contracting Party within [120][180] days, and shall promptly notify the applicant of the decision. An application shall not be considered complete until [all relevant hearings are held and] all necessary information is received. Where it is not practicable for a decision to be made within [120][180] days, the regulatory authority shall notify the applicant without undue delay and shall endeavour to make the decision within a reasonable time thereafter.

TRANSPARENCY

Nothing in this Agreement requires a Contracting Party to furnish or allow access to:

a)   information related to the financial affairs and accounts of individual customers of financial services enterprises, or

b)   any confidential or proprietary information, the disclosure of which would impede law enforcement or otherwise be contrary to the public interest or prejudice legitimate commercial interests of particular enterprises.178

INFORMATION TRANSFER AND DATA PROCESSING

1.   No Contracting Party shall take measures that prevent transfers of information or the processing of financial information outside the territory of a Contracting Party, including transfers of data by electronic means, where such transfer of information or processing of financial information is:

a)   necessary for the conduct of the ordinary business of a financial services enterprise located in a Contracting Party that is the investment of an investor of another Contracting Party; or

---

[178] The text proposed here by EG5 would be additional to the text of the General Transparency provision (see Section III, Treatment of Investors and Investments).

b) in connection with the purchase or sale by a financial services enterprise located in a Contracting Party that is the investment of an investor of another Contracting Party of:

i) financial data processing services; or

ii) financial information, including information provided to or by third parties.

2. Nothing in paragraph 1:

a) affects the financial service enterprise's obligation to comply with any record keeping and reporting requirements; or

b) restricts the right of a Contracting Party to protect privacy, including the protection of personal data and the confidentiality of individual records and accounts, so long as such right is not used to circumvent the provisions of the Agreement.

MEMBERSHIP OF SELF-REGULATORY BODIES AND ASSOCIATIONS[179]

When membership or participation in, or access to, any self-regulatory body, securities or futures exchange or market, clearing agency, or any other organisation or association is required by a Contracting Party in order for investments of investors of any other Contracting Party in a financial services enterprise established in the territory of the Contracting Party to provide financial services on an equal basis with financial services enterprises of the Contracting Party, or when the Contracting Party provides directly or indirectly such entities, privileges or advantages in providing financial services, the Contracting Party shall ensure that such entities accord national treatment to such investments.

PAYMENTS AND CLEARING SYSTEMS/LENDER OF LAST RESORT

1. Under terms and conditions that accord National Treatment, each Contracting Party shall grant to financial services enterprises that are investments of investors of any other Contracting Party established in its territory access to payment and clearing systems operated by public entities, and to official funding and refinancing facilities available in the normal course of ordinary business.

2. The provisions of this Agreement are not intended to confer access to the Contracting Party's lender of last resort facilities.

---

[179] See Commentary.

DISPUTE SETTLEMENT

DETERMINATION OF CERTAIN FINANCIAL ISSUES IN INVESTOR TO STATE PROCEEDINGS[180]

COMPOSITION OF DISPUTE SETTLEMENT PANELS IN FINANCIAL MATTERS DISPUTES[181]

"Panels for disputes on prudential issues and other financial matters shall have the necessary expertise relevant to the specific financial services under dispute."

DEFINITION OF FINANCIAL SERVICES

Financial services include all insurance and insurance-related services, and all banking and other financial services (excluding insurance). Financial services include the following activities:

Insurance and insurance-related services

    (i)   Direct insurance (including co-insurance):

        (A)   life

        (B)   non-life

    (ii)   Reinsurance and retrocession;

    (iii)   Insurance intermediation, such as brokerage and agency;

    (iv)   Services auxiliary to insurance, such as consultancy, actuarial, risk assessment and claim settlement services.

Banking and other financial services (excluding insurance)

    (v)   Acceptance of deposits and other repayable funds from the public;

    (vi)   Lending of all types, including consumer credit, mortgage credit, factoring and financing of commercial transaction;

---

[180] No text was submitted by financial services experts following their informal consultations on 11-13 February 1998 to the Negotiating Group for adoption. The group was divided as to the need for specific provisions for Investor-State dispute settlement in certain financial matters. Delegations which favoured specific provisions have suggested texts reproduced under the Commentary.

[181] A majority of delegations support this text, based on a similar provision contained in the GATS Financial Services Annex, whereas other delegations are in favour of more detailed procedures to select panellists (see Commentary). Others would prefer no specific provisions on this issue.

(vii)   Financial leasing;

(viii)   All payment and money transmission services, including credit, charge and debit cards, travellers cheques and bankers drafts;

(ix)   Guarantees and commitments;

(x)   Trading for own account or for account of customers, whether on an exchange, in an over-the-counter market or otherwise, the following:

     (A)   money market instruments (including cheques, bills, certificates of deposits);

     (B)   foreign exchange;

     (C)   derivative products including, but not limited to, futures and options;

     (D)   exchange rate and interest rate instruments, including products such as swaps, forward rate agreements;

     (E)   transferable securities;

     (F)   other negotiable instruments and financial assets, including bullion.

(xi)   Participation in issues of all kinds of securities, including underwriting and placement as agent (whether publicly or privately) and provision of services related to such issues;

(xii)   Money broking;

(xiii)   Asset management, such as cash or portfolio management, all forms of collective investment management, pension fund management, custodial, depository and trust services;

(xiv)   Settlement and clearing services for financial assets, including securities, derivative products, and other negotiable instruments;

(xv)   Provision and transfer of financial information, and financial data processing and related software by suppliers of other financial services;

(xvi)   Advisory, intermediation and other auxiliary financial services on all the activities listed in subparagraphs (v) through (xv), including credit reference and analysis, investment and portfolio research and advice, advice on acquisitions and on corporate restructuring and strategy.

VIII. TAXATION [182]

1.   Nothing in this Agreement shall apply to taxation measures except as expressly provided in paragraphs 2 to 5 below.[183]

2.   Article ... (Expropriation) shall apply to taxation measures.[184]

3.   Article ... (Transparency) shall apply to taxation measures, except that nothing in this Agreement shall require a Contracting Party to furnish or allow access to information covered by tax secrecy or any other provision or administrative practice protecting confidentiality in domestic laws or international agreements, and including information:

   a)   contained in or exchanged pursuant to any agreement or arrangement relating to taxation between governments and investors;

   b)   pursuant to any agreement with a foreign government concerning the application or interpretation of an international agreement relating to taxation in the case of an investor, including exchange of information between governments;

   c)   concerning the identity of an investor or other information which would disclose any trade, business, industrial, commercial or professional secret or trade process;

---

[182] **Political Declaration of the Contracting Parties:**

Contracting Parties recognise the importance of the principle of non-discriminatory treatment in taxation for foreign investors and their investments. In this respect, they refer to their commitments under their agreements for the avoidance of double taxation. The Contracting Parties shall pursue their efforts to conclude agreements for the avoidance of double taxation, where appropriate, with Contracting Parties with which they have not yet entered into such agreements.

[183] One delegation proposes to add an additional paragraph to the Taxation article as follows:

"This Article shall not affect the rights of a Contracting Party and its investors as contained in any other international agreement covering taxation, including bilateral investment protection treaties."

[184] Interpretative Note: When considering the issue of whether a taxation measure effects an expropriation, the following elements should be borne in mind:

   a) The imposition of taxes does not generally constitute expropriation. The introduction of a new taxation measure, taxation by more than one jurisdiction in respect to an investment, or a claim of excessive burden imposed by a taxation measure are not in themselves indicative of an expropriation.

   b) A taxation measure will not be considered to constitute expropriation where it is generally within the bounds of internationally recognised tax policies and practices. When considering whether a taxation measure satisfies this principle, an analysis should include whether and to what extent taxation measures of a similar type and level are used around the world. Further, taxation measures aimed at preventing the avoidance or evasion of taxes should not generally be considered to be expropriatory.

   c) While expropriation may be constituted even by measures applying generally (e.g., to all taxpayers), such a general application is in practice less likely to suggest an expropriation than more specific measures aimed at particular nationalities or individual taxpayers. A taxation measure would not be expropriatory if it was in force and was transparent when the investment was undertaken.

   d) Taxation measures may constitute an outright expropriation, or while not directly expropriatory they may have the equivalent effect of an expropriation (so-called "creeping expropriation"). Where a taxation measure by itself does not constitute expropriation it would be extremely unlikely to be an element of a creeping expropriation.

---

d)   pertaining to the negotiation of tax treaties or of any other international agreement relating partly or wholly to taxation or the participation by a government in the work of international organisations; or

e)   the disclosure of which would affect the assessment or collection of, the enforcement or prosecution in respect of, or the determination of appeals in relation to, taxation, or any information the disclosure of which would aid or assist in the avoidance or evasion of taxes.

4.   The provisions of Article [C] (State to State Dispute Settlement) and Article [D] (Investor to State Dispute Settlement), [except for paragraph 1b of Article [D]], and only those provisions, shall apply to a dispute under paragraph 2 or 3 of this Article. [185] [186]

5.   For the purposes of this Article:

a)   A Competent Tax Authority means the minister or ministry responsible for taxes or their authorised representatives.

b)   "Taxation measures" include

i)   any provision relating to taxes of the law of the Contracting Party or of a political subdivision thereof or a local authority therein, or any administrative practices of the Contracting Party relating to taxes; and

ii)   any provision relating to taxes of any convention for the avoidance of double taxation or of any other international agreement or arrangement by which the Contracting Party is bound.

Taxes shall be taken for this purpose to include direct taxes, indirect taxes and social security contributions.[187]

---

[185]   Interpretative Note: "For greater certainty regarding the application of Articles (C)(5) and (D)(13), the terms "scientific or technical" in those provisions shall refer to taxation; and the written report of such a board shall be obtained on request of a disputing party. The written report of such a board regarding paragraph 2 of this Article shall include an analysis of whether the measure falls within one or more of the elements of footnote [2] (Interpretative Note on the Application of Expropriation to Taxation); and a conclusion of the board that the measure falls within one or more of the elements described in subparagraph (b) or (c), shall be taken into account by the tribunal in the preparation of its award. Paragraph 4 of this Article shall not apply to claims arising out of events that occurred, or claims that have been settled, prior to the entry into force of this Agreement for the Contracting Party applying the taxation measure." One delegatoin wishes to see the second and third sentences of this note in square brackets. Another delegation would delete the interpretative note entirely.

[186]   Interpretative Note: For greater certainty, Article XX (most favoured nation treatment) shall not be invoked to avoid the provisions of paragraph ... (dispute settlement) of this Article. Several delegations maintain a scrutiny reservation on the text of this Note.

[187]   One delegation has a scrutiny reserve on the treatment of social security. Another delegation proposes that social security benefits be carved out of the agreement. One delegation proposes a general carve-out of social security and proposed the following separate article: "Nothing in this Agreement shall apply to social security."

IX.   COUNTRY SPECIFIC EXCEPTIONS

LODGING OF COUNTRY SPECIFIC EXCEPTIONS[188] [189]

A.[190]   *Articles X (National Treatment), Y (Most Favoured Nation Treatment), [Article Z, ..., ... and Article ...]*[191]*, do not apply to:*

   (a)   *any existing non-conforming measure as set out by a Contracting Party in its Schedule to Annex A of the Agreement, to the extent that the measure is maintained, continued or promptly renewed*[192] *in its legal system* [193] [194]*;*

---

[188] It is generally agreed to replace the term "reservations" by the term "exceptions". Under treaty law, "reservations" normally have reciprocal effect unless otherwise specified. This is clearly not intended to be the case with respect to Country Schedules. Any possible confusion with general exceptions could be taken care of by the qualification "country-specific". The use of the term "exception" would not prevent the listing of a measure with a reciprocity requirement. It would help avoid confusion in the case of any genuine "reservations" in the treaty law sense were to be made and called as such.

[189] The draft article to address existing measures should be examined in conjunction with the proposed introduction to Annex A of the Agreement and the standard presentation suggested for the lodging of country specific reservations (reproduced in footnote 12). These three elements combined provide the methodology for lodging country specific exceptions under the MAI.

[190] It is agreed that part A of the draft article is needed as the core provision to "grandfather" existing non-conforming measures and prevent the introduction of more restrictive measures ("standstill").

[191] It is agreed that the disciplines listed in the chapeau text of parts A and B of the draft Article should remain incomplete for the time being pending political decisions by the Negotiating Group. The text could also be reviewed after negotiators have decided how measures by sub-national entities and regional economic integration organisations should be treated across the MAI.

[192] All delegations agree that foreign investors should benefit from any liberalisation measure as soon as the relevant law, regulation or practice ... enters into force. The words "continued or promptly renewed in its legal system" at the end of the sentence are intended to make this clear. One delegation maintains a scrutiny reserve on this addition, notably in order to examine its potential implications for this delegation's obligations under other international agreements such as GATS.

[193] It is generally agreed to include the following explanatory note to the article A (a): "It is understood that the term "legal system" includes government policies enunciated under the framework of domestic legislation and subordinate measures." One delegation proposes to add to this explanatory note the phrase " which creates rights or obligations to investors or investments"; this would make it clear that "legal system" does not include, for instance, political declarations with no effect on investors and their investments.

[194] Two delegations seek the opinion of the Group whether and how Part A of Article A can take care of temporary liberalisation undertakings. Some delegations consider that this possibility should be provided only if the temporary liberalisation measures are announced prior to the entry into force of the MAI. Some other delegations consider that a temporary liberalisation measure could be consistent with Part A (a) if the temporary nature of the liberalisation and its duration were clearly reflected in the legal system at the time the liberalisation was put into effect. Some delegations consider that this delegation's question relates to the issue of the implementation of a non-conforming measure . They feel that Part A would provide the possibility to temporarily implement a measure in a more liberal way than the way described in a country schedule. Other delegations, believe on the contrary that this interpretation is not compatible with the ratchet effect built in Part A, namely that a return to a more restrictive regime should not be possible. Such an interpretation is also bound to create legal uncertainty for the investor and even encourage a proliferation of temporary measures. Delegations are invited to reflect further on this issue. One delegation may also wish to develop a text proposal.

> *(b)*   *an amendment to any non-conforming measure referred to in subparagraph (a) to the extent that the amendment does not increase the non-conformity of the measure, as it existed immediately before the amendment, with Articles X (National Treatment), Article Y (Most Favoured Nation), [Article Z, ..., and Article ...]*[195].

> [*B.*[196]   *Articles X; Y, [Article Z, ...,and Article ...] do not apply to any measure that a Contracting Party [adopts] or [maintains] with respect to sectors, subsectors or activities, as set out in its Schedule to Annex B of the Agreement.*]

---

[195]   Delegations agree that notification of a reduction in the non-conformity of a measure would not be necessary for its effective application under the MAI. Notification is a matter of transparency and should be addressed separately.

It is agreed that article 79 of the Vienna Convention concerning Corrections of Errors in texts or Certified Copies of Treaties would do away with the need of a notification obligation for rectifications of errors.

Delegations identified three policy issues for consideration by the Negotiating Group:

a)   First, whether there is a need for a notification obligation for modifications in the non-conformity of measures.

Some delegations consider that a mandatory notification obligation for changes in country exceptions lists would be too cumbersome. Update of the country lists could be a result of a possible review mechanism. Some other delegations consider that it would be highly desirable to ensure that country lists of exceptions are kept up to date as this would enhance the usefulness of the MAI for foreign investors. This could, according to some delegations, be done at regular intervals (for instance once a year).

The Group recalls in this context by way of illustration the following proposal in page 108 the Consolidated Text and Commentary:

> "Each Contracting Party shall notify (the "Parties Group") promptly and in any case no later than 60 days after their entry into force, of any change in the non-conformity of its measures with obligations under the Agreement, including the motivation or purpose of the change."

b)   Second, whether such notification obligation would have implications for the role of the Parties Group and, if so, what should be the role of the Parties Group on this regard; and

c)   Third, whether it would be allowed to rectify errors or omissions made in good faith. Delegations note the following proposal made by one delegation to address this issue:

> "Modifications made to take care of errors or omissions made in good faith relating to Annex ..., along with information about the likely circumstances of the change, shall be notified to the Parties Group and shall become effective provided there is no objection within 30 days after their notification."

Several delegations support this proposal given the complexity and novelty of the MAI as regards the top down approach to the lodging of country exceptions. They consider that the safeguard provided by the possibility to object is sufficiently dissuasive to prevent an abusive recourse to this provision. Some delegations, on the contrary, have serious misgivings about the proposal. Some of them point out to the difficulty of defining the terms "good faith". Others feel the proposal is too broad. Others stress the moral hazards. Two delegations also wonder whether it is necessary to have an explicit provision in this article given existing practice.

The Group notes the technical issue raised by one delegation on how to relate a Contracting Party's notification to a modification of its Schedule to the Agreement. It also notes one delegation's proposal for a possible solution to this issue.

> *"(c) A Contracting Party shall notify a change to its Schedule to Annex A of the Agreement to reflect any changes to the non-conformity of measures as provided for in paragraph (b) above."*

[196]   There are different views with respect to Part B of the draft article which would allow new non-conforming measures to be introduced after the Agreement comes into force. One view is that such a provision might undermine the MAI disciplines to which it applied. The opposite view is that Part B would make it easier to preserve high standards in the disciplines of the agreement by allowing flexibility to countries in lodging their exceptions.

[C.   *No Contracting Party may, under any measure adopted after the date of entry into force of this Agreement and covered by its Schedule to Annex B[197], require an investor of another Contracting Party, by reason of its nationality, to sell or otherwise dispose of an investment existing at the time the measure becomes effective.*]

Introduction to Annex A[198] of the Agreement listing country-specific exceptions[199]

1.   The Schedule of a Contracting Party sets out, pursuant to Article ... [on the lodging of country specific exceptions], the exceptions taken by that Party with respect to existing measures that do not conform with obligations imposed by:

(a)   *Article X (National Treatment),*

(b)   *Article Y (Most-Favoured-Nation Treatment),*

(c)   *Article Z (...), or*

(...)   *Article (...).*

together with any commitment to eliminate or reduce the non-conformity of any of the measures.[200]

---

[197] It is agreed that Part C is applicable only to non-conforming measures referred to in Part B. The objective of Part C is to protect existing rights of foreign investors against discriminatory treatment resulting from measures permitted under Part B. This situation is different from that of expropriation of assets of established enterprises which is addressed in the expropriation chapter of the MAI. This favourable reaction to the proposed wording does not prejudge acceptance of Part B, however. One delegation can accept Part C subject to an interpretative note which would read as follows:

> "A Contracting Party may, under this Article, take steps that seek to ensure compliance with any measure notified under Annex A or Annex B. Any such action shall not be taken as reducing the conformity of the measure notified in Annex A or Annex B."

[198] It was agreed to withhold the drafting of the introduction of "Annex B" until the Negotiating Group had taken a political decision on the status and coverage of Part B of the Article. Moreover, a number of delegations felt that the wording of such introduction might need to be drafted in a limited way (i.e. to cover only cases of privatisation or demonopolisation). Two delegations circulated a proposal for text on the introduction of Annex B which was not discussed by the Group.

[199] The following format has been followed by delegations for submitting their initial lists of country specific exceptions :

> "Sector:
>
> Sub-Sector:
>
> Obligation or MAI article in respect of which an Exception is taken:
>
> Level of Government:
>
> Legal source or authority of the Measure:
>
> Succinct Description of the Measure:
>
> Motivation or purpose of the Measure:"

2.   *Each exception sets out the following elements[201]:*

    (a)   *Sector refers to the general sector in which the exception is taken;*

    (b)   *Sub-Sector refers to the specific sector in which the exception is taken;*

    (c)   *Obligation specifies the MAI provision referred to in paragraph 1 for which an exception is taken;*

    (d)   *Level of Government indicates the level of government maintaining the measure for which an exception is taken;*

    (e)   *Legal source or authority of the measure identifies the specific legal source of the exception, whether in the form of a law, regulation, rule, decision, or any other form;[202]*

    (f)   *Succinct Description of the Measure sets out [the][203] non-conforming aspects of the existing measures for which the exception is taken, together with any commitment to eliminate or reduce the non-conformity of the measure [204]; [and*

    (g)   *Motivation or purpose describes the rationale for a given measure].[205]*

---

[200]   One delegation reserves its position on the issue of future liberalisation commitments.

[201]   A large majority of delegations consider that the presentation would gain in transparency by incorporating an "industry classification" element into the reservation. Both the Common Product Classification (CPC) or Standard Industrial Classification (ISIC) could provide a useful reference for identifying non-conforming measures. The CPC system may perhaps be more appropriate to services sectors given the GATS precedent. But this should not detract from delegations' ongoing efforts to finalise country exceptions. Delegations thus should feel free to provide such entries on a voluntary basis using the relevant international or comparable domestic classifications. The introduction of an "industry classification" could also be taken up in the context of future updates or negotiations on country schedules.

[202]   In order to clarify the automatic ratchet effect of List A measures, the Chairman proposed the addition of the following phrase at the end of paragraph (e): "as of the date of entry into force of the Agreement, or as continued, renewed or amended after that date."

This issue is solved by the revised paragraph (a) of Part A or the Article but this language may be relevant to the discussion of a notification obligation.

[203]   The bracketed text, proposed by one delegation, is supported by several delegations. Other delegations wish to maintain a scrutiny reserve.

[204]   As in footnote 13, one delegation maintains a full reservation with regard to commitments for future liberalisation.

[205]   A majority of delegations can support the inclusion of element (g) since it would give the reasons for the non-conformity of a given measure. Some of this support is based on the condition that the information provided under element (g) would not be considered in the context of dispute settlement. Some delegations consider that this information should be provided on a voluntary basis only. Some delegations consider that this information should be provided in the context of the MAI negotiations but should not be retained in the final text of exceptions. Some delegations believe that element (g) should be deleted altogether: the purpose or motivation of an exception, even it could be fully and accurately described, is not relevant to the scope of the exception. It is agreed that this issue should be submitted to the Negotiating Group for its consideration.

3. In the interpretation of an exception, elements (a) to (f)[206] shall be considered. In the event of a discrepancy between the non-conformity of the measure as set out in the legal source or authority identified and the non-conformity as set out in the other elements in their totality, the exception shall be deemed to apply to the non-conformity of the measure as set out in the legal source or authority. However if the non-conformity of the measure as set out in the legal source or authority exceeds the scope of non-conformity as set out in the other elements in so substantial and material a manner that it would be unreasonable to conclude that the legal source or authority element should prevail, the other elements shall prevail to the extent of that discrepancy.

X. RELATIONSHIP TO OTHER INTERNATIONAL AGREEMENTS

OBLIGATIONS UNDER THE ARTICLES OF AGREEMENT OF THE INTERNATIONAL MONETARY FUND

Nothing in this Agreement shall be regarded as altering the obligations undertaken by a Contracting Party as a Signatory of the Articles of Agreement of the International Monetary Fund.[207]

THE OECD GUIDELINES FOR MULTINATIONAL ENTERPRISES

1. The following draft text was developed on associating the Guidelines with the MAI:[208]

    1. The OECD Guidelines for Multinational Enterprises are set out in Annex (xx).

    2. The Contracting Parties at the invitation of the Organisation for Economic Co-operation and Development are encouraged to participate in the Guidelines work of the Organisation in order to promote co-operation on the application, clarification, interpretation and revision of the Guidelines and to facilitate the maintenance of consensus among the Contracting Parties and the members of the Organisation on the matters addressed in the Guidelines.

    3. The Contracting Parties [shall] [are encouraged to] set up National Contact Points for undertaking promotional activities, handling enquiries and for discussions with the parties concerned on all matters related to the Guidelines so that they can contribute to the solution of problems which may arise in this connection. The business community, employee organisations and other interested parties should be informed of the availability of such facilities.

---

[206] Three delegations consider that only elements (a) to (e) should be taken into account. Some delegations want element (g) to be taken into account as well.

[207] The coverage of this article would include, for example, cases where the Fund would request the imposition of capital controls in accordance with the Fund's Articles of Agreement.

[208] EG4 delegations differ on whether this text should be placed in the Final Act or the Agreement.

4.   Annexation of the Guidelines shall not bear on the interpretation or application of the Agreement, including for the purpose of dispute settlement; nor change their non-binding character.

2.   Several delegations proposed that the following additional text be added to the list of powers given to the Parties Group under Section XI of the Consolidated Text, paragraph 2:

(e)   consider revision of the Guidelines referred to in Article (xx) of the [Agreement] [Final Act] by adoption of any revised Guidelines developed in the OECD.

3.   Finally, delegations developed draft text that would be placed in an annex[209] immediately before the Guidelines, as follows:

The following Guidelines for Multinational Enterprises are a joint recommendation by participating Governments to multinational enterprises operating in their territory. Their purpose is to help multinational enterprises ensure that their operations are in harmony with the national policies of the countries in which they operate. The Guidelines include recommendations on general policies, disclosure of information, competition, financing, taxation, employment and industrial relations, environmental protection and science and technology. The Guidelines are part of the OECD Declaration on International Investment and Multinational Enterprises of 21 June 1976 as amended. Background and official clarifications are found in the publication "The OECD Guidelines for Multinational Enterprises".

[The text of the preamble to the Declaration on International Investment and Multinational Enterprises, Part I of the Declaration, and the full Annex 1 text of the Guidelines would be set out verbatim]

XI. IMPLEMENTATION AND OPERATION

THE PREPARATORY GROUP

(Text to be included in the Final Act)

1.   The Signatories to the Final Act and the Signatories to the Agreement shall meet in a Preparatory Group. A Signatory to the Final Act shall cease to be eligible to attend these meetings if it fails to become a Signatory to the Agreement by the closing date for signature of the Agreement.

2.   In the Preparatory Group, the participating Signatories shall:

(a)   prepare for entry into force of the Agreement and the establishment of the Parties Group;

---

[209] Delegations differ on whether the annex should be placed in the Final Act or the Agreement.

(b)   conduct discussions with non-signatories to the Final Act;

(c)   conduct negotiations with interested non-signatories to the Final Act with a view to their becoming signatories to the Agreement.

3.   The participating Signatories shall elect a Chair, who shall serve in a personal capacity. Meetings shall be held at intervals to be determined by participating Signatories under rules and procedures they shall determine.

4.   Except where otherwise provided, the Preparatory Group shall make decisions by consensus. A Signatory may abstain and express a differing view without barring consensus.

5.   Decisions under paragraph 4 may include a decision to adopt a different voting rule for a particular question or category of questions.[210]

6.   Where a decision cannot be made by consensus, the decision shall be made by a majority comprising [three quarters] [two thirds] of the Signatories.

7.   Paragraph 6 shall not apply to the following decisions:

(a)   decisions under paragraph 5; [and]

(b)   decisions under Article ... [see section XI of the Consolidated Text on decisions by the Preparatory Group on the eligibility of non-signatories to the Final Act to become a Signatory to the Agreement], which shall be made by [consensus] [a majority comprising ...]; [and]

8.   Where the European Community exercises its right to vote, it shall have a number of votes equal to the number of its Member States which are Contracting Parties to this Agreement. The number of votes of the European Community and its Member States shall in no case exceed the number of the Member States of the European Community which are Contracting Parties to this Agreement.211

---

[210] Delegations discussed the question of whether this paragraph should be deleted and concluded that the question requires further consideration.

[211] This text is a proposal by one delegation. Some delegations indicate that they want to consider whether the MAI should contain such a provision. Assuming that it should, two questions were raised: whether the provision should apply only in cases where this delegation has competence and whether this delegation should be restricted to casting a number of votes equal to the number of its Member States that are present when the vote takes place. It is also suggested that a provision might be drafted that applied to Regional Economic Integration Organisations rather than specifically to the European Community.

8. *THE PARTIES GROUP*[212]

1. There shall be a Parties Group comprised of the Contracting Parties.

2. The Parties Group shall facilitate the operation of this Agreement. To this end, it shall:

 (a) carry out the functions assigned to it under this Agreement;

 (b) [at the request of a Contracting Party, clarify [by consensus] the interpretation or application of this Agreement]213;

 (c) consider any matter that may affect the operation of this Agreement; and

 (d) take such other actions as it deems necessary to fulfil its mandate.

3. In carrying out the functions specified in paragraph 2, the Parties Group may consult governmental and non-governmental organisations or persons.

4. The Parties Group shall elect a Chair, who shall serve in a personal capacity. Meetings shall be held at intervals to be determined by the Parties Group. The Parties Group shall establish its rules and procedures.

5. Except where otherwise provided, the Parties Group shall make decisions by consensus. A Contracting Party may abstain and express a differing view without barring consensus.

6. Decisions under paragraph 5 may include a decision to adopt a different voting rule for a particular question or category of questions.[214]

7. Where a decision cannot be made by consensus, the decision shall be made by a majority comprising [three quarters] [two thirds] of the Contracting Parties.

---

[212] Institutional experts also consider the issue of *decision-making in the MAI*, including contributions by Delegations and a proposal by the Chairman of the informal consultations. There is no consensus on this matter nor on the related question of *voting by the European Community*. These issues, and other outstanding questions concerning the *Depositary* and *Authentic Texts of the MAI*, need to be considered by the Negotiating Group at an appropriate time.

[213] Expert Group No. 1 is considering the role of the Parties Group with respect to Dispute Settlement; this sub-paragraph would address clarification of interpretation and application outside the Dispute Settlement context. Delegations have varying views on the question of whether it is appropriate that the Parties Group expressly be given a formal role in clarifying the interpretation or application of the MAI. On a point of detail, one delegation has expressed the view that the Parties Group should have such authority, but only if more than one Contracting Party makes a request.

[214] See footnote 3.

8.   Paragraph 7 shall not apply to the following decisions:

(a)   decisions under paragraph 6;

(b)   decisions under Article ... [see section XII of the Consolidated Text on amendment], which shall be made by consensus;

(c)   decisions under Article ... [see Section XII of the Consolidated Text on accession], [which shall be made by consensus] [which shall be made, failing consensus, by a [three quarters] [two thirds] majority] [which shall be made by a [three quarters] [two thirds] majority]; and

(d)   decisions on budgetary matters, which shall be made by [consensus] [a [three quarters] [two thirds] majority] [of Contracting Parties whose assessed contributions represent, in combination, at least two thirds of the total assessed contributions].

9.   The Parties Group shall be assisted by a Secretariat.

10.   [Parties Group and Secretariat costs shall be borne by the Contracting Parties as approved and apportioned by the Parties Group.] [215]

11.   Where the European Community exercises its right to vote, it shall have a number of votes equal to the number of its Member States which are Contracting Parties to this Agreement. The number of votes of the European Community and its Member States shall in no case exceed the number of the Member States of the European Community which are Contracting Parties to this Agreement.216

XII.   FINAL PROVISIONS

SIGNATURE

This Agreement shall be open for signature at the Depositary, until [date], by Signatories of the Final Act and thereafter until entry into force by any State, or separate customs territory which possesses full autonomy on the matters covered by this Agreement, which is

---

[215] Further work is required on paragraphs 9 and 10. Some delegations note that funding of the MAI will need to be addressed by delegations in advance of ratification and that there may be a need to include a formula in the Agreement.

[216] This text is a proposal by one delegation. Some delegations want to consider whether the MAI should contain such a provision. Assuming that it should, two questions have been raised: whether the provision should apply only in cases where the Commission has competence and whether the Commission should be restricted to casting a number of votes equal to the number of its Member States that are present when the vote takes place. It has also been suggested that a provision might be drafted that applied to Regional Economic Integration Organisations rather than specifically to the European Community.

willing and able to take on its obligations on terms agreed between it and the Signatories of this Agreement.[217]

ACCEPTANCE AND ENTRY INTO FORCE

In the Final Act

1.   The Signatories to this Final Act agree to submit the Agreement for the consideration of their respective competent authorities with a view to seeking approval of the Agreement in accordance with their procedures.

2.   The Signatories to this Final Act agree on the desirability of acceptance of the Agreement by all signatories with a view to its entry into force by [date] or as early as possible thereafter.

In the MAI

3.   Not later than [date], the Signatories to this Agreement will meet to determine the date for entry into force and related matters[218]. Decisions shall be made by [consensus] [a [two-thirds] majority[219] of the Signatories].

4.   This Agreement shall enter into force on the date determined by the Signatories to this Agreement in accordance with paragraph 3 for the Signatories that have accepted this Agreement as of that date. An acceptance following the entry into force of this Agreement shall enter into force on the 30th day following the deposit of its instrument of acceptance.

ACCESSION[220]

---

[217]   Under this formulation, all signatories of the Agreement must agree the terms of a new signatory.

[218]   Delegations agree that there should be an interpretative note as follows: "Related matters" includes such matters as whether there is a critical mass to proceed with entry into force of the Agreement, but not changes to the Agreement.

[219]   There are additional possibilities for a majority voting rule, including consensus minus one (or some number greater than one), three quarters and a critical mass of delegations comprising a certain percentage of investment flows.

[220]   It was generally agreed that an appropriate clause to address the situation of non-Members could provide a strong political message that such participation was welcome. Delegations agree to put forward the following text for consideration by the Negotiating Group. There are different views on where to place such a clause, including in the Preamble, in a Final Act, or in the text of the MAI dealing with Accession. Some delegations are concerned about the political visibility of the clause and it is noted that delegations would have the option of highlighting it in individual national statements:

"In reviewing applications for adherence to the MAI, the Parties will give full consideration to the particular circumstances of each applicant, including the possible need for country specific exceptions to accommodate the applicant's development interests. Where appropriate, the Parties will consider requests for such exceptions in the context of the applicant's overall reform of its domestic investment regime, including the possibility of time-limited exceptions where a transitional period is necessary to implement such reform."

1.　　　　This Agreement shall be open for accession by any State, regional economic integration organisation[221], and any separate customs territory which possesses full autonomy in the conduct of matters covered by this agreement, which is willing and able to undertake its obligations on terms agreed between it and the Contracting Parties acting through the Parties Group.

2.　　　　Decisions on accession shall be taken by the Parties Group.[222]

3.　　　　Accession shall take effect on the thirtieth day following the deposit of the instruments of accession with the Depositary.

NON-APPLICABILITY

This Agreement shall not apply as between any Contracting Party and any acceding Party if, at the time of accession, the Contracting Party does not consent to such application.

REVIEW

The Parties Group may review this Agreement as and when it determines.

AMENDMENT

Any Contracting Party may propose to the Parties Group an amendment to this Agreement. Any amendment adopted by the Parties Group[223] shall enter into force on the deposit of an instrument of ratification by all of the Contracting Parties, or at such later date as may be specified by the Parties Group at the time of adoption of the amendment.

REVISIONS TO THE OECD GUIDELINES FOR MULTINATIONAL ENTERPRISES[224]

For Guidelines Annex changes any Contracting Party may make a unilateral statement upon signature:

---

[221]　A definition of this term will need to be agreed.

[222]　See Consolidated Text, Section XI, Preparatory Group, paragraph 7 and Parties Group, paragraph 8.

[223]　Delegations agree that when the Parties Group considers a proposed amendment, the Group will need to consider both the extent to which reservations will be allowed and any proposed reservations themselves. Delegations will consider how best to reflect this thought in the Agreement. It might be reflected in an interpretative note or in the provision on lodging country specific exceptions.

[224]　Delegations considered the need for a provision on how to take account of revisions to the Guidelines without the necessity of formal amendment of the MAI. They agreed to recommend to the Negotiating Group that any Contracting Party could, upon signature of the MAI, make one of two unilateral statements describing how it would take account of modification of the Guidelines. These two alternative statements are presented in the text.

In the event of modification of the Guidelines, Annex -- will be modified accordingly with respect to (Contracting Party name) provided that it has not made a declaration to the contrary within 180 days of notification by the depositary of the adoption of the modification.

or

In the event of modification of the Guidelines, Annex -- will be modified accordingly with respect to (Contracting Party name) provided that it has made a declaration to that effect to the depositary.

WITHDRAWAL

1.   At any time after five years from the date on which this Agreement has entered into force for a Contracting Party, that Contracting Party may give written notice to the Depositary of its withdrawal from this Agreement.

2.   Any such withdrawal shall take effect on the expiry of six months from the date of the receipt of the notice by the Depositary, or on such later date as may be specified in the notice of withdrawal. If a Contracting Party withdraws, the Agreement shall remain in force for the remaining Contracting Parties.

3.   The provisions of this Agreement shall continue to apply for a period of fifteen years from the date of notification of withdrawal to an investment existing at that date.

DEPOSITARY

The [...............] shall be the Depositary of this Agreement.

STATUS OF ANNEXES

The Annexes to this Agreement are [an integral part of the Agreement].[225]

AUTHENTIC TEXTS

The English and French [and ....] texts of this Agreement are equally authentic.[226]

DENIAL OF BENEFITS

a.   [Subject to prior notification to and consultation with the Contracting Party of the investor,] a Contracting Party may deny the benefits of the Agreement to an investor [as defined in 1 (ii)] and to its investments if investors of a non-Party own or control the first mentioned

---

[225]   This provision will need to be revisited when the content of the Annexes is known.

[226]   The question arises as to whether the MAI text should be in a language or languages additional to English and French. It should be noted that this question has budgetary implications.

investor and that investor has no substantial business activities in the territory of the Contracting Party under whose law it is constituted or organised.

or

a.   [Subject to prior notification and consultation in accordance with Articles XXX (Transparency) and XXX (Consultations), a Contracting Party may deny the benefits of this Agreement to an investor of another Contracting Party that is an enterprise of such Contracting Party and to investments of such investors if investors of a non-Contracting Party own or control the enterprise and the enterprise has no substantial business activities in the territory of the Contracting Party under whose law it is constituted or organised.][227]

---

[227]   Possible additional text not discussed by DG3

[A Contracting Party may deny the benefits of the Agreement to an investor of another Contracting Party that is an enterprise of such Contracting Party and to investment of such investor if investors of a non-Contracting Party own or control the enterprise and the denying Contracting Party:

(a) does not maintain diplomatic relations with the non-Contracting Party; or

(b) adopts or maintains measures with respect to the non-Contracting Party that prohibit transactions with the enterprise or that would be violated or circumvented if the benefits of this Chapter were accorded to the enterprise or to its investments.]

Some delegations also proposed a wider denial of benefits clause, in particular, to allow denial in cases where the parent was a national or enterprise of a country with which the investment host state lacked diplomatic relations. DG3 agreed that this matter should be considered in the wider context of "general exceptions".

ANNEX 1

COUNTRY SPECIFIC PROPOSALS FOR DRAFT TEXTS

SCOPE

(Contribution from one delegation)

1.   This delegation notes that while the draft text of the MAI contains Part II which is entitled "Scope and Application", there is no scope provisions other than provisions that relate to geographical scope. Accordingly, it is not obvious from the preliminary provisions of the text to what precisely the agreement purport to apply.

2.   Other recent trade agreements such as the General Agreement on Trade in Services (the "GATS") and the North American Free Trade Agreement ("NAFTA") set out the extent of the scope of the agreement.

3.   Article I:1 of the GATS states that it applies to "...measures by Members affecting trade in services." The investment chapter of NAFTA states that it chapter applies to measures of a Party relating to "...investors of another Party... (and) investments of another Party in the territory of the Party..."[228]

4.   This delegation believes that a provision setting out the scope of the agreement is important in order to identify the extent of the obligation being undertaken. This delegation notes that many of the contributions made by participants have implicitly assumed that the agreement applies to government measures.[229] In addition, the draft format for the lodging of country-specific reservations uses the concept of measures in describing the reservation.

5.   This delegation, as a signatory to both the GATS and NAFTA, submits that the concept of obligations applying to government measures is the correct approach. Stating so explicitly in the text of the agreement is good practice and allows countries to make a clear evaluation of their obligation and further permits them to reach a clear judgement as to what matters need to be reserved.

6.   Countries should only be bound with respect to their measures. Not all actions, statements or actions of a government necessarily constitutes a measure and the proposition that all such matters could be adjudicated is a matter that should be of some concern to governments. While it is perhaps unlikely that another government or a dissatisfied investor might initiate dispute settlement over, for example, a statement that in and of itself has no legal effect, it is possible that such a matter could be raised in dispute settlement in addition to a more substantive claim. In this delegation's view this would be wrong as being outside the scope to which we envisage the agreement applying. This is not to say that some actions by government that are not

---

[228] See: Article 1101(1) of Chapter 11 of NAFTA for full text.

[229] See, for example, the contribution on Secondary Investment Boycotts, the contribution from France on an Exception Clause for Cultural Industries and the contribution on Social Security Contributions.

measures could not be placed before an arbitral panel as, for example, being evidence that a measure has violated a provision of the agreement.

7.   This delegation proposes that a scope and application provision could be drafted as follows:

> "This Agreement applies to measures adopted or maintained by Contracting Party relating to investors of another Contracting Party and investments of investors of another Contracting Party in the territory of the Contracting Party."

> "measure" includes any law, regulation, procedure, requirement or practice;"

GEOGRAPHICAL SCOPE

(Contribution from one delegation)

I.   Introduction

The main objective of the multilateral international agreements must be to assist governments in their efforts to maintain the international peace and security, since no international agreement can be drafted in a way to disregard the existing international peace and security.

No agreement can include provisions which may violate the rights and interests of a party or parties, or upset the sensitive balance of international order.

This delegation would like to highlight the fact that there was a broad acceptance, during MAI negotiations of the principle that international peace and security shall be respected.

II.   Perspective of MAI

The aim of MAI should be to provide a comprehensive protection for investors and investments. However if it diverges from the existing definition of territory under international law this may raise legal complications. On this Delegation's view, it is not the intention of the OECD members to raise new international legal complications.

III.   Some Comments on the Draft Provision on Geographical Scope

Regarding the draft article MAI shall apply not only in the land territory, the internal waters and the territorial sea of each party, (the definition of "territory" already comprises with respect to international law), but also in the maritime areas beyond the territorial sea as well as the archipelagic waters.

None of the OECD members is an archipelagic State. In addition to this fact, it has not been taken into consideration that without contemplating all maritime issues between archipelagic states and their views on draft article, such a provision may produce contingencies between the relevant states as well as on investors and investments.

It should be recalled that not every state has ratified the 1982 UNCLOS. Furthermore, this Convention does not include any specific investment-related provisions. In the light of these facts, establishment of a relationship between MAI and the UNCLOS should be avoided. Consequently if a reference to the UNCLOS is going to be preferred, it is our view that a broader view should be followed in order to avoid discrepancies.

It should not be overlooked that there are many jurisdictional issues between the opposite or adjacent coastal states, even regarding the air territory above maritime areas, arising from the claims to extend the air territory beyond the frontiers of territorial sea. Therefore the area of application of MAI should be defined in a way so as not to produce negative effects on the nature and extent of already existing maritime issues and increase the number of countries involved to such cases. Extending the scope to the maritime areas to which a new international agreement shall apply will certainly aggravate the already existing disputes. This will also be a risk for the third countries and investors into which they never wanted to be involved.

IV.   Conclusion

This Delegation should like to reiterate their opposition to the extension of the scope of MAI to cover maritime areas and offer the following text:

"This Agreement shall apply in the land territory, internal waters and the territorial sea of a Contracting Party."

APPLICATION TO OVERSEAS TERRITORIES AND NON-APPLICABILITY IN THE MULTILATERAL AGREEMENT INVESTMENT
(Contribution from one delegation)

1.   The clause on application to overseas territories stipulates that any State may, at any time, notify the depositary of the Agreement of the extension of such State to one or more territories for whose foreign relations it is responsible.

2.   The consequences of such clause are as follows:

–   Any State can unilaterally modify the territorial scope of the Agreement at any time.

–   It is bound to notify the depositary only; the other states are not informed thereof either by the party in question or by the depositary.

3.   The outcome is imbalance among the Contracting Parties, since they cannot react to a unilateral declaration of territorial application by any one of them. The territorial clause should be amended in order to reach a balance in the obligations assumed by the Contracting Parties. The territorial clause should provide that:

- The depository must notify such territorial extension to the other States party to the Agreement.

- The latter should be afforded a reasonable period of time from receipt of the notice from the depositary in which to comment or declare that they deem such extension unsuitable.

- The extension should become effective once the above period lapses, excluding their application to any State party to the Agreement lodging its opposition to such extension.

4.   The clause should then be re-worded as follows:

"A State may at any time declare in writing to the Depositary **and to the other Contracting Parties** that this Agreement shall apply to all or one or more of the territories for the international relations of which it is responsible. **The Contracting Parties, once so informed may within 30 days after receipt of the declaration lodge any comment they wish, including their opposition to the extension of the Agreement to the above-mentioned territories.   In the latter case, the non applicability clause shall apply.** The declaration, made prior to or upon ratification, accession or acceptance, shall take effect upon entry into force of this Agreement for that State.   A subsequent declaration shall take effect with respect to the territory or territories concerned on the ninetieth day **after the conclusion of the third day period for comments**".

5.   Furthermore, the non-applicability clause should provide not only for the non-application of the MAI between a Contracting Party and the Party adhering to the Agreement, but also for the possibility that, when a Contracting Party extends the Agreement to a territory for whose foreign relations it is responsible, other Contracting Parties may oppose or refrain from applying the Agreement to such territory (in respect of both direct investment originating in such territory and indirect investment channelled through it).

6.   The non-applicability clause would be re-worded as follows:
This Agreement shall not apply as between any Contracting Party and any acceding Party if, at the time of accession, the Contracting Party does not consent to such application. **This Agreement shall not apply as between any Contracting Party and any territory or territories for the international relations of which a Contracting Party is responsible if, at the time of the declaration, the former Contracting Party does not consent to such application.**

SCOPE OF APPLICATION

(Contribution from one delegation)

1.   This Agreement shall apply:

   a)   in the land territory, internal waters, and the territorial sea of a Contracting Party, and, in the case of a Contracting Party which is an archipelagic state, its archipelagic waters; and

   b)   beyond the territorial sea with respect to the exercise by a Contracting Party of its sovereign rights or jurisdiction in accordance with international law.

2.   This Agreement applies to measures adopted or maintained by a Contracting Party relating to investors of another Contracting Party and to their investments in accordance with its provisions.

3.   This Agreement does not apply to measures taken by a Contracting Party in exercising its rights and performing its duties under international law with respect to the conservation, management and utilisation of the living resources in the sea.

4.   Nothing in this Agreement shall prejudice the positions of the Contracting Parties with respect to:

   a)   issues related to sea boundary delimitations, or

   b)   which of them is entitled to exercise sovereignty, sovereign rights or jurisdiction within a particular geographical area, or with respect to a particular activity within a particular geographical area.

The Contracting Parties recognise that such questions are governed by international law and relevant international agreements.

SCOPE OF APPLICATION - EXPLANATORY NOTE TO THIS DELEGATION'S PROPOSAL

This proposal is based on and elaborates further Article 2 in the proposals by the Chairman.

Paragraph 1(a) of this proposal is identical with paragraph 1(a) of Article 2 in the proposal by the Chairman.

Paragraph 1(b) of this proposal is based on paragraph 1(b) of Article 2 in the proposal of the Chairman. However, the text has been redrafted with a view to ensure consistency with the law of the sea, and notably with Articles 55, 56 and 77 of the United Nations Convention on the Law of the Sea of 1982 (UNCLOS).

Paragraph 2 of this proposal is inspired by Article 1.1 of the GATS and Article 1101 of the NAFTA.   Reference is also made to the proposal of one delegation contained in the

Consolidated Text. Like another delegation, this delegation believes that such a provision is important in order to clarify the extent of the obligations being undertaken.

Paragraph 3 of this proposal aims at ensuring that the conservation, management and utilisation of the living resources in the sea are excluded from the scope of application of MAI. it is the firm conviction of the Government of this delegation that these issues, which are regulated in UNCLOS Part V and in bilateral and regional fisheries agreements, should not be covered by MAI.

Paragraph 4 of this proposal is based on paragraph 2 of Article 2 in the proposal of the Chairman. It is a disclaimer to deal with concerns expressed by some delegations. In subparagraph (a) the Norwegian proposal uses the language "sea boundary delimitations" as used in UNCLOS Article 298 (1)(a)(i) instead of the language "the delimitation of maritime zones" as used in the proposal of the Chairman. The reason is that it is understood that references to "maritime zones" and "maritime areas" may cause difficulties to some delegations. Furthermore, in the proposal the following sentence is added: "The Contracting Parties recognise that such questions are governed by international law and relevant international agreements".

Like in the proposal of the Chairman, with a view to accommodate the concerns of some delegations references to the UNCLOS have been avoided in this delegation's proposal.

GOVERNMENT PROCUREMENT OF SERVICES

(Contribution from one delegation)

1.   Negotiators have been conscious of the need to ensure that the MAI is compatible with other international agreements, including those of the IMF and WTO. The MAI should not create obligations on Parties that conflict with their obligations under those agreements.

2.   In this regard, this delegation considers it important to make clear that the MAI does not apply to government procurement of services, or to the provision of social services.

3.   The whole rationale for the negotiations to develop a Multilateral Agreement on Investment rests on ensuring fair, transparent and predictable investment regimes. The rules and disciplines applying to services were negotiated in detail during the Uruguay Round resulting in the General Agreement on Trade in Services. This latter agreement specifically excludes services supplied in the exercise of governmental authority. GATS Article XIII also states that the MFN, market access and national treatment provisions in Articles II, XVI and XVII "shall not apply to laws, regulations or requirements governing the procurement by governmental agencies of services purchased for governmental purposes and not with a view to commercial resale or with a view to use in the supply of services for commercial sale." A further set of negotiations on services will take place in the WTO in 2000. Furthermore, the WTO Agreement on Government Procurement deals specifically with government procurement of services.

4.   This delegation holds the view that it is not appropriate, nor consistent with agreements negotiated in the WTO, for the MAI to extend its coverage to government procurement of services or the provision of social services. We believe that other delegations share this view.

This is reflected in the fact that experts have sought to preserve existing obligations on government procurement in various places in the text, such as in the draft articles on Monopolies and Performance Requirements. In addition, some countries have tabled draft reservations relating to existing and future measures pertaining to government procurement and to provision of social services.

5.   This delegation believes a generic solution in the text would be the most appropriate way to clarify the issue. Accordingly, this delegation proposes that an Article on Government Procurement be added to the MAI as follows:

> "Nothing in this Agreement applies to the government procurement of services, or the provision of social services."

SUBSTANTIVE APPROACH TO THE RESPECT CLAUSE

(Contribution from one delegation)

Each Contracting Party shall observe any other obligation in writing, it has assumed with regard to investments in its territory by investors of another Contracting Party.

Disputes arising from such obligations shall only be settled under the terms of the contracts underlying the obligations.

RESPECT CLAUSE

(Contribution from one delegation)

Each Contracting Party shall observe any obligation it has entered into with regard to a specific investment of an investor of another Contracting Party.

CLAUSE FOR REGIONAL ECONOMIC INTEGRATION ORGANISATIONS (REIO-CLAUSE)

(Contribution from one delegation)

This delegation has presented the principle reasons for the inclusion of a clause for Regional Economic Integration Organisations in the Multilateral Agreement on Investment at the April meeting of the Negotiating Group.

Building on this contribution, this delegation herewith submits its proposal for such a REIO-clause.

Article X
on
Regional Economic Integration Organisations (REIOs)

1.   For the purpose of this Agreement, a REIO is an organisation of sovereign States which have committed themselves to abolish in substance all barriers to investment among themselves and to which these States have transferred competence on a range of matters within the purview of this Agreement, including the authority to adopt legislation and to make decisions binding on them in respect of those matters.

2.   Article ..... (MFN clause) shall not prevent a Contracting Party which is a Member State of a REIO from according more favourable treatment to investors and their investments from other Member States of the organisation as a result of the measures applied within the framework of that organisation than it accords to investors and their investments from other Contracting Parties.

3.   Nothing in this Agreement shall prevent a REIO and its Member States from applying, consistent with the objectives of this Agreement, new harmonised measures adopted within the framework of such organisation and which replace the measures previously applied by these States.

4.   A Contracting Party which joins a REIO shall not be prevented from applying in place of its previous national legislation the corresponding legislation of the said organisation from the day of its accession to it. If a Contracting Party has concluded an agreement with a REIO and its Member States in preparation for its accession to it, nothing in this Agreement shall prevent it from aligning its national legislation to the measures applied in the framework of such organisation, nor shall this Agreement prevent Member States of a REIO from extending to the investors and their investments of such a Contracting Party more favourable treatment as referred to in paragraph 2.

CLAUSE FOR REGIONAL ECONOMIC INTEGRATION
ORGANISATIONS (REIO - CLAUSE)

(Contribution from three delegations)

Hereby three delegations, supporting in principle the draft text of REIO-Clause proposed by another delegation in the wording contained in Annex of the "Multilateral Agreement on Investment: Consolidated text and commentary", do submit , for the sake of clarity, their proposal for modification of last sentence of the paragraph 4 of the mentioned REIO-Clause, which should read as follows:

„ A Contracting Party which joins a REIO shall not be prevented from applying in place of its previous national legislation the corresponding legislation of the said organisation from the day of its accession to it.

If a Contracting Party has concluded an agreement with a REIO and its Member States in preparation for its accession to it, nothing in this Agreement shall prevent it from aligning its national legislation to the measures applied in the framework of such Organisation. *This Agreement shall prevent neither this Contracting Party nor a Member State of that REIO from according more favourable treatment resulting from such an alignment to each other's investors and their investments than they accord to investors and their investments from other Contracting Parties."*

PACKAGE OF ADDITIONAL ENVIRONMENTAL PROPOSALS

(Contribution by one delegation)

In addition to the environmental elements in the preamble, the article based on NAFTA 1114, and the association of the OECD Guidelines for Multinational Enterprises, this delegation proposes the following additional language to address environmental issues in the MAI.

1)   **Health, Safety and Environment**

Two new paragraphs, to add to the already tabled NAFTA 1114.2-type provision (regarding the lowering of standards for the purpose of attracting investment).

a)   **"Nothing in this Agreement shall be construed to prevent a Party from adopting, maintaining or enforcing any measure otherwise consistent with this Agreement that it considers appropriate to ensure that investment activity in its territory is undertaken in a manner sensitive to environmental concerns."** (Text same as NAFTA 1114.1)

b)   " **Parties, through the cooperation of relevant international organizations and industry, where appropriate, should encourage investors wherever they operate to introduce policies and make commitments to follow environmentally protective standards regarding toxic chemicals and hazardous waste generation and disposal."**

2.)   **Maintaining and Enforcing High Environmental Standards**

"Recognizing the right of each Party to establish its own levels of domestic environmental protection and environmental development policies and priorities, and to adopt or modify accordingly its environmental laws and regulations, each Party should ensure that its laws and regulations provide for high levels of environmental protection and should continue to improve those laws and regulations. Moreover, each Party should effectively enforce its environmental laws and regulations through appropriate governmental action."

3)   **Environmental Impact Assessments**

"Each Party should require or undertake, as appropriate, and consistent with Articles ** on most-favoured national and national treatment, environmental impact assessments for proposed investment in its territory that is likely to have a significant adverse impact on health or the environment and is subject to a decision of a competent national authority."

In addition, we propose the following additional language. While this language is not strictly environmental, it addresses some environmental concerns that were identified during our analysis of the potential environmental implications of the MAI.

4) "In Like Circumstances"

The following language already tabled for a footnote or interpretive note to "in like circumstances" in the national and MFN treatment articles would also include new language **in bold**:

> "National Treatment and most favoured nation treatment are relative standards requiring a comparison between treatment of a foreign investor and its investment and treatment of domestic or third country investors and investments. The goal of both standards is to prevent discrimination in fact or in law compared with domestic investors or investments of those of a third country. At the same time, however, governments may have legitimate policy reasons to accord differential treatment to different types of investments. **Similarly, governments may have legitimate policy reasons to accord differential treatment as between domestic and foreign investors and their investments in certain circumstances, for example where needed to secure compliance with domestic laws that are not inconsistent with national treatment and most favoured nation treatment. Moreover, the fact that a measure applied by a government has a different effect on an investment or investor of another Party would not in itself render the measure inconsistent with national treatment and most favoured nation treatment.**
>
> " 'In like circumstances' ensures that comparisons are made between investors and investment on the basis of characteristics that are relevant for the purposes of the comparison. The objective is to permit the consideration of all relevant circumstances, including those relating to a foreign investor and its investment, in deciding to which domestic or third country investors and investments they should appropriately be compared, while excluding from consideration those characteristics that are not germane to such a comparison."

5) Transparency

A new phrase **(in bold)** would be added to the already tabled articles on Transparency. The brackets in the text below are presently in the draft MAI text itself.

> "2.3 Nothing in this Agreement shall prevent a Contracting Party from requiring an investor of another Contracting Party, or its investment, **to provide or allow the verification of information to ensure compliance with the first Contracting Party's laws and regulations, or** to provide routine information concerning that investment solely for information or statistical purposes. No contracting Party shall be required to furnish or allow access to information concerning particular investors or investments the disclosure of which would impede law enforcement or would be contrary to its laws [policies, or practices] protecting confidentiality."

In addition, this delegation is continuing to consider the need to address other environmental concerns in the text. In particular, we are continuing to review the expropriation and general treatment articles to ensure concerns in that area are addressed. We also note that we will need to ensure that MAI obligations do not conflict with the Climate Change Convention.

DRAFT ARTICLE ON CONFLICTING REQUIREMENTS

(Amendment of the proposal introduced by one delegation)[230]

(Contribution from one delegation)

Paragraph 1. A Contracting Party shall not prohibit outside its territory, directly or indirectly, or cause to refrain, an investor from another Contracting Party from acting in accordance with the latter Contracting Party's laws, regulations or express policies unless those laws, regulations or express policy are contrary to international law (conflicting requirement).

"Express policy" means a situation in which the conduct of an investor is not explicitly regulated but allowed on the basis of general principles of law or general policy in the relevant country

REASONS FOR REFORMULATING PARAGRAPH 1 OF THE PROPOSAL BY ONE DELEGATION

1. It appears to be necessary to cover not only cases where a contracting party is (directly) requiring an investor to behave in a certain way but also cases where the Contracting Party enjoins sanctions on investors when they behave in that way (e.g. loss of rights or advantages that would otherwise be granted).

2. The wording proposed by one delegation *"to act in conflict"* seems to be unduly narrow as it implies that there is an open conflict between two legal orders, one imposing to do X, the other to do Y in the same situation. Those cases exist, but are extremely rare (e.g. a Saudi Arabian law imposes on investors not to export to or invest in Israel/a US law imposes on American investors abroad not to accept boycott against Israel). The normal situation is, however, that the legal order of a Contracting Party simply allows certain activities (e.g. this delegation permits whaling) whilst the legal order of another Contracting Party prohibits investors such activities, even abroad (e.g. another delegation would not allow its investors at home and abroad to invest in whaling).

In this case there would be no real conflict according to the proposal by one delegation as the investor can abide by the rule of anothe delegation without entering in conflict with this country's laws.

Thus, there is a choice to make between the two concepts. The *"open conflict"* rule does in the view of one delegation not serve much purpose.

---

[230] Original proposal by one delegation included in is reproduced at the end of this contribution.

Moreover, a *"conflict"* in the meaning of requirements that are really opposed to one another is not possible between a law on the one hand and a *"policy"* on the other as a pure policy measure is not mandatory. If one would choose the narrow approach (open conflict), the reference to such policy measure would have to be deleted.

3.   It seems to be useful to require that the measures of the Contracting party concerned are not contrary to international law otherwise they do not merit protection (e.g. a country exploits unlawfully the continental shelf of another country; measures against investors contributing to such behaviour can be sanctioned).

4.   As the term *"conflicting requirement"* reappears more often in the text it is preferable to give it the form of a definition.

5.   The term *"express policy"* is new and it seems useful, for reasons of legal clarity, to define it.

Paragraph 2.   The Parties Group may receive notice of conflicting requirements from :

a)   A Contracting Party which considers that [.......] another Contracting Party imposes or enforces, or intends to do so, conflicting requirements on investors or investments of investors in respect of conduct within its territory;

b)   A Contracting Party which is considering imposing or enforcing or which has imposed or enforced conflicting requirements on investors or investments of investors in respect of conduct within the territory of another Contracting Party.

Commentary

Simple streamlining of the text.

Paragraph 3.   A Contracting Party may at any time advise the Parties Group that it does not regard a conflicting requirement that has been notified by another Contracting Party pursuant to paragraph 2 as objectionable. In such cases, paragraph 1 [...] does not apply to such requirements *in the relation between the Contracting Parties concerned.*

Commentary

Some amendments are necessary to align the wording to the amended paragraph 1.

In addition, it should be made clear that the non-objection of one Contracting Party to the measure has no legal effect for other Contracting Parties.

Paragraph 4   (Unchanged).

Paragraph 5   (Unchanged until the third stroke; the third stroke contains a full concept in itself and should become a new paragraph 6).

Paragraph 6   If the conflicting requirements have been imposed consistent with international law in order to minimise or avoid substantial effects within a Contracting Party of actions outside that Contracting Party, the waiver shall be granted unless the Contracting Party in whose territory the conduct occurs has taken reasonable measures to ensure that such effects do not recur.

Commentary

Paragraph 6 introduces a useful concept of legitimate "self defence", applicable e.g. in case a Contracting Party would allow drug production or far reaching and serious pollution of the environment; there may be however also cases where the decision is not so easy to find (e.g. advertising directed from one country to the other using methods not allowed in the latter; investment in border shops selling articles which are not authorised in a contracting party etc.).

Draft Article on Conflicting Requirements[1]

1.   A Contracting Party shall not impose or enforce measures that require an investor or an investment of an investor to act in conflict with the laws, regulations or express policies of another Contracting Party in whose territory such acts occur.

2.   The MAI Parties Group may receive notice of conflicting requirements from:

   a)   A Contracting Party which considers that measures or proposed measures of another Contracting Party impose or enforce conflicting requirements on investors or investments of investors in respect of conduct within its territory;

   b)   A Contracting Party which is considering imposing or enforcing, or which has imposed or enforced conflicting requirements on investors or investments of investors in respect of conduct within the territory of another Contracting Party.

3.   A Contracting Party in whose territory conduct occurs may at any time advise the Parties Group that it does not regard a requirement that has been notified pursuant to paragraph 2 as objectionable. In such cases, paragraph 1 of this Article does not apply to such requirements.

4.   If a conflicting requirement has been notified to the Parties Group, and the Contracting Party in whose territory the conduct occurs has not provided the notification provided for by paragraph 3, the Parties Group may, at the request of the state which exercises jurisdiction outside its territory, consider whether a waiver should be granted from the prohibition on conflicting requirements set out in paragraph 1.

5.   In considering whether to grant a waiver from paragraph 1, the Parties Group shall have regard to the following considerations:

---

[1]   Taken from a contribution by one delegation.

- The results of consultations between the affected states regarding the manner in which the conflict could be minimized or avoided.

- Whether, as a result of the conflicting requirement any investor or investment of an investor has been or may be subjected to treatment that is unfair or inequitable.

- If the conflicting requirement has been imposed consistent with international law in order to minimize or avoid substantial effects within a Contracting Party of actions outside that Contracting Party, the waiver shall be granted unless the Contracting Party in whose territory the conduct occurs has taken reasonable measures to ensure that such effects do not recur.

DRAFT ARTICLE ON SECONDARY INVESTMENT BOYCOTTS
(Based on the proposal by one delegation, [2] *drafting changes are indicated and explained in the footnotes)*

No Contracting Party may take measures that

   i)   either[3] impose or may be used to impose liability on investors or investments of investors of another Contracting Party;

   ii)   *or* prohibit, or *impose sanctions*[4] for, dealing with investors or investment of investors of another Contracting Party;

because of investments an investor of another Contracting Party makes, owns or controls, directly or indirectly, in a third country in accordance with [*international law*[5] *and*] regulations of such third country.

---

  [2]   Original proposal by one delegation is reproduced as follows:

"Draft Article on Secondary Investment Boycotts

No Contracting Party may take measures that

(i) impose or may be used to impose liability on investors or investments of investors of another Contracting Party; or

(ii) prohibit dealing with investors or investments of investors of another Contracting Party

because of investments they own or control, directly or indirectly, in a third country in accordance with the laws and regulations of such third country."

  [3]   Purely a drafting amendment.

  [4]   Broader wording is suggested because in some cases a sanction can be applied without explicit prohibition. There is a danger of circumvention.

  [5]   Consistency with international law should be required because a measure merits protection by an international agreement only if this measure is consistent with international law.

INTRODUCTION OF AN EXCEPTION CLAUSE
FOR CULTURAL INDUSTRIES

(Contribution from one delegation)

After in-depth analysis of the implications of the MAI, this delegation has come to the conclusion that the basic principles of this agreement raise application problems for cultural industries (notably the printing, press and audio-visual sectors). In fact, policies designed to preserve cultural and linguistic diversity may not be entirely compatible with the disciplines of the agreement and so could be endangered.

As regards direct restrictions on foreign investment, the standstill commitment is likely to make existing limitations ineffective, since sectors using new technologies would not be subject to such limitations. This would be unacceptable for this delegation and would undermine the results of the Uruguay Round for the audio-visual sector. On completion of the Round, only three OECD Members undertook specific commitments in the audio-visual sector. The other signatories - including the European Union and its Member States - did not agree to a standstill commitment with respect to mode 3 of the GATS ("establishment of a commercial presence") in this sector.

As regards indirect restrictions on investment, the type of disciplines to be included in the MAI are not yet precisely known. However, the audio-visual and press sectors are governed by specific regulations in which linguistic and/or nationality criteria play a central role. In this respect, it should be clear in MAI that a State may treat two enterprises of these sectors differently, in particularly according to the linguistic content of the goods produced or the services supplied.

The Most Favoured Nation clause and National Treatment principle would also be difficult to apply to these sectors. In fact, various international agreements, including coproduction agreements, make exceptions to the Most Favoured Nation clause and offer foreign enterprises of third countries preferential or even national treatment.

The MAI should allow the Signatories to implement policies designed to promote cultural and linguistic diversity and consequently, to protect and promote industries ensuring such diversity.

Only a cultural exception would make it possible to protect cultural industries from the disciplines covered by the agreement. This general exception could be drafted as follows:

> "Nothing in this agreement shall be construed to prevent any Contracting Party to take any measure to regulate investment of foreign companies and the conditions of activity of these companies, in the framework of policies designed to preserve and promote cultural and linguistic diversity."

SUBNATIONAL MEASURES

(Contribution from one delegation)

The application of the MAI to sub-federal entities raises a particular issue with regard to the application of national treatment. Delegations will recall that Commentary number 7, on the MAI's national treatment article, page 100 of the Consolidated Texts and Commentary reads:

"The question was asked whether the treatment accorded to foreign investors by a <u>sub-federal state or province</u> would meet the national treatment test only if it were no less favourable than the treatment accorded to the investors of the <u>same</u> state or province, or whether it would be sufficient to accord treatment no less favourable than that accorded to the investors from <u>any</u> other state or province. The question will need to be answered by the Negotiating Group in due course."

The MAI intends to set high standards of liberalisation, and it is therefore believed that foreign investors would benefit most if the sub-federal entity would accord to them "in state" treatment.

This issue has been the subject of debate in other fora, lately notably in the GATS context. These discussions have shown that legal clarity and certainty in this regard are of considerable importance.

It is therefore proposed to add the following language to the National Treatment Article in a separate paragraph:

1.4.   If a sub-federal entity of a Contracting Party accords to its own investors and their investments treatment more favourable than to investors and investments of other sub-federal entities of the same Contracting Party it shall in accordance with paragraphs 1 to 3 extend the more favourable treatment to investors of other Contracting Parties and to their investments.

We would appreciate the view of other Delegations with regard to inclusion of the principle as well as the proposed language in the MAI.

THE RELATIONSHIP BETWEEN THE SVALBARD TREATY AND THE MAI

(Contribution from one delegation)

Draft Article to be included in Part X (Other Provisions)

In the event of a conflict between the Treaty concerning Spitsbergen of 9 February 1920 (the Svalbard Treaty) and this Agreement, the Svalbard Treaty shall prevail to the extent of the conflict, without prejudice to the positions of the Contracting Parties with respect to the

Svalbard Treaty. In the event of such a conflict or a dispute as to whether there is such a conflict or as to its extent, Part V (Dispute Settlement) and Part VII (Relationship to other International Agreements) of this Agreement shall not apply.

LABOUR MARKETS INTEGRATION AGREEMENTS

(Contribution from five delegations)

During the MAI negotiations in Paris delegations have agreed on the inclusion of a provision regarding "key personnel".[6] The basic provision is that the Contracting Parties are obliged to permit certain groups of natural persons to enter into and stay in a Contracting State in connection with investments covered by the MAI, subject to the application of Contracting Parties' national laws, regulations and procedures affecting the entry, stay and work of natural persons. Under the stated condition, the same groups of natural persons are entitled to work permits in connection with covered investments. A Contracting Party may make the issue of such permits conditional on the submission of formal written applications for such permits in accordance with its relevant laws and regulations.

For more than 40 years the Nordic countries have maintained a special legal regime for the entry by their nationals into their respective employment markets.[7] Under this regime nationals of the Nordic countries may move freely from one country to another and are not required to obtain residence permits and/or work permits from the relevant national authorities. It goes without saying that this also covers nationals of the five countries in their capacity as investors or key personnel. The regime covers all groups of workers and also provides for certain social benefits regardless of nationality. The rules of the Nordic common labour market are thus more favourable to nationals of the Nordic countries than the rules applicable to nationals of third countries.[8]

The historical, economic and political ties between the five Nordic countries as well as the similarities in their welfare systems have motivated the integration of their labour markets and have been the rationale for the intergovernmental agreements on the subject. Thus, the motivation for the Nordic Labour Market agreements goes far beyond purely economic considerations.

---

[6]   **For the latest draft text see document DAFFE/MAI/ST(97)4, p. 3-4.**

[7]   The rules are contained in an Agreement of May 22, 1954 concerning exemption from requirements of passport, residence and work permits, an Agreement of July 12, 1957 concerning the suspension of passport control at the common Nordic borders and in the Nordic Convention on Social Security of 1955 (new Convention 1992). The Agreement of May 22, 1954 has been replaced by a subsequent agreement which entered into force on August 1, 1983. The duration of the Agreement is indefinite.

[8]   Another distinct legal regime is applicable to nationals of the EU and EEA states.

While it would seem clear that the MAI is not intended to interfere with integrated labour markets, such as the Nordic Labour Market, it cannot be excluded that the Most Favoured Nation provision of the MAI[9] to some extent interferes with the Nordic Labour Market.

Even if there are important differences between the scope of MAI and the WTO General Agreement on Trade in Services, which e.g. directly covers movement of natural persons, it is worth recalling that the Nordic countries obtained special coverage for integrated labour markets in GATS, through the insertion of article V bis of that agreement. This provision allows Contracting Parties to enter into labour markets integration agreements without having to extend to nationals of third countries by means of MFN treatment an benefits deriving from such an agreement.

In order to obtain complete legal certainty concerning the relationship between the MAI and substantially integrated labour markets the Nordic Countries propose the insertion of a provision similar to GATS art. V bis in the MAI. This would not in any way derogate from the binding MAI obligation regarding key personnel.

Based on the above these five delegations suggest the insertion of a GENERAL labour markets integration provision in the MAI with the following wording[10]:

"Labour markets integration agreements

Paragraph 1

Nothing in this Agreement shall prevent any of the Contracting Parties from being a party to an agreement establishing full integration of the labour markets between the parties to such an agreement.

Paragraph 2

For the purpose of this Agreement the term "labour markets integration agreements" means agreements which allow citizens of the parties to such agreements a right of free entry to the employment markets of the parties concerned and which exempts citizens of parties to the agreement from requirements concerning residency and work permits. Labour markets integration agreements may also include measures concerning conditions of pay, other conditions of employment and social benefits."

---

[9] See document Consolidated Text, p. 11.

[10] The wording is based on the GATS article V bis.

MAI: PROPOSED ANNEX ON THE SAMI PEOPLE

(Contribution by three delegations)

THE CONTRACTING PARTIES,

RECOGNIZING the obligations and commitments of these countries with regard to the Sami people under national and international law,

NOTING, in particular, that these countries are committed to preserving and developing the means of livelihood, language, culture and way of life of the Sami people,

CONSIDERING the dependence on traditional Sami culture and livelihood on primary economic activities, such as reindeer husbandry in the traditional areas of Sami settlement,

HAVE AGREED on the following provisions.

Article 1

Notwithstanding the provisions of this Agreement, exclusive rights to reindeer husbandry within traditional Sami areas may be granted to the Sami people.

Article 2

This Annex may be extended to take account of any further development of exclusive Sami rights linked to their traditional means of livelihood. The Parties Group may adopt the necessary amendments to this Annex.

DISPUTE SETTLEMENT

(Contribution from one delegation)

Investor-State Procedures

Article D, paragraph 3 - Contracting Party Consent

Paragraph 3a should be amended to read:

     a)   Subject only to paragraphs 3b <u>and 3c</u>, each Contracting Party hereby gives ......

Add a new paragraph 3c:

     c)   On the basis of reciprocity a Contracting Party may, by notifying the depositary upon deposit of its instrument of ratification or accession declare that:

(i)   it does not give its consent under paragraph 3a to the submission of a dispute to international arbitration under the ICSID Convention in accordance with this Article; and

(ii)   it does not give its consent under paragraph 3a to the submission of a dispute to international arbitration in cases where under the provisions of the New York Convention recognition and enforcement of the award may be refused by its competent authority.

DISPUTE SETTLEMENT

PROPOSAL FOR INTERPRETATIVE NOTE ON THE ARTICLE ON FINAL AWARDS IN INVESTOR-STATE PROCEDURES (Article D 16(a) (iii))

(Contribution from one delegation)

"Restitution in kind means factual restoration of property and property rights".

Dispute Settlement

Response to Non-compliance

(Contribution from one delegation)

a)   If a Contracting Party fails within a reasonable period of time to comply with its obligations as determined in the award, such Contracting Party shall, at the request of any Contracting Party in whose favour the award was rendered, enter into consultations with a view to reaching a mutually acceptable solution. If no satisfactory solution has been agreed within thirty days after the date of the request for consultations, any Contracting Party in whose favour the award was rendered, shall notify the other Contracting Party and the Parties Group if it intends to suspend the application to the other CP of obligations under this agreement.

b)   The effect of any such suspension must be proportionate to the effect of the other Party's non-compliance. Such suspension may not include suspension of the application of Articles -- (General Treatment) and -- (Expropriation) and should not include denial of other protections to established investment.

c)   At the request of any Party to the award upon conclusion of the thirty-day period for consultation, the Parties Group shall consider the matter. Until twenty days after the decision by the Parties Group set out in iii below suspension shall not be put into effect. The Parties Group may:

i.   make recommendations, by consensus minus the disputing Contracting Parties;

      ii.   suspend the non-complying Party's right to participate in decisions of the Parties Group, by consensus minus the non-complying Contracting Party; and

      iii.   by consensus minus the non-complying Contracting Party, decide that suspension may be carried out. The Contracting Party shall comply with that decision.

d)   Any dispute concerning the alleged failure of a Contracting Party to comply with its obligations as determined in an award or the lawfulness of any responsive measures shall, at the request of any Contracting Party that is party to the dispute, be submitted for decision to the arbitral tribunal which rendered the award or, if the original tribunal is unavailable, to a single member or three member arbitral tribunal designated by the Secretary-General. The request shall be submitted in the same fashion, and the proceedings carried out in accordance with the same rules as are applicable to a request made under paragraph 1.a of this Article, with such modifications as the tribunal deems appropriate, and the final award shall be issued no later than 60 days after the date of the request, in case of the original tribunal, or after the date of its formation, in the case of a new tribunal. No suspension may be carried out from the time of submission of a dispute unless authorised by the tribunal as an interim measure or found lawful.

Article ___[1]

Advisory Opinion

Suggestion for MAI dispute settlement or institutional matter experts

1.   The Parties Group may set up a legal advisory body, on either an ad hoc or permanent basis, on the interpretation and application of the Agreement.

2.   Members of the legal advisory group may include a national of parties which have substantial interests in the issue under consideration.

3.   The legal advisory group should, unless otherwise decided by the Parties Group, conclude its legal opinion no later than 90 days following the submission by the Parties Group.

4.   A Contracting Party may request the Parties Group to consider whether it will ask a legal opinion of the legal advisory body, regarding the compatibility of another Contracting Party's measures with the Agreement.

---

[1] This suggested Article might be included in the provisions with regard to the Parties Group's competence.

Maintaining the Overall Level of Liberalisation

(Contribution from one delegation)

1.   During the latest stages of the MAI-negotiations it became evident that the strict application of the standstill-principle without allowing for any exceptions would be difficult because of problems with respect to certain

*   disciplines,

*   sectors,

*   internal policies, and

*   future developments.

2.   Means suggested to address these concerns are, inter alia:

*   general exceptions,

*   broadly formulated country specific reservations,

*   "List B"-reservations, and

*   specific provisions on, e.g., demonopolization and privatisation.

3.   Without a corrective element all these approaches

*   complicate the assessment of and/or may lead to future distortions in the overall balance of commitments among Contracting Parties, and, more generally,

*   tend to favour "bad" guys having lodged such reservations and/or willing to introduce new non-conforming measures,

thereby considerably deteriorating the legal quality of the agreement (which would then fall short of what was achieved in GATS) and the benefits to be gained from the MAI by Contracting Parties in general and the "good" guys in particular.

4.   This delegation has therefore on earlier occasions proposed to introduce the concept of a legally binding and enforceable "substantive standstill" (the "maintain-the-overall-level-of liberalisation-rule")[11], which would, while allowing for some flexibility, apply without exception and therefore avoid the problems mentioned in Para 4.

---

[11]   The corresponding "substantive rollback-principle" could be formulated as a "enhancing the overall level of liberalisation rule".

5.   The Annex contains a suggestion for such an article on "Maintaining the overall level of liberalisation".

Annex

ARTICLE XX
MAINTAINING THE OVERALL LEVEL OF LIBERALISATION

(1)   A Contracting Party intending to take or taking a nonconforming measure under Articles xy, ..., xz ["list B", all general exceptions] shall do so only consistent with the objectives of this Agreement and in accordance with the provisions of this Article. It shall ensure that the overall level of liberalisation is maintained, if necessary through compensatory adjustments.

(2)   Compensatory adjustments shall be made on a most-favoured-nation basis.

(3)   A Contracting Party shall notify its intent to take such a nonconforming measure to the Parties Group as soon as possible and not later than 3 months before the intended date of implementation of the nonconforming measure. The notification shall contain a description of the nonconforming measure, its likely impact on the overall level of liberalisation and envisaged compensatory adjustments.

(4)   At the request of any Contracting Party the benefits of which under this Agreement may be affected by the intended nonconforming measure, the Parties Group shall take up the subject with a view to reaching agreement on any compensatory adjustments necessary to maintain the overall level of liberalisation.

(5)   If such agreement is not reached within [...] months, any Contracting Party may, within a further [...] days, refer the matter to an arbitral tribunal in accordance with [Part C of State-State Dispute Settlement Procedures].

(6)   The arbitral tribunal may, in its award, state that

     (i)   the overall level of liberalisation is maintained and no compensatory adjustments are necessary;

     (ii)   the overall level of liberalisation is not maintained and the compensatory adjustments proposed or implemented are adequate and sufficient;

     or

     (iii)   the overall level of liberalisation is not maintained and the compensatory adjustments proposed or implemented by the modifying Contracting Party are inadequate or insufficient.

(7)   Necessary procedural rules shall be established by the Parties Group within [...] months after the entry into force of the Agreement.

ANNEX 2

CHAIRMAN'S PROPOSALS ON ENVIRONMENT AND RELATED MATTERS AND ON LABOUR[1]

1.   The approach to the environment and to labour has evolved to achieve balance between MAI disciplines and other important areas of public policy of concern to MAI Parties and to avoid unintended consequences on normal regulatory practices. Details of the three anchors of preamble, text and association of the OECD Guidelines for Multinational Enterprises, are still under consideration. Annexed to this Chairman's Note is a package of proposals for text on environment and labour that in comprehensive fashion brings together the outstanding aspects of our work.[2]

2.   Some portions of this package of proposals address more general concerns than just environmental or labour implications of the MAI, including the proposal for the national treatment and most favoured nation treatment articles and the proposal for the expropriation and general treatment articles.

Environment and Related Matters

3.   The portions of this package of proposals that address environmental concerns in a specific manner are the Preamble, the affirmation of the right of Contracting Parties to regulate in a non-discriminatory manner, the "not lowering measures" provision and the exception to the performance
requirements disciplines.

4.   To respect the need for balance, the proposal for the environmental language in the Preamble seeks as concise a formulation as possible while making the key explicit references. Any additional proposals for preambular language currently before the Negotiating Group could be reconsidered in the context of a political declaration or associated with the MAI in some other way.

5.   The inclusion of "in like circumstances" in the national treatment and most favoured nation treatment provisions, plus the interpretative note, would address concerns about the practical implementation of the "de facto" discrimination principle and preserve the necessary scope for non-discriminatory regulation.

---

[1]   This text reproduces the content of the Note by the Chairman dated 9 March 1998. When this Note was discussed by the Negotiating Group in April 1998, a large majority expressed support for the overall approach and believed that it could be a basis for further work.

[2]   The dispute settlement procedures also take account of environmental and labour concerns through the possibility of appointment to panels of individuals with special expertise (Article V.C.2(c) for State-State proceedings), panel recourse to environmental and other necessary expertise (Articles V.C.5 and V.D.13) and through proposals for transparency of panel proceedings through the Parties Group. Furthermore, a review of the OECD Guidelines for Multinational Enterprises is scheduled to begin this year. The environment and employment and industrial relations chapters of the Guidelines will receive a thorough scrutiny during the review process.

6.   A specific affirmation that the MAI does not inhibit normal non-discriminatory government regulatory activity seems necessary in the environmental field. Combined with the other elements of this package of proposals, this represents a targeted approach. Another approach would be a general exception inspired by GATT Article XX, which would eliminate the need for some other elements of this package, notably the exception to the provisions on performance requirements.

7.   The proposal for binding "not lowering measures" language is limited to domestic measures and the circumstances of a particular investment. The interpretative note spells out the widely-shared views that governments must have the ability to adjust their overall environmental standards over time, and that investment should not be enticed by relaxing standards. Further consideration of the implications of binding language for the dispute settlement procedures may be required.

8.   The proposal for an interpretative note for the expropriation and general treatment articles responds to the agreement at the High Level Meeting that it needs to be made clear that the MAI will not inhibit the exercise of the normal regulatory powers of government and that the exercise of such powers will not amount to expropriation.

9.   The exception article for the provisions on performance requirements is needed because they go beyond non-discrimination. The exception covers those performance requirements that could affect compliance with laws and regulations, or that could affect health, safety or the environment.

10.   The package of proposals includes annexation of the OECD Guidelines to the text of the MAI, without changing their non-binding character.

Labour

11.   The portions of this package of proposals that address labour concerns in a specific manner are the Preamble and the binding "not lowering measures" provision.

12.   As with environment, the proposal sets out a concise formulation that maintains the key explicit references supported by the large majority of MAI Parties. As with environment, any additional proposals for preambular language currently before the Negotiating Group could be reconsidered in the context of a political declaration or associated with the MAI in some other way.

13.   The inclusion of "in like circumstances" in the national treatment and most favoured nation treatment provisions, plus the interpretative note, would address concerns about the practical implementation of the "de facto" discrimination principle and preserve the necessary scope for non-discriminatory regulation. This could be as true for labour concerns as for environmental concerns.

14.	A specific affirmation that the MAI does not inhibit normal non-discriminatory government regulatory activity, to the extent that it addresses health and safety concerns, could cover measures that set labour standards.

15.	The proposal for binding "not lowering measures" language is limited to domestic measures and the circumstances of a particular investment. "Domestic" is chosen as the main qualifier because approaches to "core" or "core international" labour standards appear to vary greatly among MAI Parties. "Measures" has been chosen for consistency with MAI drafting where there is a need to refer to the means by which governments take action (by domestic legislation, regulation, directives, policy, etc).[3] The interpretative note spells out the widely-shared views that governments must have the ability to adjust their overall labour market policies as appropriate over time, and that investment should not be enticed by relaxing standards. Further consideration of the implications of binding language for dispute settlement may be required.

16.	As stated above, the exception article for the provisions on performance requirements is needed because they go beyond the non-discrimination. The exception covers performance requirements that could affect compliance with laws and regulations, or that could affect health, safety or the environment.

17.	Finally, the package of proposals includes annexation of the OECD Guidelines to the text of the MAI, without changing their non-binding character.

ANNEX: PACKAGE OF PROPOSALS FOR TEXT ON ENVIRONMENT AND LABOUR

### *1.	Preamble*

"Recognising that investment, as an engine of economic growth, can play a key role in ensuring that economic growth is sustainable, when accompanied by appropriate environmental and labour policies;

"Re-affirming their commitment to the Rio Declaration on Environment and Development, and Agenda 21 and the Programme for its Further Implementation, including the principles of the polluter pays and the precautionary approach; and resolving to implement this Agreement in a manner consistent with sustainable development and with environmental protection and conservation;

"Renewing their commitment to the Copenhagen Declaration of the World Summit on Social Development and the observance of internationally recognised core labour standards, i.e., freedom of association, the right to organise and bargain collectively, prohibition of forced

---

[3]	See the Articles on performance requirements, recognition arrangements, expropriation and compensation, transfers, exceptions, temporary safeguards, prudential measures, information transfer and data processing, and taxation.

labour, the elimination of exploitative forms of child labour, and non-discrimination in employment, and noting that the International Labour Organisation is the competent body to set and deal with core labour standards world-wide;"

2. *National Treatment and Most Favoured Nation Treatment*

"1. Each Contracting Party shall accord to investors of another Contracting Party and to their investments, treatment no less favourable that the treatment it accords in like circumstances to its own investors and their investments with respect to the establishment, acquisition, expansion, operation, management, maintenance, use, enjoyment and sale or other disposition of investments.

2. Each Contracting Party shall accord to investors of another Contracting Party and to their investments, treatment no less favourable that the treatment it accords in like circumstances to investors of any other Contracting Party or of a non-Contracting Party, and to the investments of investors of any other Contracting Party or of a non-Contracting Party, with respect to the establishment, acquisition, expansion, operation, management, maintenance, use, enjoyment and sale or other disposition of investments.

3. Each Contracting Party shall accord to investors of another Contracting Party and to their investments the better of the treatment required by Articles 1.1 and 1.2, whichever is the more favourable to those investors or investments.*"

---

*Interpretative Note: National Treatment and most favoured nation treatment are relative standards requiring a comparison between treatment of a foreign investor and investments and treatment of domestic or third country investors and investments. Governments may have legitimate policy reasons to accord differential treatment to different types of investments. Similarly, governments may have legitimate policy reasons to accord differential treatment as between domestic and foreign investors and their investments in certain circumstances, for example where needed to secure compliance with domestic laws that are not inconsistent with national treatment and most favoured nation treatment. The fact that a measure applied by a government has a different effect on an investment or investor of another Party would not in itself render the measure inconsistent with national treatment and most favoured nation treatment. The objective of "in like circumstances" is to permit the consideration of all relevant circumstances, including those relating to a foreign investor and its investments, in deciding to which domestic or third country investors and investments they should appropriately be compared.

3. *Affirmation of Right to Regulate*

"A Contracting Party may adopt, maintain or enforce any measure that it considers appropriate to ensure that investment activity is undertaken in a manner sensitive to health, safety or environmental concerns, provided such measures are consistent with this agreement."

4. *"Not Lowering Measures"*

"A Contracting Party shall not waive or otherwise derogate from, or offer to waive or otherwise derogate from, its domestic health, safety, environmental, or labour measures, as an encouragement to the establishment, acquisition, expansion, operation, management, maintenance, use, enjoyment and sale or other disposition of an investment of an investor.*"

"*Interpretative Note: The Parties recognise that governments must have the flexibility to adjust their overall health, safety, environmental or labour standards over time for public policy reasons other than attracting foreign investment."

5. *Expropriation and General Treatment**

"1.   GENERAL TREATMENT

1.   Each Contracting Party shall accord to investments in its territory of investors of another Contracting Party fair and equitable treatment and full and constant protection and security.   Such treatment shall also apply to the operation, management, maintenance, use, enjoyment or disposal of such investments.   In no such case shall a Contracting Party accord treatment less favourable than that required by international law.

"2.   EXPROPRIATION AND COMPENSATION

"1.   A Contracting Party shall not expropriate or nationalise an investment in its territory of an investor of another Contracting Party or take any measure tantamount to expropriation or nationalisation except: ..."

"*Interpretative Note: Articles -- on General Treatment, and -- on Expropriation and Compensation, are intended to incorporate into the MAI existing international legal norms. The reference in Article IV.2.1 to expropriation or nationalisation and "measures tantamount to expropriation or nationalisation" reflects the fact that international law requires compensation for an expropriatory taking without regard to the label applied to it, even if title to the property is not taken. It does not establish a new requirement that Parties pay compensation for losses which an investor or investment may incur through regulation, revenue raising and other normal activity in the public interest undertaken by governments. Nor would such normal and non-discriminatory government activity contravene the standards in Article --.1 (General Treatment)."

6. *Performance Requirements*

"4.   Provided that such measures are not applied in an arbitrary or unjustifiable manner, or do not constitute a disguised restriction on investment, nothing in paragraphs 1(b) and 1(c) shall be construed to prevent any Contracting Party from adopting or maintaining measures, including environmental measures:

(a)   necessary to secure compliance with measures that are not inconsistent with the provisions of this Agreement;

(b)   necessary to protect human, animal or plant life or health; or

(c)   necessary for the conservation of living or non-living exhaustible natural resources."

7.   *OECD Guidelines for Multinational Enterprises*

The OECD Guidelines for Multinational Enterprises will be annexed to the text of the MAI.

*   *   *

PROTOCOL AMENDING THE TREATY ESTABLISHING THE CARIBBEAN COMMUNITY (PROTOCOL III : INDUSTRIAL POLICY)*
[excerpts]

(CARIBBEAN COMMUNITY)

The Protocol Amending the Treaty Establishing the Caribbean Community (Protocol III: Industrial Policy) was opened for signature in Castries (Saint Lucia) on 30 June 1998 and entered into provisional application on 27 October 1999, pending ratification by all parties. The Protocol was signed by the member States of the Caribbean Community (CARICOM), namely, Antigua and Barbuda, Barbados, Belize, Dominica, Grenada, Guyana, Jamaica, Monserrat, Saint Kitts and Nevis, Saint Lucia, Saint Vincent and the Grenadines, and Trinidad and Tobago. The Bahamas, a member of the Caribbean Community, is not a party to this Protocol.

PREAMBLE

The Parties to the Treaty Establishing the Caribbean Community (hereinafter referred to as "the Member States"),

Convinced that market-driven industrial development in the production of goods and services is essential to the economic and social development of the peoples of the Community;

Conscious that trade liberalisation and globalisation have operated to underscore the importance of international competitiveness as an essential condition of survival in the national, regional and international market place;

Recognising the potential of micro, small, and medium enterprise development to contribute to the expansion and viability of national economies of the Community;

Recognising further the importance of large enterprises for achieving economies of scale in the production process;

Mindful of the imperatives of research and development and technology transfer and adaptation for the competitiveness of Community enterprises on a sustainable basis;

Desirous of establishing and maintaining a sound and stable macro-economic environment that is conducive to investment, including cross-border investments, and the competitive production of goods and services in the Community;

---

* *Source*: The Caribbean Community secretariat (1998). "Protocol Amending the Treaty Establishing the Caribbean Community (Protocol III: Industrial Policy)"; available on the Internet (http://www.caricom.org/expframes.htm). [Note added by the editor.]

Aware that differences in resource endowment and in the levels of economic development of Member States, may affect the implementation of the Community Industrial Policy;

Determined to promote and establish a sustainable balance between industrial development and environmental integrity;

Have agreed as follows:

ARTICLE II
Amendment

The provisions of this Protocol shall replace the Articles in Chapter Six of the Caribbean Common Market Annex (except Articles 43, 48 and 49) to the Treaty and shall take effect as hereinafter provided.

ARTICLE III

Replace Article 39 with the following:

"Article 39

Objectives of the Community Industrial Policy

1.   The goal of the Community Industrial Policy shall be market-led, internationally competitive and sustainable production of goods and services for the promotion of the Region's economic and social development.

2.   In fulfilment of the goal set out in paragraph 1 of this Article, the Community shall pursue the following objectives:

   (a)   cross-border employment of natural resources, human resources, capital, technology and management capabilities for the production of goods and services on a sustainable basis;

   (b)   linkages among economic sectors and enterprises within and among Member States of the Single Market and Economy;

   (c)   regional economic enterprises capable of achieving scales of production to facilitate successful competition in domestic and extra-regional markets;

   (d)   a viable micro and small economic enterprise sector;

   (e)   enhanced and diversified production of goods and services for both export and domestic markets;

   (f)   public and private sector collaboration in order to secure market-led production of goods and services;

(g)   industrial production on an environmentally sustainable basis;

(h)   balanced economic and social development in the CARICOM Single Market and Economy bearing in mind the special needs of disadvantaged countries, regions and sectors within the meaning of Article I of the Protocol amending the Treaty providing for disadvantaged countries, regions and sectors; and

(i)   stable industrial relations."

ARTICLE IV

Insert new Article to read as follows:

"Article 39a Implementation of Community Industrial Policy

1.   In order to achieve the objectives of its industrial policy, the Community shall promote, inter alia:

(a)   the co-ordination of national industrial policies of Member States;

(b)   the establishment and maintenance of an investment-friendly environment, including a facilitative administrative process;

(c)   the diversification of the products and markets for goods and services with a view to increasing the range and value of exports;

(d)   the organisation and development of product and factor markets;

(e)   the development of required institutional, legal, technical, financial, administrative and other support for the establishment or development of micro and small economic enterprises throughout the Community; and

(f)   in collaboration with the social partners, the advancement of production integration.

2.   The Community shall establish a special regime for disadvantaged countries, regions and sectors.

3.   The Council for Trade and Economic Development (hereinafter referred to as "the COTED") shall, in collaboration with competent organs and bodies of the Community and the private sector, establish criteria for according special consideration to particular industries and sectors. Such criteria shall include, in particular, arrangements relating to the prospects of the industry for successful production integration.

4.   The COTED shall collaborate with competent agencies to assist Member States in designing appropriate policy instruments to support industries, which may include effective export promotion policies, financing policies, incentives and technology policies.

5.   In implementing the Community Industrial Policy, the COTED shall have regard to the provisions of the Treaty relating to environmental protection.

6.   Member States shall undertake to establish and maintain appropriate macro-economic policies supportive of efficient production in the Community. In addition, they shall undertake to put in place arrangements for, inter alia:

(a)   effective payment mechanisms;

(b)   arrangements for the avoidance of double taxation;

(c)   harmonised legislation in relevant areas;

(d)   the elimination of bureaucratic impediments to deployment of investments in industrial enterprises;

(e)   the improvement of infrastructure and co-operation in the areas of air and maritime transport;

(f)   communications systems; and

(g)   disputes settlement.

7   In order to facilitate the implementation of the Community Industrial Policy, the COTED shall, in collaboration with competent organs and agencies:

(a)   develop strategies for the development and dissemination of market information and appropriate mechanisms to facilitate acquisition, storage and retrieval of such information;

(b)   promote the establishment and development of capital markets in Member States; and

(c)   encourage Member States to establish and develop export markets, especially in non-traditional sectors, through the development of sector-specific incentives and appropriate policy instruments.

8.   For the purpose of this Article, "production integration" includes:

(a)   the direct organisation of production in more than one Member State by a single economic enterprise;

(b)   complementary production involving collaboration among several economic enterprises operating in one or more Member States to produce and use required inputs in the production chain; and

(c)   co-operation among economic enterprises in areas such as purchasing, marketing, and research and development."

ARTICLE VI

Replace Article 41 with the following:

"Article 41 Development of the Services Sector

1.   The COTED shall, in collaboration with the appropriate Councils, promote the development of the services sector in the Community in order to stimulate economic complementarities among, and accelerate economic development in, Member States. In particular, the COTED shall promote measures to achieve:

(a)   increased investment in services;

(b)   increased volume, value and range of trade in services within the Community and with third States;

(c)   competitiveness in the modes of delivering services; and

(d)   enhanced enterprise and infrastructural development, including that of micro and small service enterprises.

2.   In order to achieve the objectives set out in paragraph 1, Member States shall, through the appropriate Councils, collaborate in:

(a)   designing programmes for the development of human resources to achieve competitiveness in the provision of services;

(b)   establishing a regime of incentives for the development of and trade in services; and

(c)   adopting measures to promote the establishment of an appropriate institutional and administrative framework and, in collaboration with the Legal Affairs Committee, promote the establishment of the appropriate legal framework to support the services sector in the Community.

3.   In the establishment of programmes and policies of the Community for the development of the services sector, the relevant Councils shall give priority to:

(a)   the efficient provision of infrastructural services including telecommunications, road, air, maritime and riverain transportation, statistical data generation and financial services;

(b)   the development of capacity-enhancing services including education services, research and development services;

(c)   the development of services which enhance cross-sector competitiveness;

(d)   the facilitation of cross-border provision of services which enhance the competitiveness of the services sector; and

(e)   the development of informatics and other knowledge-based services."

ARTICLE XIII

Replace Article 50 with the following:

"Article 48 Community Investment Policy

The COTED in collaboration with the Council for Finance and Planning (hereinafter referred to as "the COFAP") and the COHSOD shall establish a Community Investment Policy which shall include sound national macro-economic policies, a harmonised system of investment incentives, stable industrial relations, appropriate financial institutions and arrangements, supportive legal and social infrastructure and modernisation of the role of public authorities."

ARTICLE XIV

Insert new Article to read as follows:

"Article 49 Harmonisation of Investment Incentives

1.   Member States shall harmonise national incentives to investments in the industrial, agricultural and services sectors.

2.   The COFAP shall, consistent with relevant international agreements, formulate proposals for the establishment of regimes for the granting of incentives to enterprises in the sectors mentioned in paragraph 1. In particular, such proposals shall accord support for industries considered to be of strategic interest to the Community.

3.   In formulating the proposals mentioned in paragraph 2, the COFAP shall give due consideration to the peculiarities of the industries concerned and, without prejudice to the generality of the foregoing, may provide for the following:

(a)   national incentives to investment designed to promote sustainable, export-led industrial and service-oriented development;

(b)   investment facilitation through the removal of bureaucratic impediments; and

(c)   non-discrimination in the granting of incentives among Community nationals."

ARTICLE XVIII

Insert new Article to read as follows:

"Article 49d Legal Infrastructure

1.   The Legal Affairs Committee shall co-operate with competent organs of the Community to advise Member States on the legal infrastructure required to promote investments in the Member States, including cross-border investments, bearing in mind the provisions of Article 49c.

2.   Member States shall harmonise their laws and administrative practices in respect of, inter alia:

(a)   companies or other legal entities;

(b)   intellectual property rights;

(c)   standards and technical regulations;

(d)   labelling of food and drugs;

(e)   sanitary and phytosanitary measures;

(f)   restrictive business practices;

(g)   dumping;

(h)   subsidies and countervailing measures; and

(i)   commercial arbitration."

ARTICLE XIX

Insert new Article to read as follows:

"Article 49e Double Taxation Agreements

1.   Member States shall conclude among themselves an agreement for the avoidance of double taxation in order to facilitate the free movement of capital in the Community.

2.   Member States shall conclude their double taxation agreements with third States on the basis of mutually agreed principles which shall be determined by COFAP."

ARTICLE XXI

Insert new Article to read as follows:

"Article 50a Role of Public Authorities

The COTED shall promote the modernisation of government bureaucracies by, inter alia:

(a)   encouraging the development of closer contacts between public sector administrations, industry and other stakeholders to ensure that challenges presented by the global environment are understood and co-operative solutions developed;

(b)   removing impediments and improving the regulatory framework for economic enterprises at national and regional levels;

(c)   encouraging cost-effectiveness in the delivery of services to the public; and

(d)   proposing adequate arrangements to address the changes in the business environment and future challenges to industry."

ARTICLE XXII

Insert new Article to read as follows:

"Article 50b Special Provisions for Less Developed Countries

Where in this Protocol Member States or competent Organs are required to adopt measures for the achievement of the Community Industrial Policy, the special needs and circumstances of the Less Developed Countries shall be taken into account."

*   *   *

FRAMEWORK AGREEMENT ON THE ASEAN INVESTMENT AREA[*]

(ASSOCIATION OF SOUTHEAST ASIAN NATIONS)

> The Framework Agreement on the ASEAN Investment Area (AIA) was signed in Manila (the Philippines) during the 30th ASEAN Economic Ministers Meeting, on 7 October 1998. The Agreement entered into force on 21 June 1999, having been ratified by all member countries of ASEAN, namely, Brunei Darussalam, Cambodia, Indonesia, Lao People's Democratic Republic, Malaysia, Myanmar, the Philippines, Singapore, Thailand and Viet Nam.

The Governments of Brunei Darussalam, the Republic of Indonesia, the Lao People's Democratic Republic, Malaysia, the Union of Myanmar, the Republic of the Philippines, the Republic of Singapore, the Kingdom of Thailand and the Socialist Republic of Vietnam, Member States of the Association of South-East Asian Nations (ASEAN);

REAFFIRMING the importance of sustaining economic growth and development in all Member States through joint efforts in liberalising trade and promoting intra-ASEAN trade and investment flows enshrined in the Framework Agreement on Enhancing ASEAN Economic Co-operation signed in Singapore on 28 January 1992;

RECALLING the decision of the Fifth ASEAN Summit held on 15 December 1995 to establish an ASEAN Investment Area (hereinafter referred to as "AIA"), in order to enhance ASEAN's attractiveness and competitiveness for promoting direct investments;

AFFIRMING their commitment to the 1987 ASEAN Agreement for the Promotion and Protection of Investments and its 1996 Protocol to enhance investor confidence for investing in ASEAN;

MINDFUL of the decision to establish an ASEAN Free Trade Area (AFTA) and the implementation of the ASEAN Industrial Co-operation (AICO) Scheme, to encourage greater investment flows into the region;

RECOGNISING that direct investment is an important source of finance for sustaining the pace of economic, industrial, infrastructure and technology development; hence, the need to attract higher and sustainable level of direct investment flows in ASEAN;

DETERMINED to realise the vision of ASEAN to establish a competitive ASEAN Investment Area through a more liberal and transparent investment environment by 1st January 2010; and

---

[*] *Source*: Association of Southeast Asian Nations (1998). "Framework Agreement on the ASEAN Investment Area", *Handbook of Investment Agreements in ASEAN* (Jakarta: ASEAN Secretariat), pp. 51-65; also available on the Internet (http://www.asean.or.id/economic/aem/30/frm_aia.htm). [Note added by the editor.]

BEARING IN MIND that the measures agreed upon to establish a competitive ASEAN Investment Area by 2010 shall contribute towards ASEAN Vision 2020.

HAVE AGREED AS FOLLOWS:

ARTICLE 1
Definition

For the purpose of this Agreement:

"ASEAN investor " means -

    i.   a national of a Member State; or

    ii. any juridical person of a Member State,

making an investment in another Member State, the effective ASEAN equity of which taken cumulatively with all other ASEAN equities fulfills at least the minimum percentage required to meet the national equity requirement and other equity requirements of domestic laws and published national policies, if any, of the host country in respect of that investment.

For the purpose of this definition, equity of nationals or juridical persons of any Member State shall be deemed to be the equity of nationals or juridical persons of the host country.

"effective ASEAN equity" in respect of an investment in an ASEAN Member State means ultimate holdings by nationals or juridical persons of ASEAN Member States in that investment. Where the shareholding/equity structure of an ASEAN investor makes it difficult to establish the ultimate holding structure, the rules and procedures for determining effective equity used by the Member State in which the ASEAN investor is investing may be applied. If necessary, the Co-ordinating Committee on Investment shall prepare guidelines for this purpose.

"juridical person" means any legal entity duly constituted or otherwise organised under applicable law of a Member State, whether for profit or otherwise, and whether privately-owned or governmentally-owned, including any corporation, trust, partnership, joint venture, sole proprietorship or association.

"measures" means laws, regulations, rules, procedures, decisions, administrative actions, or any other actions affecting investments taken by Member States.

"national" means a natural person having the citizenship of a Member State in accordance with its applicable laws.

ARTICLE 2
Coverage

This Agreement shall cover all direct investments other than -

    a.   portfolio investments; and

b. matters relating to investments covered by other ASEAN Agreements, such as the ASEAN Framework Agreement on Services.

ARTICLE 3
Objectives

The objectives of this Agreement are:

a. to establish a competitive ASEAN Investment Area with a more liberal and transparent investment environment amongst Member States in order to -

   i. substantially increase the flow of investments into ASEAN from both ASEAN and non-ASEAN sources;

   ii. jointly promote ASEAN as the most attractive investment area;

   iii. strengthen and increase the competitiveness of ASEAN's economic sectors;

   iv. progressively reduce or eliminate investment regulations and conditions which may impede investment flows and the operation of investment projects in ASEAN; and

b. to ensure that the realisation of the above objectives would contribute towards free flow of investments by 2020.

ARTICLE 4
Features

The AIA shall be an area where:

a. there is a co-ordinated ASEAN investment co-operation programme that will generate increased investments from ASEAN and non-ASEAN sources;

b. national treatment is extended to ASEAN investors by 2010, and to all investors by 2020, subject to the exceptions provided for under this Agreement;

c. all industries are opened for investment to ASEAN investors by 2010 and to all investors by 2020, subject to the exceptions provided for under this Agreement;

d. the business sector has a larger role in the co-operation efforts in relation to investments and related activities in ASEAN; and

e. there is freer flow of capital, skilled labour and professionals, and technology amongst Member States.

ARTICLE 5
General Obligations

To realise the objectives referred to in Article 3, the Member States shall:

a. ensure that measures and programmes are undertaken on a fair and mutually beneficial basis;

b. undertake appropriate measures to ensure transparency and consistency in the application and interpretation of their investment laws, regulations and administrative procedures in order to create and maintain a predictable investment regime in ASEAN;

c. begin the process of facilitation, promotion and liberalisation which would contribute continuously and significantly to achieving the objective of a more liberal and transparent investment environment;

d. take appropriate measures to enhance the attractiveness of the investment environment of Member States for direct investment flows; and

e. take such reasonable actions as may be available to them to ensure observance of the provisions of this Agreement by the regional and local governments and authorities within their territories.

ARTICLE 6
Programmes and Action Plans

1. Member States shall, for the implementation of the obligations under this Agreement, undertake the joint development and implementation of the following programmes:

a. co-operation and facilitation programme as specified in Schedule I;

b. promotion and awareness programme as specified in Schedule II; and

c. liberalisation programme as specified in Schedule III.

2. Member States shall submit Action Plans for the implementation of the programmes in paragraph 1 to the AIA Council established under Article 16 of this Agreement.

3. The Action Plans shall be reviewed every 2 years to ensure that the objectives of this Agreement are achieved.

ARTICLE 7
Opening Up of Industries and National Treatment

1. Subject to the provisions of this Article, each Member State shall:

a. open immediately all its industries for investments by ASEAN investors;

b. accord immediately to ASEAN investors and their investments, in respect of all industries and measures affecting investment including but not limited to the admission, establishment, acquisition, expansion, management, operation and disposition of investments, treatment no less favourable than that it accords to its own like investors and investments ("national treatment").

ARTICLE 8
Most Favoured Nation Treatment

1. Subject to Articles 7 and 9 of this Agreement, each Member State shall accord immediately and unconditionally to investors and investments of another Member State, treatment no less favourable than that it accords to investors and investments of any other Member State with respect to all measures affecting investment including but not limited to the admission, establishment, acquisition, expansion, management, operation and disposition of investments.

2. In relation to investments falling within the scope of this Agreement, any preferential treatment granted under any existing or future agreements or arrangements to which a Member State is a party shall be extended on the most favoured nation basis to all other Member States.

3. The requirement in paragraph 2 shall not apply to existing agreements or arrangements notified by Member States to the AIA Council within 6 months after the date of signing of this Agreement.

4. Nothing in paragraph 1 shall prevent any Member State from conferring special treatment or advantages to adjacent countries under growth triangles and other sub- regional arrangements between Member States.

ARTICLE 9
Waiver of Most Favoured Nation Treatment

5. Where a Member State is temporarily not ready to make concessions under Articles 7 of this Agreement, and another Member State has made concessions under the said Article, then the first mentioned Member State shall waive its rights to such concessions. However, if a Member State which grants such concessions is willing to forego the waiver, then the first mentioned Member State can still enjoy these concessions.

6. Having regard to the late entry into ASEAN of the Socialist Republic of Vietnam, the Lao People's Democratic Republic and the Union of Myanmar, the provisions of paragraph 1 of this Article shall only apply to the Socialist Republic of Vietnam for a period of 3 years, and the Lao People's Democratic Republic and the Union of Myanmar for a period of 5 years from the date this Agreement comes into force.

ARTICLE 10
Modification of Schedules, Annexes and Action Plans

7. Any modification to Schedules I and II, and Action Plans thereof shall be subject to the approval of the Co-ordinating Committee on Investments (CCI) established under Article 16(4) of this Agreement.

8. Any modification to or withdrawal of any commitments in Schedule III and Action Plans thereof and the Annexes shall be subject to the consideration of the AIA Council in accordance with the provisions of the ASEAN Protocol on Notification Procedures.

ARTICLE 11
Transparency

9. Each Member State shall make available to the AIA Council through publication or any other means, all relevant measures, laws, regulations and administrative guidelines which pertain to, or affect, the operation of this Agreement. This shall also apply to international agreements pertaining to or affecting investment to which a Member State is also a signatory.

10. Each Member State shall promptly and at least annually inform the AIA Council of the introduction of any new or any changes to existing laws, regulations or administrative guidelines which significantly affect investments or its commitments under this Agreement.

11. Nothing in this Agreement shall require any Member State to provide confidential information, the disclosure of which would impede law enforcement, or otherwise be contrary to the public interest, or which would prejudice legitimate commercial interests of particular enterprises, public or private.

ARTICLE 12
Other Agreements

1. Member States affirm their existing rights and obligations under the 1987 ASEAN Agreement for the Promotion and Protection of Investments and its 1996 Protocol. In the event that this Agreement provides for better or enhanced provisions over the said Agreement and its Protocol, then such provisions of this Agreement shall prevail.

2. This Agreement or any action taken under it shall not affect the rights and obligations of the Member States under existing agreements to which they are parties.

3. Nothing in this Agreement shall affect the rights of the Member States to enter into other agreements not contrary to the principles, objectives and terms of this Agreement.

ARTICLE 13
General Exceptions

Subject to the requirement that such measures are not applied in a manner which would constitute a means of arbitrary or unjustifiable discrimination between countries where like conditions prevail, or a disguised restriction on investment flows, nothing in this Agreement shall be construed to prevent the adoption or enforcement by any Member State of measures;

a. necessary to protect national security and public morals;

b. necessary to protect human, animal or plant life or health;

c. necessary to secure compliance with laws or regulations which are not inconsistent with the provisions of this Agreement including those relating to:

>   i. the prevention of deceptive and fraudulent practices or to deal with the effects of a default on investment agreement.
>
>   ii. the protection of the privacy of individuals in relation to the processing and dissemination of personal data and the protection of confidentiality of individual records and accounts.
>
>   iii. safety.

d. aimed at ensuring the equitable or effective imposition or collection of direct taxes in respect of investments or investors of Member States.

ARTICLE 14
Emergency Safeguard Measures

1. If, as a result of the implementation of the liberalisation programme under this Agreement, a Member state suffers or is threatened with any serious injury and threat, the Member State may take emergency safeguard measures to the extent and for such period as may be necessary to prevent or to remedy such injury. The measures taken shall be provisional and without discrimination.

2. Where emergency safeguard measures are taken pursuant to this Article, notice of such measure shall be given to the AIA Council within 14 days from the date such measures are taken.

3. The AIA Council shall determine the definition of serious injury and threat of serious injury and the procedures of instituting emergency safeguards measures pursuant to this Article.

ARTICLE 15
Measures to Safeguard the Balance of Payments

1. In the event of serious balance of payments and external financial difficulties or threat thereof, a Member State may adopt or maintain restrictions on investments on which it has undertaken specific commitments, including on payments or transfers for transactions related to such commitments. It is recognised that particular pressures on the balance of payments of a Member State in the process of economic development or economic transition may necessitate the use of restrictions to ensure, inter alia, the maintenance of a level of financial

reserves adequate for the implementation of its programme of economic development or economic transition.

2. Where measures to safeguard balance of payments are taken pursuant to this Article notice of such measures shall be given to the AIA Council within 14 days from the date such measures are taken.

3. The measures referred to in paragraph (1):

   a. shall not discriminate among Member States;

   b. shall be consistent with the Articles of Agreement of the International Monetary Fund;

   c. shall avoid unnecessary damage to the commercial, economic and financial interests of any other Member State;

   d. shall not exceed those necessary to deal with the circumstances described in paragraph I; and

   e. shall be temporary and be phased out progressively as the situation specified in paragraph 1 improves.

4. The Member States adopting the balance of payments measures shall commence consultations with the AIA Council and other Member States within 90 days from the date of notification in order to review the balance of payment measures adopted by it.

5. The AIA Council shall determine the rules applicable to the procedures under this Article.

ARTICLE 16
Institutional Arrangements

1. The ASEAN Economic Ministers (AEM) shall establish an ASEAN Investment Area Council (in this Agreement referred to as "the AIA Council") comprising the Ministers responsible for investment and the Secretary-General of ASEAN. The ASEAN Heads of Investment Agencies shall participate in the AIA Council meetings.

2. Notwithstanding Article 21 of this Agreement, the AIA Council shall be established upon the signing of this Agreement.

3. The AIA Council shall supervise, co-ordinate and review the implementation of this Agreement and assist the AEM in all matters relating thereto.

4. In the performance of its functions, the AIA Council shall establish a Co-ordinating Committee on Investment (CCI) comprising senior officials responsible for investment and other senior officials from relevant government agencies.

5. The Co-ordinating Committee on Investment shall report to the AIA Council through the Senior Economic Officials Meeting (SEOM).

6. The ASEAN Secretariat shall be the secretariat to the AIA Council and the Co-ordinating Committee on Investment (CCI).

ARTICLE 17
Settlement of Disputes

1. The Protocol on Dispute Settlement Mechanism for ASEAN shall apply in relation to any dispute arising from, or any differences between Member States concerning the interpretation or application of this Agreement or any arrangement arising therefrom.

2. If necessary, a specific dispute settlement mechanism may be established for the purpose of this Agreement which shall form an integral part of this Agreement.

ARTICLE 18
Amendments

Any amendments to this Agreement shall be made by consensus and shall become effective upon the deposit of instruments of ratification or acceptance by all signatory governments with the Secretary-General of ASEAN.

ARTICLE 19
Supplementary Agreements or Arrangements

The Schedules, Action Plans, Annexes, and any other arrangements or agreements arising under this Agreement shall form an integral part of this Agreement.

ARTICLE 20
Accession of New Members

New members of ASEAN shall accede to this Agreement on terms and conditions agreed between them and signatories to this Agreement and by depositing the instrument of accession with the Secretary-General of ASEAN.

ARTICLE 21
Final Provisions

1. This Agreement shall enter into force upon the deposit of instruments of ratification or acceptance by all signatory governments with the Secretary-General of ASEAN. The signatory governments undertake to deposit their instruments of ratification or acceptance within 6 months after the date of signing of this Agreement.
2. This Agreement shall be deposited with the Secretary-General of ASEAN, who shall promptly furnish a certified copy thereof to each Member State.

IN WITNESS WHEREOF, the undersigned being duly authorised by their respective Governments, have signed this Framework Agreement on the ASEAN Investment Area.

Done at Manila, Philippines this 7th day of October 1998, in a single copy in the English language.

*   *   *

RESOLUTION OF THE EUROPEAN PARLIAMENT ON EUROPEAN UNION STANDARDS FOR EUROPEAN ENTERPRISES OPERATING IN DEVELOPING COUNTRIES: TOWARDS A EUROPEAN CODE OF CONDUCT[*]

(EUROPEAN PARLIAMENT)

On 15 January 1999, the European Parliament adopted a resolution in which it made a number of recommendations including proposals for voluntary codes of conduct adopted by companies to include independent monitoring and verification; a new legal base for a statutory European framework governing companies' operations worlwide; the setting up of an independent European monitoring and verification body with public hearings in the European Parliament to highlight good and bad conduct; a mechanism to cut off European funding where companies operating on European contracts breach fundamental rights; and new international investment agreements to include duties as well as rights for European enterprises.

Resolution on EU Standards for European Enterprises Operating in Developing Countries: towards a European Code of Conduct

The European Parliament;

- having regard to its resolution of 9 February 1994 on the introduction of a social clause in the unilateral and multilateral trading system[1],

- having regard to its resolution of 12 December 1996 on human rights throughout the world in 1995/96 and the Union's human rights policy[2],

- having regard to its resolution of 15 January 1998 on relocation and foreign direct investment in third countries[3],

- having regard to its resolutions on Indigenous peoples[4],

---

[*] *Source*: European Parliament (1999). "Resolution on EU standards for European enterprises operating in developing Countries: towards a European Code of Conduct", [A4-508/98], *Official Journal of the European Communities*, C 104, Part II, 14 April 1999, pp. 180-184. [Note added by the editor.]

[1] OJ C 61, 28.2.1994, p.89.
[2] OJ C 20, 20.1.1997, p. 161.
[3] OJ C 34, 2.2.1998, p. 156.
[4] OJ C 61, 28.2.1994, p. 69; OJ C 43, 20.2.1995, p. 85; OJ C 323, 4.12.1995,p.117; OJ C 141, 13.5.1996, p. 212.

-   having regard to its resolution of 11 March 1998 containing its recommendation to the Commission on negotiations in the framework of the OECD on a multilateral agreement on investments (MAI)[5],

-   having regard to its resolution of 2 July 1998 on fair trade[6],

-   having regard to its resolution of 17 December 1998 on human rights in the world in 1997 and 1998 and European Union human rights policy[7]

-   having regard to the two most authoritative internationally agreed standards for corporate conduct adopted by the ILO: the 1977 "Tripartite Declaration of Principles concerning Multinational Enterprises and Social Policy" and the 1976 OECD "Guidelines for Multinational Enterprises", and to codes of conduct agreed under the aegis of international organisations such as the FAO, WHO and World Bank and efforts under the auspices of UNCTAD with regard to the activities of enterprises in developing countries,

-   having regard to the ILO Declaration on Fundamental Principles and Rights at Work, 18 June 1998, and its agreement of universal core labour standards: Abolition of forced labour (Conventions 29 and 105), Freedom of association and the right to collective bargaining (Conventions 87 and 98), Abolition of child labour (Convention 138), and Non-Discrimination in Employment (Conventions 100 and 111),

-   having regard to the United Nations Universal Declaration of Human Rights and in particular its call to every individual and every organ of society to contribute to securing universal observance of human rights, the 1966 International Covenant on Civil and Political Rights, the 1966 Covenant on Economic, Social and Cultural Rights, the 1979 Convention of the Elimination of All Forms of Discrimination Against Women, the 1994 Draft United Nations Declaration on the Rights of Indigenous Peoples,

-   having regard to the decision of the European social partners to contribute to the implementation of actions aimed at eradicating all forms of child labour exploitation and to promote the rights of these children throughout the world,

-   having regard to Article 220 of the EC Treaty regarding reciprocal recognition of court judgments, to the 1968 Convention on jurisdiction and the enforcement of judgments in civil and commercial matters[8], usually known as the Brussels Convention, and to the Joint Action of 24 February 1997 adopted by the Council on the basis of Article K.3 of the Treaty on European Union concerning action to combat trafficking in human beings and sexual exploitation of children[9],

-   having regard to the 1997 OECD Convention on Combating Bribery of Foreign Public Officials in International Business Transactions,

---

[5] OJ C 104, 6.4.1998, p. 143.
[6] OJ C 226, 20.7.1998, p. 73.
[7] OJ Minutes of that sitting, Part II, Item 9(b).
[8] OJ L 299, 31.12.1972, p. 32
[9] OJ L 63, 4.3.1997, p. 2.

- having regard to Council Regulation (EC) No 1154/ 98 of 25 May 1998 applying the special incentive arrangements concerning labour rights and environmental protection provided for in Articles 7 and 8 of Regulations (EC) No 3281/94 and (EC) No 1256/96 applying multiannual schemes of generalised tariff preferences in respect of certain industrial and agricultural products originating in developing countries[10], and to Parliament's resolution of 14 May 1998 on a code of conduct for arms exports[11],

- having regard to numerous initiatives on the part of individual enterprises, their associations, trade unions and non-governmental organisations, together with international voluntary standards such as Social Accountability 8000,

- having regard to the Hearing on 'EU standards for European Enterprises operating in developing countries' of 2 September 1998 in the Committee on Development and Cooperation,

- having regard to Rule 148 of its Rules of Procedure,

- having regard to the report of the Committee on Development and Cooperation and the Opinion of the Committee on External Economic Relations (A4-0508/98),

A.   whereas the EU as the largest development aid donor, and European enterprises, as the largest direct investors in developing countries, can play a decisive role in global sustainable social and economic development,

B.   deeply concerned about numerous cases where intense competition for investment and markets and lack of application of international standards and national laws, have led to cases of corporate abuse, particularly in countries where human rights are not upheld,

C.   stressing that no company should profit from any competitive advantage resulting from disregarding basic labour laws and social and environmental standards; and recognising increasing evidence that corporate social responsibility is linked to good financial performance,

D.   bearing in mind that there is increasing consensus amongst business and industry, trade unions, NGOs and governments both from developing countries and from the industrialised world, to improve business practices through voluntary codes of conduct,

E.   whereas in this connection a process of review is currently under way in the OECD, in consultation with representatives of companies, labour and other components of civil society, to strengthen the guiding principles set out by the Organisation for multinational companies,

F.   stressing that voluntary and binding approaches to corporate Regulation are not mutually exclusive, and adopting an evolutionary approach to the question of standard-setting for European enterprises,

---

[10]   OJ L 160, 4.6.1998, p. 1.
[11]   OJ L 167, 1.6.1998, p. 226.

Voluntary codes of conduct

1.   Welcomes and encourages voluntary initiatives by business and industry, trade unions and coalitions of NGOs to promote codes of conduct, with effective and independent monitoring and verification, and stakeholder participation in the development, implementation and monitoring of these Codes of Conduct; emphasises, however, that codes of conduct cannot replace or set aside national or international rules or the jurisdiction of governments; considers that codes of conduct must not be used as instruments for putting multinational enterprises beyond the scope of governmental and judicial scrutiny;

2.   Reiterates its calls on the Council to develop a joint position on voluntary codes of conduct, on the lines of the code of conduct for arms exporters, taking due account of the fact that "self-policing" is not always the answer;

3.   Stresses that the content of a code, and the process by which it is determined and implemented, must involve those in developing countries who are covered by it;

4.   Believes that special attention must be paid to implementing codes in respect of workers in the informal sector, sub-contractors and in free trade zones, notably concerning recognition of the right to form independent trade unions; and against corporate collusion in violations of human rights;

5.   Believes that a code should recognise the responsibilities of companies operating in conflict situations by ensuring that a Code covers the Amnesty International Human Rights Principles for Companies, Human Rights Watch recommendations to companies, and the UN Code of Conduct for Law Enforcement Officials;

6.   Believes that under the voluntary codes of conduct European companies should comply with EU environmental, animal welfare and health standards;

7.   Stresses that indigenous peoples and their communities should benefit from such codes of conduct recognizing their important role for sustainable development;

8.   Welcomes the fact that in the present context of globalisation of trade flows and communications as well as of increased vigilance of NGO's and consumer associations, it seems to be increasingly in the interest of multinational undertakings to adopt and implement voluntary codes of conduct, if they want to avoid negative publicity campaigns, sometimes leading to boycotts, public relation costs and consumer complaints;

9.   Considers that enterprises should contribute economically and socially to the development process in the affected areas, in compliance with the guidelines laid down by the public authorities concerned;

10.   Recommends that an 'evolutionary approach' be weighted towards a continuous and gradual improvement of standards; takes the view that this must reflect the enterprises' own obligations to make improvements;

European enforcement mechanism

11.   Reiterates its request to the Commission and the Council to make proposals, as a matter of urgency, to develop the right legal basis for establishing a European multilateral framework governing companies' operations worldwide and to organise for this purpose consultations with companies' representatives, the social partners and those groups in society which would be covered by the code;

12.   Recommends, that a model Code of Conduct for European businesses should comprise existing minimum applicable international standards:

-       the ILO Tripartite Declaration of Principles concerning MNEs and Social Policy and the OECD Guidelines for Multinational Enterprises;

-       in the field of labour rights: the ILO core Conventions;

-       in the field of human rights: the UN Declaration and different Covenants on Human Rights;

-       in the field of minority and indigenous peoples' rights: ILO Convention 169, Chapter 26 of Agenda 21, 1994 Draft United Nations Declaration on the Rights of Indigenous Peoples, UN Declaration on the Elimination of All Forms of Racial Discrimination;

-       in the field of environmental standards: UN Convention on Biological Diversity, the Rio Declaration and the European Commission proposal for the development of a code of conduct for European logging companies (COM(89)0410) and the relevant UN Conventions in the fields of protection of the environment, animal welfare and public health;

-       in the field of security services: Common Article 3 of the Geneva Conventions and Protocol II, and the UN Code of Conduct for Law Enforcement Officials;

-       in the field of corruption: the OECD anti-bribery convention and the European Commission communication on legislative measures against corruption (COM(97) 0192);

but should also include consideration of new international standards which are currently being developed;

13.   Reaffirms its support for the creation of a 'Social Label';

14.   Calls on the Commission to study the possibility of setting up a European Monitoring Platform (EMP), (already proposed by some trade associations) in close collaboration with the social partners, NGO's from North and South and representatives of indigenous and local communities;

15.   Calls on the Commission and the Member States to take coordinated action within the OECD, the ILO and other international fora to promote the establishment of a truly independent and impartial monitoring mechanism which is internationally accepted;

16.   Believes that an independent monitoring and verification body could only prove useful if it is highly skilled, if it has appropriate procedures and, above all, if it is widely accepted as being objective and impartial;

17.   Recommends that business and industry provide dissemination of information about their voluntary initiatives and conduct to the monitoring mechanism so that their compliance with a European Code of conduct, international standards and private voluntary codes of practice (if adopted) could be properly assessed;

18.   Recommends that the monitoring mechanism promote dialogue on standards met by European enterprises, the identification of best practice, as well as being open to receiving complaints about corporate conduct from community and/or workers' representatives and the private sector in the host country, NGOs or consumer organisations, from individual victims or from any other source;

European Parliamentary action

19.   Proposes that during the new legislative period, special rapporteurs are appointed for a period of one year and annual hearings are held in the European Parliament, inviting the social partners and NGOs from the South and the North until such a time as a European Monitoring Platform is established by the Commission;

20.   Recommends that public hearings be organised regularly in the European Parliament in order to discuss specific cases, of both good and bad conduct, and that all persons concerned (including enterprises) be invited to attend them;

Role of European development cooperation

21.   Recognises that a responsibility for applying internationally agreed standards rests with the governments of the developing countries themselves; therefore welcomes recent EU initiatives to strengthen and extend the coverage of political dialogue with developing countries and to make "good governance" an essential element of EU cooperation policy;

22.   Considers that resources must be set aside to support the governments of developing countries, so as to help ensure that international standards are incorporated in those countries' laws, and that technical and financial assistance must be granted to monitoring groups in the host countries;

23.   Calls on the Commission to enforce the requirement that all private companies carrying out operations in third countries on behalf of the Union, and financed out of the Commission's budget or the European Development Fund, act in accordance with the Treaty on European Union in respect of fundamental rights, failing which such companies would not be entitled to continue to receive European Union funding, in particular from its instruments for assistance with investment in third countries; calls on the Commission to prepare a report on the extent to which private companies to which it awards contracts have been made aware of these obligations; further recognises that private companies acting as agents of the Commission in the

field of development cooperation are already obliged to adhere to OECD standards concerning best aid practice and human rights and sustainable development principles enshrined in the Lomé Convention;

24.   Calls on the Commission to ensure that the development strategy to strengthen the private sector environment in developing countries, should specifically integrate the role of European-based multinational enterprises, and take forward an investment agreement with the ACP to promote economic growth and poverty reduction;

Other actions at European level

25.   Calls on the Commission to improve consultation and monitoring of European companies' operations in third countries through the mechanisms of the Social Dialogue within Europe, and the operation of democracy and human rights clauses in trade agreements with third countries outside Europe;

26.   Recommends as a matter of urgency that at least the ILO Declaration of Fundamental Principles and Rights at Work, of 18 June 1998, be an explicit part of any future agreement the EU negotiates with third countries;

27.   Calls on the Commission to ensure that consideration is given, with an appropriate legal base, to incorporating core labour, environmental and human rights international standards when reviewing European company law including the new EU Directive on a European-incorporated company;

28.   Calls on the Commission to bring forward proposals for a system of incentives for companies complying with international standards developed in close consultation and cooperation with consumer groups and human rights and environmental NGOs - such as in procurement, fiscal incentives, access to EU financial assistance and publication in the Official Journal;

Actions within international institutions

29.   Recommends that the European Union seeks to work en bloc to strengthen existing ILO and OECD instruments, in particular in the review now underway in the OECD, and within the United Nations, to ensure more powerful and effective monitoring and enforcement mechanisms, and that EU efforts notably go into reviving the UN Commission on TNCs for it to be entrusted with concrete tasks in the context of the monitoring and implementation of Codes, along with the OECD Committee for International Investment and Multinational Enterprises and the ILO's Department for Multinational Enterprises;

30.   Strongly recommends that in connection with negotiations on investment agreements which could be concluded in either the OECD or the WTO, the European Union not only contribute to establishing the legitimate rights of multinational enterprises, but also their duties - with due regard to the present minimum applicable international standards - in the field of

environment, labour and human rights; recommends that a monitoring mechanism affording every guarantee of impartiality and independence be incorporated in such an agreement;

*

*   *

31.   Instructs its President to forward this resolution to the Commission, the Council, the ILO, the WTO, the OECD and the governments and parliaments of the Member States.

*   *   *

CRIMINAL LAW CONVENTION ON CORRUPTION[*]

(COUNCIL OF EUROPE)

The Council of Europe Criminal Law Convention on Corruption was opened for signature by the member States of the Council of Europe and by non-members which had participated in its elaboration, in Strasbourg on 27 January 1999. As of 15 October 1999, the following countries had signed the Convention: Albania, Belgium, Bulgaria, Croatia, Cyprus, Czech Republic, Denmark, Finland, France, Georgia, Germany, Greece, Hungary, Iceland, Ireland, Italy, Latvia, Lithuania, Luxembourg, Moldova, Norway, Poland, Portugal, Romania, Russia, Slovakia, Slovenia, Sweden, the former Yugoslav Republic of Macedonia, Ukraine, and the United Kingdom. After its entry into force, other non-member States and the European Community may be invited by the Committee of Ministers of the Council of Europe to accede to the Convention.

Preamble

The member States of the Council of Europe and the other States signatory hereto,

Considering that the aim of the Council of Europe is to achieve a greater unity between its members;

Recognising the value of fostering co-operation with the other States signatories to this Convention;

Convinced of the need to pursue, as a matter of priority, a common criminal policy aimed at the protection of society against corruption, including the adoption of appropriate legislation and preventive measures;

Emphasising that corruption threatens the rule of law, democracy and human rights, undermines good governance, fairness and social justice, distorts competition, hinders economic development and endangers the stability of democratic institutions and the moral foundations of society;

Believing that an effective fight against corruption requires increased, rapid and well-functioning international co-operation in criminal matters;

Welcoming recent developments which further advance international understanding and co-operation in combating corruption, including actions of the United Nations, the World Bank, the

---

[*] *Source*: Council of Europe (1999). "Criminal Law Convention on Corruption", *European Treaty Series* No. 173; available also on the Internet (http://www.coe.fr/eng/legaltxt/173e.htm). [Note added by the editor.]

International Monetary Fund, the World Trade Organisation, the Organisation of American States, the OECD and the European Union;

Having regard to the Programme of Action against Corruption adopted by the Committee of Ministers of the Council of Europe in November 1996 following the recommendations of the 19th Conference of European Ministers of Justice (Valletta, 1994);

Recalling in this respect the importance of the participation of non-member States in the Council of Europe's activities against corruption and welcoming their valuable contribution to the implementation of the Programme of Action against Corruption;

Further recalling that Resolution No. 1 adopted by the European Ministers of Justice at their 21st Conference (Prague, 1997) recommended the speedy implementation of the Programme of Action against Corruption, and called, in particular, for the early adoption of a criminal law convention providing for the co-ordinated incrimination of corruption offences, enhanced co-operation for the prosecution of such offences as well as an effective follow-up mechanism open to member States and non-member States on an equal footing;

Bearing in mind that the Heads of State and Government of the Council of Europe decided, on the occasion of their Second Summit held in Strasbourg on 10 and 11 October 1997, to seek common responses to the challenges posed by the growth in corruption and adopted an Action Plan which, in order to promote co-operation in the fight against corruption, including its links with organised crime and money laundering, instructed the Committee of Ministers, inter alia, to secure the rapid completion of international legal instruments pursuant to the Programme of Action against Corruption;

Considering moreover that Resolution (97) 24 on the 20 Guiding Principles for the Fight against Corruption, adopted on 6 November 1997 by the Committee of Ministers at its 101st Session, stresses the need rapidly to complete the elaboration of international legal instruments pursuant to the Programme of Action against Corruption;

In view of the adoption by the Committee of Ministers, at its 102nd Session on 4 May 1998, of Resolution (98) 7 authorising the partial and enlarged agreement establishing the "Group of States against Corruption - GRECO", which aims at improving the capacity of its members to fight corruption by following up compliance with their undertakings in this field,

Have agreed as follows:

Chapter I - Use of terms

Article 1 - Use of terms

For the purposes of this Convention:

a)   **"public official"** shall be understood by reference to the definition of **"official"**, **"public officer"**, **"mayor "**, **"minister"** or **"judge"** in the national law of the State in which the person in question performs that function and as applied in its criminal law;

b)   the term **"judge"** referred to in sub-paragraph a above shall include prosecutors and holders of judicial offices;

c)   in the case of proceedings involving a public official of another State, the prosecuting State may apply the definition of public official only insofar as that definition is compatible with its national law;

d)   **"legal person"** shall mean any entity having such status under the applicable national law, except for States or other public bodies in the exercise of State authority and for public international organisations.

Chapter II - Measures to be taken at national level

Article 2 - Active bribery of domestic public officials

Each Party shall adopt such legislative and other measures as may be necessary to establish as criminal offences under its domestic law, when committed intentionally, the promising, offering or giving by any person, directly or indirectiy, of any undue advantage to any of its public officials, for himself or herself or for anyone else, for him or her to act or refrain from acting in the exercise of his or her functions.

Article 3 - Passive bribery of domestic public officials

Each Party shall adopt such legislative and other measures as may be necessary to establish as criminal offences under its domestic law, when committed intentionally, the request or receipt by any of its public officials, directly or indirectly, of any undue advantage, for himself or herself or for anyone else, or the acceptance of an offer or a promise of such an advantage, to act or refrain from acting in the exercise of his or her functions.

Article 4 - Bribery of members of domestic public assemblies

Each Party shall adopt such legislative and other measures as may be necessary to establish as criminal offences under its domestic law the conduct referred to in Articles 2 and 3, when involving any person who is a member of any domestic public assembly exercising legislative or administrative powers.

Article 5 - Bribery of foreign public officials

Each Party shall adopt such legislative and other measures as may be necessary to establish as criminal offences under its domestic law the conduct referred to in Articles 2 and 3, when involving a public official of any other State.

Article 6 - Bribery of members of foreign public assemblies

Each Party shall adopt such legislative and other measures as may be necessary to establish as criminal offences under its domestic law the conduct referred to in Articles 2 and 3, when involving any person who is a member of any public assembly exercising legislative or administrative powers in any other State.

Article 7 - Active bribery in the private sector

Each Party shall adopt such legislative and other measures as may be necessary to establish as criminal offences under its domestic law, when committed intentionally in the course of business activity, the promising, offering or giving, directly or indirectly, of any undue advantage to any persons who direct or work for, in any capacity, private sector entities, for themselves or for anyone else, for them to act, or refrain from acting, in breach of their duties.

Article 8 - Passive bribery in the private sector

Each Party shall adopt such legislative and other measures as may be necessary to establish as criminal offences under its domestic law, when committed intentionally, in the course of business activity, the request or receipt, directly or indirectly, by any persons who direct or work for, in any capacity, private sector entities, of any undue advantage or the promise thereof for themselves or for anyone else, or the acceptance of an offer or a promise of such an advantage, to act or refrain from acting in breach of their duties.

Article 9 - Bribery of officials of international organisations

Each Party shall adopt such legislative and other measures as may be necessary to establish as criminal offences under its domestic law the conduct referred to in Articles 2 and 3, when involving any official or other contracted employee, within the meaning of the staff regulations, of any public international or supranational organisation or body of which the Party is a member, and any person, whether seconded or not, carrying out functions corresponding to those performed by such officials or agents.

Article 10 - Bribery of members of international parliamentary assemblies

Each Party shall adopt such legislative and other measures as may be necessary to establish as criminal offences under its domestic law the conduct referred to in Article 4 when involving any members of parliamentary assemblies of international or supranational organisations of which the Party is a member.

Article 11 - Bribery of judges and officials of international courts

Each Party shall adopt such legislative and other measures as may be necessary to establish as criminal offences under its domestic law the conduct referred to in Articles 2 and 3 involving any holders of judicial office or officials of any international court whose jurisdiction is accepted by the Party.

Article 12 - Trading in influence

Each Party shall adopt such legislative and other measures as may be necessary to establish as criminal offences under its domestic law, when committed intentionally, the promising, giving or offering, directly or indirectly, of any undue advantage to anyone who asserts or confirms that he or she is able to exert an improper influence over the decision-making of any person referred to in Articles 2, 4 to 6 and 9 to 11 in consideration thereof, whether the undue advantage is for himself or herself or for anyone else, as well as the request, receipt or the acceptance of the offer or the promise of such an advantage, in consideration of that influence, whether or not the influence is exerted or whether or not the supposed influence leads to the intended result.

Article 13 - Money laundering of proceeds from corruption offences

Each Party shall adopt such legislative and other measures as may be necessary to establish as criminal offences under its domestic law the conduct referred to in the Council of Europe Convention on Laundering, Search, Seizure and Confiscation of the Products from Crime (ETS No. 141), Article 6, paragraphs 1 and 2, under the conditions referred to therein, when the predicate offence consists of any of the criminal offences established in accordance with Articles 2 to 12 of this Convention, to the extent that the Party has not made a reservation or a declaration with respect to these offences or does not consider such offences as serious ones for the purpose of their money laundering legislation.

Article 14 - Account offences

Each Party shall adopt such legislative and other measures as may be necessary to establish as offences liable to criminal or other sanctions under its domestic law the following acts or omissions, when committed intentionally, in order to commit, conceal or disguise the offences referred to in Articles 2 to 12, to the extent the Party has not made a reservation or a declaration:

a)   creating or using an invoice or any other accounting document or record containing false or incomplete information;

b)   unlawfully omitting to make a record of a payment.

Article 15 - Participatory acts

Each Party shall adopt such legislative and other measures as may be necessary to establish as criminal offences under its domestic law aiding or abetting the commission of any of the criminal offences established in accordance with this Convention.

Article 16 - Immunity

The provisions of this Convention shall be without prejudice to the provisions of any Treaty, Protocol or Statute, as well as their implementing texts, as regards the withdrawal of immunity.

Article 17 - Jurisdiction

1.   Each Party shall adopt such legislative and other measures as may be necessary to establish jurisdiction over a criminal offence established in accordance with Articles 2 to 14 of this Convention where:

a)   the offence is committed in whole or in part in its territory;

b)   the offender is one of its nationals, one of its public officials, or a member of one of its domestic public assemblies;

c)   the offence involves one of its public officials or members of its domestic public assemblies or any person referred to in Articles 9 to 11 who is at the same time one of its nationals.

2.   Each State may, at the time of signature or when depositing its instrument of ratification, acceptance, approval or accession, by a declaration addressed to the Secretary General of the Council of Europe, declare that it reserves the right not to apply or to apply only in specific cases or conditions the jurisdiction rules laid down in paragraphs 1 b and c of this article or any part thereof.

3.   If a Party has made use of the reservation possibility provided for in paragraph 2 of this article, it shall adopt such measures as may be necessary to establish jurisdiction over a criminal offence established in accordance with this Convention, in cases where an alleged offender is present in its territory and it does not extradite him to another Party, solely on the basis of his nationality, after a request for extradition.

4.   This Convention does not exclude any criminal jurisdiction exercised by a Party in accordance with national law.

Article 18 - Corporate liability

1.   Each Party shall adopt such legislative and other measures as may be necessary to ensure that legal persons can be held liable for the criminal offences of active bribery, trading in influence and money laundering established in accordance with this Convention, committed for their benefit by any natural person, acting either individually or as part of an organ of the legal person, who has a leading position within the legal person, based on:

- a power of representation of the legal person; or

- an authority to take decisions on behalf of the legal person; or

- an authority to exercise control within the legal person;

as well as for involvement of such a natural person as accessory or instigator in the above-mentioned offences.

2.   Apart from the cases already provided for in paragraph 1, each Party shall take the necessary measures to ensure that a legal person can be held liable where the lack of supervision or control by a natural person referred to in paragraph 1 has made possible the commission of the criminal offences mentioned in paragraph 1 for the benefit of that legal person by a natural person under its authority.

3.   Liability of a legal person under paragraphs 1 and 2 shall not exclude criminal proceedings against natural persons who are perpetrators, instigators of, or accessories to, the criminal offences mentioned in paragraph 1.

Article 19 - Sanctions and measures

1.   Having regard to the serious nature of the criminal offences established in accordance with this Convention, each Party shall provide, in respect of those criminal offences established in accordance with Articles 2 to 14, effective, proportionate and dissuasive sanctions and measures, including, when committed by natural persons, penalties involving deprivation of liberty which can give rise to extradition.

2. Each Party shall ensure that legal persons held liable in accordance with Article 18, paragraphs 1 and 2, shall be subject to effective, proportionate and dissuasive criminal or non-criminal sanctions, including monetary sanctions.

3. Each Party shall adopt such legislative and other measures as may be necessary to enable it to confiscate or otherwise deprive the instrumentalities and proceeds of criminal offences established in accordance with this Convention, or property the value of which corresponds to such proceeds.

Article 20 - Specialised authorities

Each Party shall adopt such measures as may be necessary to ensure that persons or entities are specialised in the fight against corruption. They shall have the necessary independence in accordance with the fundamental principles of the legal system of the Party, in order for them to be able to carry out their functions effectively and free from any undue pressure. The Party shall ensure that the staff of such entities has adequate training and financial resources for their tasks.

Article 21 - Co-operation with and between national authorities

Each Party shall adopt such measures as may be necessary to ensure that public authorities, as well as any public official, co-operate, in accordance with national law, with those of its authorities responsible for investigating and prosecuting criminal offences:

a) by informing the latter authorities, on their own initiative, where there are reasonable grounds to believe that any of the criminal offences established in accordance with Articles 2 to 14 has been committed, or

b) by providing, upon request, to the latter authorities all necessary information.

Article 22 - Protection of collaborators of justice and witnesses

Each Party shall adopt such measures as may be necessary to provide effective and appropriate protection for:

a) those who report the criminal offences established in accordance with Articles 2 to 14 or otherwise co-operate with the investigating or prosecuting authorities;

b) witnesses who give testimony concerning these offences.

Article 23 - Measures to facilitate the gathering of evidence and the confiscation of proceeds

1. Each Party shall adopt such legislative and other measures as may be necessary, including those permitting the use of special investigative techniques, in accordance with national law, to enable it to facilitate the gathering of evidence related to criminal offences established in accordance with Article 2 to 14 of this Convention and to identify, trace, freeze and seize instrumentalities and proceeds of corruption, or property the value of which corresponds to such proceeds, liable to measures set out in accordance with paragraph 3 of Article 19 of this Convention.

2.	Each Party shall adopt such legislative and other measures as may be necessary to empower its courts or other competent authorities to order that bank, financial or commercial records be made available or be seized in order to carry out the actions referred to in paragraph 1 of this article.

3.	Bank secrecy shall not be an obstacle to measures provided for in paragraphs 1 and 2 of this article.

Chapter III - Monitoring of implementation

Article 24 - Monitoring

The Group of States against Corruption (GRECO) shall monitor the implementation of this Convention by the Parties.

Chapter IV - International co-operation

Article 25 - General principles and measures for international co-operation

1.	The Parties shall co-operate with each other, in accordance with the provisions of relevant international instruments on international co-operation in criminal matters, or arrangements agreed on the basis of uniform or reciprocal legislation, and in accordance with their national law, to the widest extent possible for the purposes of investigations and proceedings concerning criminal offences established in accordance with this Convention.

2.	Where no international instrument or arrangement referred to in paragraph 1 is in force between Parties, Articles 26 to 31 of this chapter shall apply.

3.	Articles 26 to 31 of this chapter shall also apply where they are more favourable than those of the international instruments or arrangements referred to in paragraph 1.

Article 26 - Mutual assistance

1.	The Parties shall afford one another the widest measure of mutual assistance by promptly processing requests from authorities that, in conformity with their domestic laws, have the power to investigate or prosecute criminal offences established in accordance with this Convention.

2.	Mutual legal assistance under paragraph 1 of this article may be refused if the requested Party believes that compliance with the request would undermine its fundamental interests, national sovereignty, national security or ordre public.

3.	Parties shall not invoke bank secrecy as a ground to refuse any co-operation under this chapter. Where its domestic law so requires, a Party may require that a request for co-operation which would involve the lifting of bank secrecy be authorised by either a judge or another judicial authority, including public prosecutors, any of these authorities acting in relation to criminal offences.

Article 27 - Extradition

1.   The criminal offences established in accordance with this Convention shall be deemed to be included as extraditable offences in any extradition treaty existing between or among the Parties. The Parties undertake to include such offences as extraditable offences in any extradition treaty to be concluded between or among them.

2.   If a Party that makes extradition conditional on the existence of a treaty receives a request for extradition from another Party with which it does not have an extradition treaty, it may consider this Convention as the legal basis for extradition with respect to any criminal offence established in accordance with this Convention.

3.   Parties that do not make extradition conditional on the existence of a treaty shall recognise criminal offences established in accordance with this Convention as extraditable offences between themselves.

4.   Extradition shall be subject to the conditions provided for by the law of the requested Party or by applicable extradition treaties, including the grounds on which the requested Party may refuse extradition.

5.   If extradition for a criminal offence established in accordance with this Convention is refused solely on the basis of the nationality of the person sought, or because the requested Party deems that it has jurisdiction over the offence, the requested Party shall submit the case to its competent authorities for the purpose of prosecution unless otherwise agreed with the requesting Party, and shall report the final outcome to the requesting Party in due course.

Article 28 - Spontaneous information

Without prejudice to its own investigations or proceedings, a Party may without prior request forward to another Party information on facts when it considers that the disclosure of such information might assist the receiving Party in initiating or carrying out investigations or proceedings concerning criminal offences established in accordance with this Convention or might lead to a request by that Party under this chapter.

Article 29 - Central authority

1.   The Parties shall designate a central authority or, if appropriate, several central authorities, which shall be responsible for sending and answering requests made under this chapter, the execution of such requests or the transmission of them to the authorities competent for their execution.

2.   Each Party shall, at the time of signature or when depositing its instrument of ratification, acceptance, approval or accession, communicate to the Secretary General of the Council of Europe the names and addresses of the authorities designated in pursuance of paragraph 1 of this article.

Article 30 - Direct communication

1.   The central authorities shall communicate directly with one another.

2.   In the event of urgency, requests for mutual assistance or communications related thereto may be sent directly by the judicial authorities, including public prosecutors, of the requesting Party to such authorities of the requested Party. In such cases a copy shall be sent at the same time to the central authority of the requested Party through the central authority of the requesting Party.

3.   Any request or communication under paragraphs 1 and 2 of this article may be made through the International Criminal Police Organisation (Interpol).

4.   Where a request is made pursuant to paragraph 2 of this article and the authority is not competent to deal with the request, it shall refer the request to the competent national authority and inform directly the requesting Party that it has done so.

5.   Requests or communications under paragraph 2 of this article, which do not involve coercive action, may be directly transmitted by the competent authorities of the requesting Party to the competent authorities of the requested Party.

6.   Each State may, at the time of signature or when depositing its instrument of ratification, acceptance, approval or accession, inform the Secretary General of the Council of Europe that, for reasons of efficiency, requests made under this chapter are to be addressed to its central authority.

Article 31 - Information

The requested Party shall promptly inform the requesting Party of the action taken on a request under this chapter and the final result of that action. The requested Party shall also promptly inform the requesting Party of any circumstances which render impossible the carrying out of the action sought or are likely to delay it significantly.

Chapter V - Final provisions

Article 32 - Signature and entry into force

1.   This Convention shall be open for signature by the member States of the Council of Europe and by non-member States which have participated in its elaboration. Such States may express their consent to be bound by:

> a)   signature without reservation as to ratification, acceptance or approval; or

> b)   signature subject to ratification, acceptance or approval, followed by ratification, acceptance or approval.

2.   Instruments of ratification, acceptance or approval shall be deposited with the Secretary General of the Council of Europe.

3.   This Convention shall enter into force on the first day of the month following the expiration of a period of three months after the date on which fourteen States have expressed their consent to be bound by the Convention in accordance with the provisions of paragraph 1.

Any such State, which is not a member of the Group of States against Corruption (GRECO) at the time of ratification, shall automatically become a member on the date the Convention enters into force.

4.   In respect of any signatory State which subsequently expresses its consent to be bound by it, the Convention shall enter into force on the first day of the month following the expiration of a period of three months after the date of the expression of their consent to be bound by the Convention in accordance with the provisions of paragraph 1. Any signatory State, which is not a member of the Group of States against Corruption (GRECO) at the time of ratification, shall automatically become a member on the date the Convention enters into force in its respect.

Article 33 - Accession to the Convention

1.   After the entry into force of this Convention, the Committee of Ministers of the Council of Europe, after consulting the Contracting States to the Convention, may invite the European Community as well as any State not a member of the Council and not having participated in its elaboration to accede to this Convention, by a decision taken by the majority provided for in Article 20d of the Statute of the Council of Europe and by the unanimous vote of the representatives of the Contracting States entitled to sit on the Committee of Ministers.

2.   In respect of the European Community and any State acceding to it under paragraph 1 above, the Convention shall enter into force on the first day of the month following the expiration of a period of three months after the date of deposit of the instrument of accession with the Secretary General of the Council of Europe. The European Community and any State acceding to this Convention shall automatically become a member of GRECO, if it is not already a member at the time of accession, on the date the Convention enters into force in its respect.

Article 34 - Territorial application

1.   Any State may, at the time of signature or when depositing its instrument of ratification, acceptance, approval or accession, specify the territory or territories to which this Convention shall apply.

2.   Any Party may, at any later date, by a declaration addressed to the Secretary General of the Council of Europe, extend the application of this Convention to any other territory specified in the declaration. In respect of such territory the Convention shall enter into force on the first day of the month following the expiration of a period of three months after the date of receipt of such declaration by the Secretary General.

3.   Any declaration made under the two preceding paragraphs may, in respect of any territory specified in such declaration, be withdrawn by a notification addressed to the Secretary General of the Council of Europe. The withdrawal shall become effective on the first day of the month following the expiration of a period of three months after the date of receipt of such notification by the Secretary General.

Article 35 - Relationship to other conventions and agreements

1.   This Convention does not affect the rights and undertakings derived from international multilateral conventions concerning special matters.

2.   The Parties to the Convention may conclude bilateral or multilateral agreements with one another on the matters dealt with in this Convention, for purposes of supplementing or strengthening its provisions or facilitating the application of the principles embodied in it.

3.   If two or more Parties have already concluded an agreement or treaty in respect of a subject which is dealt with in this Convention or otherwise have established their relations in respect of that subject, they shall be entitled to apply that agreement or treaty or to regulate those relations accordingly, in lieu of the present Convention, if it facilitates international co-operation.

Article 36 - Declarations

Any State may, at the time of signature or when depositing its instrument of ratification, acceptance, approval or accession, declare that it will establish as criminal offences the active and passive bribery of foreign public officials under Article 5, of officials of international organisations under Article 9 or of judges and officials of international courts under Article 11, only to the extent that the public official or judge acts or refrains from acting in breach of his duties.

Article 37 - Reservations

1.   Any State may, at the time of signature or when depositing its instrument of ratification, acceptance, approval or accession, reserve its right not to establish as a criminal offence under its domestic law, in part or in whole, the conduct referred to in Articles 4, 6 to 8, 10 and 12 or the passive bribery offences defined in Article 5.

2.   Any State may, at the time of signature or when depositing its instrument of ratification, acceptance, approval or accession declare that it avails itself of the reservation provided for in Article 17, paragraph 2.

3.   Any State may, at the time of signature or when depositing its instrument of ratification, acceptance, approval or accession declare that it may refuse mutual legal assistance under Article 26, paragraph 1, if the request concerns an offence which the requested Party considers a political offence.

4.   No State may, by application of paragraphs 1, 2 and 3 of this article, enter reservations to more than five of the provisions mentioned thereon. No other reservation may be made. Reservations of the same nature with respect to Articles 4, 6 and 10 shall be considered as one reservation.

Article 38 - Validity and review of declarations and reservations

1.   Declarations referred to in Article 36 and reservations referred to in Article 37 shall be valid for a period of three years from the day of the entry into force of this Convention in respect of the State concerned. However, such declarations and reservations may be renewed for periods of the same duration.

2.   Twelve months before the date of expiry of the declaration or reservation, the Secretariat General of the Council of Europe shall give notice of that expiry to the State concerned. No later than three months before the expiry, the State shall notify the Secretary General that it is upholding, amending or withdrawing its declaration or reservation. In the absence of a

notification by the State concerned, the Secretariat General shall inform that State that its declaration or reservation is considered to have been extended automatically for a period of six months. Failure by the State concerned to notify its intention to uphold or modify its declaration or reservation before the expiry of that period shall cause the declaration or reservation to lapse.

3.   If a Party makes a declaration or a reservation in conformity with Articles 36 and 37, it shall provide, before its renewal or upon request, an explanation to GRECO, on the grounds justifying its continuance.

Article 39 - Amendments

1.   Amendments to this Convention may be proposed by any Party, and shall be communicated by the Secretary General of the Council of Europe to the member States of the Council of Europe and to every non-member State which has acceded to, or has been invited to accede to, this Convention in accordance with the provisions of Article 33.

2.   Any amendment proposed by a Party shall be communicated to the European Committee on Crime Problems (CDPC), which shall submit to the Committee of Ministers its opinion on that proposed amendment.

3.   The Committee of Ministers shall consider the proposed amendment and the opinion submitted by the CDPC and, following consultation of the non-member States Parties to this Convention, may adopt the amendment.

4.   The text of any amendment adopted by the Committee of Ministers in accordance with paragraph 3 of this article shall be forwarded to the Parties for acceptance.

5.   Any amendment adopted in accordance with paragraph 3 of this article shall come into force on the thirtieth day after all Parties have informed the Secretary General of their acceptance thereof.

Article 40 - Settlement of disputes

1.   The European Committee on Crime Problems of the Council of Europe shall be kept informed regarding the interpretation and application of this Convention.

2.   In case of a dispute between Parties as to the interpretation or application of this Convention, they shall seek a settlement of the dispute through negotiation or any other peaceful means of their choice, including submission of the dispute to the European Committee on Crime Problems, to an arbitral tribunal whose decisions shall be binding upon the Parties, or to the International Court of Justice, as agreed upon by the Parties concerned.

Article 41 - Denunciation

1.   Any Party may, at any time, denounce this Convention by means of a notification addressed to the Secretary General of the Council of Europe.

2.   Such denunciation shall become effective on the first day of the month following the expiration of a period of three months after the date of receipt of the notification by the Secretary General.

Article 42 - Notification

The Secretary General of the Council of Europe shall notify the member States of the Council of Europe and any State which has acceded to this Convention of:

a)   any signature;

b)   the deposit of any instrument of ratification, acceptance, approval or accession;

c)   any date of entry into force of this Convention in accordance with Articles 32 and 33;

d)   any declaration or reservation made under Article 36 or Article 37;

e)   any other act, notification or communication relating to this Convention.

In witness whereof the undersigned, being duly authorised thereto, have signed this Convention.

Done at Strasbourg, this 27th of January 1999, in English and in French, both texts being equally authentic, in a single copy which shall be deposited in the archives of the Council of Europe. The Secretary General of the Council of Europe shall transmit certified copies to each member State of the Council of Europe, to the non-member States which have participated in the elaboration of this Convention, and to any State invited to accede to it.

*   *   *

OECD PRINCIPLES OF CORPORATE GOVERNANCE[*]

(ORGANISATION FOR ECONOMIC CO-OPERATION AND DEVELOPMENT)

> The OECD Principles of Corporate Governance constitute a set of non-binding corporate governance standards and guidelines. They were prepared by an Ad-Hoc Task Force on Corporate Governance established for that purpose in conjunction with national Governments, other relevant organizations and the private sector. The Principles, which embody the views of OECD member countries on this issue, were submitted to the OECD Council at the ministerial level at its annual meeting on 26-27 May 1999 and received its approval.

PREAMBLE

The Principles are intended to assist Member and non-Member governments in their efforts to evaluate and improve the legal, institutional and regulatory framework for corporate governance in their countries, and to provide guidance and suggestions for stock exchanges, investors, corporations, and other parties that have a role in the process of developing good corporate governance. The Principles focus on publicly traded companies. However, to the extent they are deemed applicable, they might also be a useful tool to improve corporate governance in non-traded companies, for example, privately held and state-owned enterprises. The Principles represent a common basis that OECD Member countries consider essential for the development of good governance practice. They are intended to be concise, understandable and accessible to the international community. They are not intended to substitute for private sector initiatives to develop more detailed "best practice" in governance.

Increasingly, the OECD and its Member governments have recognised the synergy between macroeconomic and structural policies. One key element in improving economic efficiency is corporate governance, which involves a set of relationships between a company's management, its board, its shareholders and other stakeholders. Corporate governance also provides the structure through which the objectives of the company are set, and the means of attaining those objectives and monitoring performance are determined. Good corporate governance should provide proper incentives for the board and management to pursue objectives that are in the interests of the company and shareholders and should facilitate effective monitoring, thereby encouraging firms to use resources more efficiently.

Corporate governance is only part of the larger economic context in which firms operate, which includes, for example, macroeconomic policies and the degree of competition in product and factor markets. The corporate governance framework also depends on the legal, regulatory, and institutional environment. In addition, factors such as business ethics and corporate

---

[*] *Source*: Organisation for Economic Co-operation and Development (1999). "OECD Principles of Corporate Governance"; available on the Internet (http://www.oecd.org/daf/governance/principles.htm). [Note added by the editor.]

awareness of the environmental and societal interests of the communities in which it operates can also have an impact on the reputation and the long-term success of a company.

While a multiplicity of factors affect the governance and decision-making processes of firms, and are important to their long-term success, the Principles focus on governance problems that result from the separation of ownership and control. Some of the other issues relevant to a company's decision-making processes, such as environmental or ethical concerns, are taken into account but are treated more explicitly in a number of other OECD instruments (including the Guidelines for Multinational Enterprises and the Convention and Recommendation on Bribery) and the instruments of other international organisations.

The degree to which corporations observe basic principles of good corporate governance is an increasingly important factor for investment decisions. Of particular relevance is the relation between corporate governance practices and the increasingly international character of investment. International flows of capital enable companies to access financing from a much larger pool of investors. If countries are to reap the full benefits of the global capital market, and if they are to attract long-term "patient" capital, corporate governance arrangements must be credible and well understood across borders. Even if corporations do not rely primarily on foreign sources of capital, adherence to good corporate governance practices will help improve the confidence of domestic investors, may reduce the cost of capital, and ultimately induce more stable sources of financing.

Corporate governance is affected by the relationships among participants in the governance system. Controlling shareholders, which may be individuals, family holdings, bloc alliances, or other corporations acting through a holding company or cross shareholdings, can significantly influence corporate behaviour. As owners of equity, institutional investors are increasingly demanding a voice in corporate governance in some markets. Individual shareholders usually do not seek to exercise governance rights but may be highly concerned about obtaining fair treatment from controlling shareholders and management. Creditors play an important role in some governance systems and have the potential to serve as external monitors over corporate performance. Employees and other stakeholders play an important role in contributing to the long-term success and performance of the corporation, while governments establish the overall institutional and legal framework for corporate governance. The role of each of these participants and their interactions vary widely among OECD countries and among non-Members as well. These relationships are subject, in part, to law and regulation and, in part, to voluntary adaptation and market forces.

There is no single model of good corporate governance. At the same time, work carried out in Member countries and within the OECD has identified some common elements that underlie good corporate governance. The Principles build on these common elements and are formulated to embrace the different models that exist. For example, they do not advocate any particular board structure and the term "board" as used in this document is meant to embrace the different national models of board structures found in OECD countries. In the typical two tier system, found in some countries, "board" as used in the Principles refers to the "supervisory board" while "key executives" refers to the "management board". In systems where the unitary board is overseen by an internal auditor's board, the term "board" includes both.

The Principles are non-binding and do not aim at detailed prescriptions for national legislation. Their purpose is to serve as a reference point. They can be used by policy makers, as they examine and develop their legal and regulatory frameworks for corporate governance that reflect their own economic, social, legal and cultural circumstances, and by market participants as they develop their own practices.

The Principles are evolutionary in nature and should be reviewed in light of significant changes in circumstances. To remain competitive in a changing world, corporations must innovate and adapt their corporate governance practices so that they can meet new demands and grasp new opportunities. Similarly, governments have an important responsibility for shaping an effective regulatory framework that provides for sufficient flexibility to allow markets to function effectively and to respond to expectations of shareholders and other stakeholders. It is up to governments and market participants to decide how to apply these Principles in developing their own frameworks for corporate governance, taking into account the costs and benefits of regulation.

The following document is divided into two parts. The Principles presented in the first part of the document cover five areas: I) The rights of shareholders; II) The equitable treatment of shareholders; III) The role of stakeholders; IV) Disclosure and transparency; and V) The responsibilities of the board. Each of the sections is headed by a single Principle that appears in bold italics and is followed by a number of supporting recommendations. In the second part of the document, the Principles are supplemented by annotations that contain commentary on the Principles and are intended to help readers understand their rationale. The annotations may also contain descriptions of dominant trends and offer alternatives and examples that may be useful in making the Principles operational.

PART ONE

OECD PRINCIPLES OF CORPORATE GOVERNANCE

I. THE RIGHTS OF SHAREHOLDERS

The corporate governance framework should protect shareholders' rights.

A. Basic shareholder rights include the right to: 1) secure methods of ownership registration; 2) convey or transfer shares; 3) obtain relevant information on the corporation on a timely and regular basis; 4) participate and vote in general shareholder meetings; 5) elect members of the board; and 6) share in the profits of the corporation.

B. Shareholders have the right to participate in, and to be sufficiently informed on, decisions concerning fundamental corporate changes such as: 1) amendments to the statutes, or articles of incorporation or similar governing documents of the company; 2) the authorisation of additional shares; and 3) extraordinary transactions that in effect result in the sale of the company.

C. Shareholders should have the opportunity to participate effectively and vote in general shareholder meetings and should be informed of the rules, including voting procedures, that govern general shareholder meetings:

    1. Shareholders should have the opportunity to anticipate in, and to be sufficiently informed on, decisions concerning fundamental corporate changes such as: 1) amendments to the statutes, or articles of incorporation or similar governing

documents of the company; 2) the authorisation of additional shares; and 3) extraordinary transactions that in effect result in the sale of the company.

2. Opportunity should be provided for shareholders to ask questions of the board and to place items on the agenda at general meetings, subject to reasonable limitations.

3. Shareholders should be able to vote in person or in absentia, and equal effect should be given to votes whether cast in person or in absentia.

D. Capital structures and arrangements that enable certain shareholders to obtain a degree of control disproportionate to their equity ownership should be disclosed.

E. Markets for corporate control should be allowed to function in an efficient and transparent manner.

1. The rules and procedures governing the acquisition of corporate control in the capital markets, and extraordinary transactions such as mergers, and sales of substantial portions of corporate assets, should be clearly articulated and disclosed so that investors understand their rights and recourse. Transactions should occur at transparent prices and under fair conditions that protect the rights of all shareholders according to their class.

2. Anti-take-over devices should not be used to shield management from accountability.

F. Shareholders, including institutional investors, should consider the costs and benefits of exercising their voting rights.

II. THE EQUITABLE TREATMENT OF SHAREHOLDERS

The corporate governance framework should ensure the equitable treatment of all shareholders, including minority and foreign shareholders. All shareholders should have the opportunity to obtain effective redress for violation of their rights.

A. All shareholders of the same class should be treated equally.

1. Within any class, all shareholders should have the same voting rights. All investors should be able to obtain information about the voting rights attached to all classes of shares before they purchase. Any changes in voting rights should be subject to shareholder vote.

2. Votes should be cast by custodians or nominees in a manner agreed upon with the beneficial owner of the shares.

3. Processes and procedures for general shareholder meetings should allow for equitable treatment of all shareholders. Company procedures should not make it unduly difficult or expensive to cast votes.

B. Insider trading and abusive self-dealing should be prohibited.

C. Members of the board and managers should be required to disclose any Material interests in transactions or matters affecting the corporation.

III. THE ROLE OF STAKEHOLDERS IN CORPORATE GOVERNANCE

The corporate governance framework should recognise the rights of stakeholders as established by law and encourage active co-operation between corporations and stakeholders in creating wealth, jobs, and the sustainability of financially sound enterprises.

A. The corporate governance framework should assure that the rights of stakeholders that are protected by law are respected.

B. Where stakeholder interests are protected by law, stakeholders should have the opportunity to obtain effective redress for violation of their rights.

C. The corporate governance framework should permit performance-enhancing mechanisms for stakeholder participation.

D. Where stakeholders participate in the corporate governance process, they should have access to relevant information.

IV. DISCLOSURE AND TRANSPARENCY

The corporate governance framework should ensure that timely and accurate disclosure is made on all material matters regarding the corporation, including the financial situation, performance, ownership, and governance of the company.

A. Disclosure should include, but not be limited to, material information on:

1. The financial and operating results of the company.

2. Company objectives.

3. Major share ownership and voting rights.

4. Members of the board and key executives, and their remuneration.

5. Material foreseeable risk factors.

6. Material issues regarding employees and other stakeholders.

7. Governance structures and policies.

B. Information should be prepared, audited, and disclosed in accordance with high quality standards of accounting, financial and non-financial disclosure, and audit.

C. An annual audit should be conducted by an independent auditor in order to provide an external and objective assurance on the way in which financial statements have been prepared and presented.

D. Channels for disseminating information should provide for fair, timely and cost-efficient access to relevant information by users.

V. THE RESPONSIBILITIES OF THE BOARD

The corporate governance framework should ensure the strategic guidance of the company, the effective monitoring of management by the board, and the board's accountability to the company and the shareholders.

A. Board members should act on a fully informed basis, in good faith, with due diligence and care, and in the best interest of the company and the shareholders.

B. Where board decisions may affect different shareholder groups differently, the board should treat all shareholders fairly.

C. The board should ensure compliance with applicable law and take into account the interests of stakeholders.

D. The board should fulfil certain key functions, including:

1. Reviewing and guiding corporate strategy, major plans of action, risk policy, annual budgets and business plans; setting performance objectives; monitoring implementation and corporate performance; and overseeing major capital expenditures, acquisitions and divestitures.

2. Selecting, compensating, monitoring and, when necessary, replacing key executives and overseeing succession planning.

3. Reviewing key executive and board remuneration, and ensuring a formal and transparent board nomination process.

4. Monitoring and managing potential conflicts of interest of management, board members and shareholders, including misuse of corporate assets and abuse in related party transactions.

5. Ensuring the integrity of the corporation's accounting and financial reporting systems, including the independent audit, and that appropriate systems of control are in place, in particular, systems for monitoring risk, financial control, and compliance with the law.

6. Monitoring the effectiveness of the governance practices under which it operates and making changes as needed.

7. Overseeing the process of disclosure and communications.

E. The board should be able to exercise objective judgement on corporate affairs independent, in particular, from management.

    1.   Boards should consider assigning a sufficient number of non-executive board members capable of exercising independent judgement to tasks where there is a potential for conflict of interest. Examples of such key responsibilities are financial reporting, nomination and executive and board remuneration.

    2.   Board members should devote sufficient time to their responsibilities.

F. In order to fulfil their responsibilities, board members should have access to accurate, relevant and timely information.

PART II

ANNOTATIONS TO THE OECD PRINCIPLES OF CORPORATE GOVERNANCE

I. THE RIGHTS OF SHAREHOLDERS

The corporate governance framework should protect shareholders' rights.

Equity investors have certain property rights. For example, an equity share can be bought, sold, or transferred. An equity share also entitles the investor to participate in the profits of the corporation, with liability limited to the amount of the investment. In addition, ownership of an equity share provides a right to information about the corporation and a right to influence the corporation, primarily by participation in general shareholder meetings and by voting.

As a practical matter, however, the corporation cannot be managed by shareholder referendum. The shareholding body is made up of individuals and institutions whose interests, goals, investment horizons and capabilities vary. Moreover, the corporation's management must be able to take business decisions rapidly. In light of these realities and the complexity of managing the corporation's affairs in fast moving and ever changing markets, shareholders are not expected to assume responsibility for managing corporate activities. The responsibility for corporate strategy and operations is typically placed in the hands of the board and a management team that is selected, motivated and, when necessary, replaced by the board.

Shareholders' rights to influence the corporation centre on certain fundamental issues, such as the election of board members, or other means of influencing the composition of the board, amendments to the company's organic documents, approval of extraordinary transactions, and other basic issues as specified in company law and internal company statutes. This Section can be seen as a statement of the most basic rights of shareholders, which are recognised by law in virtually all OECD countries. Additional rights such as the approval or election of auditors, direct nomination of board members, the ability to pledge shares, the approval of distributions of profits, etc., can be found in various jurisdictions.

A. Basic shareholder rights include the right to: 1) secure methods of ownership registration; 2) convey or transfer shares; 3) obtain relevant information on the corporation on a timely and regular basis; 4) participate and vote in general shareholder meetings; 5) elect members of the board; and 6) share in the profits of the corporation.

B. Shareholders have the right to participate in, and to be sufficiently informed on, decisions concerning fundamental corporate changes such as: 1) amendments to the statutes, or articles of incorporation or similar governing documents of the company; 2) the authorisation of additional shares; and 3) extraordinary transactions that in effect result in the sale of the company.

C. Shareholders should have the opportunity to participate effectively and vote in general shareholder meetings and should be informed of the rules, including voting procedures, that govern general shareholder meetings:

1. Shareholders should be furnished with sufficient and timely information concerning the date, location and agenda of general meetings, as well as full and timely information regarding the issues to be decided at the meeting.

2. Opportunity should be provided for shareholders to ask questions of the board and to place items on the agenda at general meetings, subject to reasonable limitations.

   In order to enlarge the ability of investors to participate in general meetings, some companies have increased the ability of shareholders to place items on the agenda by simplifying the process of filing amendments and resolutions. The ability of shareholders to submit questions in advance and to obtain replies from management and board members has also been increased. Companies are justified in assuring that frivolous or disruptive attempts to place items on the agenda do not occur. It is reasonable, for example, to require that in order for shareholder-proposed resolutions to be placed on the agenda, they need to be supported by those holding a specified number of shares.

3. Shareholders should be able to vote in person or in absentia, and equal effect should be given to votes whether cast in person or in absentia.

   The Principles recommend that voting by proxy be generally accepted. Moreover, the objective of broadening shareholder participation suggests that companies consider favourably the enlarged use of technology in voting, including telephone and electronic voting. The increased importance of foreign shareholders suggests that on balance companies ought to make every effort to enable shareholders to participate through means which make use of modern technology. Effective participation of shareholders in general meetings can be enhanced by developing secure electronic means of communication and allowing shareholders to communicate with each other without having to comply with the formalities of proxy solicitation. As a matter of transparency, meeting procedures should ensure that votes are properly counted and recorded, and that a timely announcement of the outcome be made.

D. Capital structures and arrangements that enable certain shareholders to obtain a degree of control disproportionate to their equity ownership should be disclosed.

Some capital structures allow a shareholder to exercise a degree of control over the corporation disproportionate to the shareholders' equity ownership in the company. Pyramid structures and cross shareholdings can be used to diminish the capability of non-controlling shareholders to influence corporate policy.

In addition to ownership relations, other devices can affect control over the corporation. Shareholder agreements are a common means for groups of shareholders, who individually may hold relatively small shares of total equity, to act in concert so as to constitute an effective majority, or at least the largest single block of shareholders. Shareholder agreements usually give those participating in the agreements preferential rights to purchase shares if other parties to the agreement wish to sell. These agreements can also contain provisions that require those accepting the agreement not to sell their shares for a specified time. Shareholder agreements can cover issues such as how the board or the Chairman will be selected. The agreements can also oblige those in the agreement to vote as a block.

Voting caps limit the number of votes that a shareholder may cast, regardless of the number of shares the shareholder may actually possess. Voting caps therefore redistribute control and may affect the incentives for shareholder participation in shareholder meetings.

Given the capacity of these mechanisms to redistribute the influence of shareholders on company policy, shareholders can reasonably expect that all such capital structures and arrangements be disclosed.

E. Markets for corporate control should be allowed to function in an efficient and transparent manner.

    1. The rules and procedures governing the acquisition of corporate control in the capital markets, and extraordinary transactions such as mergers, and sales of substantial portions of corporate assets, should be clearly articulated and disclosed so that investors understand their rights and recourse. Transactions should occur at transparent prices and under fair conditions that protect the rights of all shareholders according to their class.

    2. Anti-take-over devices should not be used to shield management from accountability.

        In some countries, companies employ anti-take-over devices. However, both investors and stock exchanges have expressed concern over the possibility that widespread use of anti-take-over devices may be a serious impediment to the functioning of the market for corporate control. In some instances, take-over defences can simply be devices to shield the management from shareholder monitoring.

F. Shareholders, including institutional investors, should consider the costs and benefits of exercising their voting rights.

The Principles do not advocate any particular investment strategy for investors and do not seek to prescribe the optimal degree of investor activism. Nevertheless, many investors have concluded that positive financial returns can be obtained by undertaking a reasonable amount of analysis and by exercising their voting rights. Some institutional investors also disclose their own policies with respect to the companies in which they invest.

II. THE EQUITABLE TREATMENT OF SHAREHOLDERS

The corporate governance framework should ensure the equitable treatment of all shareholders, including minority and foreign shareholders. All shareholders should have the opportunity to obtain effective redress for violation of their rights.

Investors' confidence that the capital they provide will be protected from misuse or misappropriation by corporate managers, board members or controlling shareholders is an important factor in the capital markets. Corporate boards, managers and controlling shareholders may have the opportunity to engage in activities that may advance their own interests at the expense of non-controlling shareholders. The Principles support equal treatment for foreign and domestic shareholders in corporate governance. They do not address government policies to regulate foreign direct investment.

One of the ways in which shareholders can enforce their rights is to be able to initiate legal and administrative proceedings against management and board members. Experience has shown that an important determinant of the degree to which shareholder rights are protected is whether effective methods exist to obtain redress for grievances at a reasonable cost and without excessive delay. The confidence of minority investors is enhanced when the legal system provides mechanisms for minority shareholders to bring lawsuits when they have reasonable grounds to believe that their rights have been violated.

There is some risk that a legal system, which enables any investor to challenge corporate activity in the courts, can become prone to excessive litigation. Thus, many legal systems have introduced provisions to protect management and board members against litigation abuse in the form of tests for the sufficiency of shareholder complaints, so-called safe harbours for management and board member actions (such as the business judgement rule) as well as safe harbours for the disclosure of information. In the end, a balance must be struck between allowing investors to seek remedies for infringement of ownership rights and avoiding excessive litigation. Many countries have found that alternative adjudication procedures, such as administrative hearings or arbitration procedures organised by the securities regulators or other regulatory bodies, are an efficient method for dispute settlement, at least at the first instance level.

A. All shareholders of the same class should be treated equally.

1. Within any class, all shareholders should have the same voting rights. All investors should be able to obtain information about the voting rights attached to all classes of shares before they purchase. Any changes in voting rights should be subject to shareholder vote.

    The optimal capital structure of the firm is best decided by the management and the board, subject to the approval of the shareholders. Some companies issue preferred (or preference) shares which have a preference in respect of receipt of the profits of the firm but which normally have no voting rights. Companies may also issue participation certificates or shares without voting rights, which would presumably trade at different prices than shares with voting rights. All of these structures may be effective in distributing risk and reward in ways that are thought to be in the best interest of the company and to cost-efficient financing. The Principles do not take a position on the concept of "one share one vote". However, many institutional investors and shareholder associations support this concept.

Investors can expect to be informed regarding their voting rights before they invest. Once they have invested, their rights should not be changed unless those holding voting shares have had the opportunity to participate in the decision. Proposals to change the voting rights of different classes of shares are normally submitted for approval at general shareholders meetings by a specified majority of voting shares in the affected categories.

2. Votes should be cast by custodians or nominees in a manner agreed upon with the beneficial owner of the shares.

In some OECD countries it was customary for financial institutions which held shares in custody for investors to cast the votes of those shares. Custodians such as banks and brokerage firms holding securities as nominees for customers were sometimes required to vote in support of management unless specifically instructed by the shareholder to do otherwise.

The trend in OECD countries is to remove provisions that automatically enable custodian institutions to cast the votes of shareholders. Rules in some countries have recently been revised to require custodian institutions to provide shareholders with information concerning their options in the use of their voting rights. Shareholders may elect to delegate all voting rights to custodians. Alternatively, shareholders may choose to be informed of all upcoming shareholder votes and may decide to cast some votes while delegating some voting rights to the custodian. It is necessary to draw a reasonable balance between assuring that shareholder votes are not cast by custodians without regard for the wishes of shareholders and not imposing excessive burdens on custodians to secure shareholder approval before casting votes. It is sufficient to disclose to the shareholders that, if no instruction to the contrary is received, the custodian will vote the shares in the way he deems consistent with shareholder interest.

It should be noted that this item does not apply to the exercise of voting rights by trustees or other persons acting under a special legal mandate (such as, for example, bankruptcy receivers and estate executors).

3. Processes and procedures for general shareholder meetings should allow for equitable treatment of all shareholders. Company procedures should not make it unduly difficult or expensive to cast votes.

In Section I of the Principles, the right to participate in general shareholder meetings was identified as a shareholder right. Management and controlling investors have at times sought to discourage non-controlling or foreign investors from trying to influence the direction of the company. Some companies charged fees for voting. Other impediments included prohibitions on proxy voting and the requirement of personal attendance at general shareholder meetings to vote. Still other procedures may make it practically impossible to exercise ownership rights. Proxy materials may be sent too close to the time of general shareholder meetings to allow investors adequate time for reflection and consultation. Many companies in OECD countries are seeking to develop better channels of communication and decision-making with shareholders. Efforts by companies to remove artificial barriers to participation in general meetings are encouraged.

B. Insider trading and abusive self-dealing should be prohibited.

Abusive self-dealing occurs when persons having close relationships to the company exploit those relationships to the detriment of the company and investors. Since insider trading entails manipulation of the capital markets, it is prohibited by securities regulations, company law and/or criminal law in most OECD countries. However, not all jurisdictions prohibit such practices, and in some cases enforcement is not vigorous. These practices can be seen as constituting a breach of good corporate governance inasmuch as they violate the principle of equitable treatment of shareholders.

The Principles reaffirm that it is reasonable for investors to expect that the abuse of insider power be prohibited. In cases where such abuses are not specifically forbidden by legislation or where enforcement is not effective, it will be important for governments to take measures to remove any such gaps.

C. Members of the board and managers should be required to disclose any material interests in transactions or matters affecting the corporation.

This item refers to situations where members of the board and managers have a business, family or other special relationship to the company that could affect their judgement with respect to a transaction.

III. THE ROLE OF STAKEHOLDERS IN CORPORATE GOVERNANCE

The corporate governance framework should recognise the rights of stakeholders as established by law and encourage active co-operation between corporations and stakeholders in creating wealth, jobs, and the sustainability of financially sound enterprises.

A key aspect of corporate governance is concerned with ensuring the flow of external capital to firms. Corporate governance is also concerned with finding ways to encourage the various stakeholders in the firm to undertake socially efficient levels of investment in firm-specific human and physical capital. The competitiveness and ultimate success of a corporation is the result of teamwork that embodies contributions from a range of different resource providers including investors, employees, creditors, and suppliers. Corporations should recognise that the contributions of stakeholders constitute a valuable resource for building competitive and profitable companies. It is, therefore, in the long-term interest of corporations to foster wealth-creating co-operation among stakeholders. The governance framework should recognise that the interests of the corporation are served by recognising the interests of stakeholders and their contribution to the long-term success of the corporation.

A. The corporate governance framework should assure that the rights of stakeholders that are protected by law are respected.

In all OECD countries stakeholder rights are established by law, such as labour law, business law, contract law, and insolvency law. Even in areas where stakeholder interests are not legislated, many firms make additional commitments to stakeholders, and concern over corporate reputation and corporate performance often require the recognition of broader interests.

B. Where stakeholder interests are protected by law, stakeholders should have the opportunity to obtain effective redress for violation of their rights.
The legal framework and process should be transparent and not impede the ability of stakeholders to communicate and to obtain redress for the violation of rights.

C. The corporate governance framework should permit performance-enhancing mechanisms for stakeholder participation.

Corporate governance frameworks will provide for different roles for stakeholders. The degree to which stakeholders participate in corporate governance depends on national laws and practices, and may vary from company to company as well. Examples of mechanisms for stakeholder participation include: employee representation on boards; employee stock ownership plans or other profit sharing mechanisms or governance processes that consider stakeholder viewpoints in certain key decisions. They may, in addition, include creditor involvement in governance in the context of insolvency proceedings.

D. Where stakeholders participate in the corporate governance process, they should have access to relevant information.

Where laws and practice of corporate governance systems provide for participation by stakeholders, it is important that stakeholders have access to information necessary to fulfil their responsibilities.

IV. DISCLOSURE AND TRANSPARENCY

The corporate governance framework should ensure that timely and accurate disclosure is made on all material matters regarding the corporation, including the financial situation, performance, ownership, and governance of the company.

In most OECD countries a large amount of information, both mandatory and voluntary, is compiled on publicly traded and large unlisted enterprises, and subsequently disseminated to a broad range of users. Public disclosure is typically required, at a minimum, on an annual basis though some countries require periodic disclosure on a semi-annual or quarterly basis, or even more frequently in the case of material developments affecting the company. Companies often make voluntary disclosure that goes beyond minimum disclosure requirements in response to market demand.

A strong disclosure regime is a pivotal feature of market-based monitoring of companies and is central to shareholders' ability to exercise their voting rights. Experience in countries with large and active equity markets shows that disclosure can also be a powerful tool for influencing the behaviour of companies and for protecting investors. A strong disclosure regime can help to attract capital and maintain confidence in the capital markets. Shareholders and potential investors require access to regular, reliable and comparable information in sufficient detail for them to assess the stewardship of management, and make informed decisions about the valuation, ownership and voting of shares. Insufficient or unclear information may hamper the ability of the markets to function, may increase the cost of capital and result in a poor allocation of resources.

Disclosure also helps improve public understanding of the structure and activities of enterprises, corporate policies and performance with respect to environmental and ethical standards, and companies' relationships with the communities in which they operate. The OECD Guidelines for Multinational Enterprises are relevant in this context.

Disclosure requirements are not expected to place unreasonable administrative or cost burdens on enterprises. Nor are companies expected to disclose information that may endanger their competitive position unless disclosure is necessary to fully inform the investment decision and to avoid misleading the investor. In order to determine what information should be disclosed at a minimum, many countries apply the concept of materiality. Material information can be defined as information whose omission or misstatement could influence the economic decisions taken by users of information.

The Principles support timely disclosure of all material developments that arise between regular reports. They also support simultaneous reporting of information to all shareholders in order to ensure their equitable treatment.

A. Disclosure should include, but not be limited to, material information on:

1. The financial and operating results of the company.

   Audited financial statements showing the financial performance and the financial situation of the company (most typically including the balance sheet, the profit and loss statement, the cash flow statement and notes to the financial statements) are the most widely used source of information on companies. In their current form, the two principal goals of financial statements are to enable appropriate monitoring to take place and to provide the basis to value securities. Management's discussion and analysis of operations is typically included in annual reports. This discussion is most useful when read in conjunction with the accompanying financial statements. Investors are particularly interested in information that may shed light on the future performance of the enterprise.

   It is important that transactions relating to an entire group be disclosed. Arguably, failures of governance can often be linked to the failure to disclose the "whole picture", particularly where off-balance sheet items are used to provide guarantees or similar commitments between related companies.

2. Company objectives.

   In addition to their commercial objectives, companies are encouraged to disclose policies relating to business ethics, the environment and other public policy commitments. Such information may be important for investors and other users of information to better evaluate the relationship between companies and the communities in which they operate and the steps that companies have taken to implement their objectives.

3. Major share ownership and voting rights.

   One of the basic rights of investors is to be informed about the ownership structure of the enterprise and their rights *vis-à-vis* the rights of other owners. Countries often require disclosure of ownership data once certain thresholds of ownership are passed. Such disclosure might include data on major shareholders and others that control or may control the company, including information on special voting rights, shareholder agreements, the ownership of controlling or large blocks of shares, significant cross shareholding relationships and cross guarantees. (See Section I.D) Companies are also expected to provide information on related party transactions.

4. Members of the board and key executives, and their remuneration.

   Investors require information on individual board members and key executives in order to evaluate their experience and qualifications and assess any potential conflicts of interest that might affect their judgement.
   Board and executive remuneration are also of concern to shareholders. Companies are generally expected to disclose sufficient information on the remuneration of board members and key executives (either individually or in the aggregate) for investors to properly assess the costs and benefits of remuneration plans and the contribution of incentive schemes, such as stock option schemes, to performance.

5. Material foreseeable risk factors.

   Users of financial information and market participants need information on reasonably foreseeable material risks that may include: risks that are specific to the industry or geographical areas; dependence on commodities; financial market risk including interest rate or currency risk; risk related to derivatives and off-balance sheet transactions; and risks related to environmental liabilities.

   The Principles do not envision the disclosure of information in greater detail than is necessary to fully inform investors of the material and foreseeable risks of the enterprise. Disclosure of risk is most effective when it is tailored to the particular industry in question. Disclosure of whether or not companies have put systems for monitoring risk in place is also useful.

6. Material issues regarding employees and other stakeholders.

   Companies are encouraged to provide information on key issues relevant to employees and other stakeholders that may materially affect the performance of the company. Disclosure may include management/employee relations, and relations with other stakeholders such as creditors, suppliers, and local communities.

Some countries require extensive disclosure of information on human resources. Human resource policies, such as programmes for human resource development or employee share ownership plans, can communicate important information on the competitive strengths of companies to market participants.

7.   Governance structures and policies.

Companies are encouraged to report on how they apply relevant corporate governance principles in practice. Disclosure of the governance structures and policies of the company, in particular the division of authority between shareholders, management and board members is important for the assessment of a company's governance.

B. Information should be prepared, audited, and disclosed in accordance with high quality standards of accounting, financial and non-financial disclosure, and audit.

The application of high quality standards is expected to significantly improve the ability of investors to monitor the company by providing increased reliability and comparability of reporting, and improved insight into company performance. The quality of information depends on the standards under which it is compiled and disclosed. The Principles support the development of high quality internationally recognised standards, which can serve to improve the comparability of information between countries.

C. An annual audit should be conducted by an independent auditor in order to provide an external and objective assurance on the way in which financial statements have been prepared and presented.

Many countries have considered measures to improve the independence of auditors and their accountability to shareholders. It is widely felt that the application of high quality audit standards and codes of ethics is one of the best methods for increasing independence and strengthening the standing of the profession. Further measures include strengthening of board audit committees and increasing the board's responsibility in the auditor selection process.

Other proposals have been considered by OECD countries. Some countries apply limitations on the percentage of non-audit income that the auditor can receive from a particular client. Other countries require companies to disclose the level of fees paid to auditors for non-audit services. In addition there may be limitations on the total percentage of auditor income that can come from one client. Examples of other proposals include quality reviews of auditors by another auditor, prohibitions on the provision of non-audit services, mandatory rotation of auditors and the direct appointment of auditors by shareholders.

D. Channels for disseminating information should provide for fair, timely and cost-efficient access to relevant information by users.

Channels for the dissemination of information can be as important as the content of the information itself. While the disclosure of information is often provided for by legislation, filing and access to information can be cumbersome and costly. Filing of statutory reports has been greatly enhanced in some countries by electronic filing and data retrieval systems. The Internet and other information technologies also provide the opportunity for improving information dissemination.

V. THE RESPONSIBILITIES OF THE BOARD

The corporate governance framework should ensure the strategic guidance of the company, the effective monitoring of management by the board, and the board's accountability to the company and the shareholders.

Board structures and procedures vary both within and among OECD countries. Some countries have two-tier boards that separate the supervisory function and the management function into different bodies. Such systems typically have a "supervisory board" composed of non-executive board members and a "management board" composed entirely of executives. Other countries have "unitary" boards, which bring together executive and non-executive board members. The Principles are intended to be sufficiently general to apply to whatever board structure is charged with the functions of governing the enterprise and monitoring management.

Together with guiding corporate strategy, the board is chiefly responsible for monitoring managerial performance and achieving an adequate return for shareholders, while preventing conflicts of interest and balancing competing demands on the corporation. In order for boards to effectively fulfil their responsibilities they must have some degree of independence from management. Another important board responsibility is to implement systems designed to ensure that the corporation obeys applicable laws, including tax, competition, labour, environmental, equal opportunity, health and safety laws. In addition, boards are expected to take due regard of, and deal fairly with, other stakeholder interests including those of employees, creditors, customers, suppliers and local communities. Observance of environmental and social standards is relevant in this context.

A. Board members should act on a fully informed basis, in good faith, with due diligence and care, and in the best interest of the company and the shareholders.

In some countries, the board is legally required to act in the interest of the company, taking into account the interests of shareholders, employees, and the public good. Acting in the best interest of the company should not permit management to become entrenched.

B. Where board decisions may affect different shareholder groups differently, the board should treat all shareholders fairly.

C. The board should ensure compliance with applicable law and take into account the interests of stakeholders.

D. The board should fulfil certain key functions, including:

1. Reviewing and guiding corporate strategy, major plans of action, risk policy, annual budgets and business plans; setting performance objectives; monitoring implementation and corporate performance; and overseeing major capital expenditures, acquisitions and divestitures.

2. Selecting, compensating, monitoring and, when necessary, replacing key executives and overseeing succession planning.

3. Reviewing key executive and board remuneration, and ensuring a formal and transparent board nomination process.

4. Monitoring and managing potential conflicts of interest of management, board members and shareholders, including misuse of corporate assets and abuse in related party transactions.

5. Ensuring the integrity of the corporation's accounting and financial reporting systems, including the independent audit, and that appropriate systems of control are in place, in particular, systems for monitoring risk, financial control, and compliance with the law.

6. Monitoring the effectiveness of the governance practices under which it operates and making changes as needed.

7. Overseeing the process of disclosure and communications.
   The specific functions of board members may differ according to the articles of company law in each jurisdiction and according to the statutes of each company. The above-noted elements are, however, considered essential for purposes of corporate governance.

E. The board should be able to exercise objective judgement on corporate affairs independent, in particular, from management.

The variety of board structures and practices in different countries will require different approaches to the issue of independent board members. Board independence usually requires that a sufficient number of board members not be employed by the company and not be closely related to the company or its management through significant economic, family or other ties. This does not prevent shareholders from being board members.

Independent board members can contribute significantly to the decision-making of the board. They can bring an objective view to the evaluation of the performance of the board and management. In addition, they can play an important role in areas where the interests of management, the company and shareholders may diverge such as executive remuneration, succession planning, changes of corporate control, take-over defences, large acquisitions and the audit function.

The Chairman as the head of the board can play a central role in ensuring the effective governance of the enterprise and is responsible for the board's effective function. The

Chairman may in some countries, be supported by the company secretary. In unitary board systems, the separation of the roles of the Chief Executive and Chairman is often proposed as a method of ensuring an appropriate balance of power, increasing accountability and increasing the capacity of the board for independent decision making.

1. Boards should consider assigning a sufficient number of non-executive board members capable of exercising independent judgement to tasks where there is a potential for conflict of interest. Examples of such key responsibilities are financial reporting, nomination and executive and board remuneration.

    While the responsibility for financial reporting, remuneration and nomination are those of the board as a whole, independent non-executive board members can provide additional assurance to market participants that their interests are defended. Boards may also consider establishing specific committees to consider questions where there is a potential for conflict of interest. These committees may require a minimum number or be composed entirely of non-executive members.

2. Board members should devote sufficient time to their responsibilities.

    It is widely held that service on too many boards can interfere with the performance of board members. Companies may wish to consider whether excessive board service interferes with board performance. Some countries have limited the number of board positions that can be held. Specific limitations may be less important than ensuring that members of the board enjoy legitimacy and confidence in the eyes of shareholders.

    In order to improve board practices and the performance of its members, some companies have found it useful to engage in training and voluntary self-evaluation that meets the needs of the individual company. This might include that board members acquire appropriate skills upon appointment, and thereafter remain abreast of relevant new laws, regulations, and changing commercial risks.

F. In order to fulfil their responsibilities, board members should have access to accurate, relevant and timely information.

Board members require relevant information on a timely basis in order to support their decision-making. Non-executive board members do not typically have the same access to information as key managers within the company. The contributions of non-executive board members to the company can be enhanced by providing access to certain key managers within the company such as, for example, the company secretary and the Internal auditor, and recourse to independent external advice at the expense of the company. In order to fulfil their responsibilities, board members should ensure that they obtain accurate, relevant and timely information.

*   *   *

AGREEMENT BETWEEN THE EUROPEAN COMMUNITIES AND THE GOVERNMENT OF CANADA REGARDING THE APPLICATION OF THEIR COMPETITION LAWS[*]

The Agreement between the European Communities and the Government of Canada regarding the Application of Their Competition Laws was signed in Bonn on 17 June 1999. It entered into force on the same date.

THE EUROPEAN COMMUNITY AND THE EUROPEAN COAL AND STEEL COMMUNITY (the European Communities) of the one part and THE GOVERNMENT OF CANADA (Canada) of the other part (the Parties):

Considering the close economic relations between them;

Recognising that the world's economies, including those of the parties, are becoming increasingly interrelated;

Noting that the parties share the view that the sound and effective enforcement of competition law is a matter of importance to the efficient operation of their respective markets and to trade between them;

Acknowledging their commitment to enhancing the sound and effective enforcement of their competition laws through cooperation and, in appropriate cases, coordination between them in the application of those laws;

Noting that coordination of their enforcement activities may, in certain cases, result in a more effective resolution of the Parties' respective competition concerns than would be attained through independent enforcement action by the Parties;

Acknowledging the Parties' commitment to giving careful consideration to each other's important interests in the application of their competition laws and to using their best efforts to arrive at an accommodation of those interests;

Having regard to the Recommendation of the Organisation for Economic Cooperation and Development Concerning Cooperation Between Member Countries on Restrictive Business Practices Affecting International Trade, adopted on 27 and 28 July 1995, and

Having regard to the Economic Cooperation Agreement between Canada and the European Communities adopted on 6 July 1976, to the Declaration on European Community-

---

[*] *Source*: European Communities (1999). "Agreement between the European Communities and the Government of Canada regarding the Application of Their Competition Laws", *Official Journal of the European Communities*, L 175, 10 July 1999, pp. 50-60; available also on the Internet (http://www.europa.eu.int/eurlex /en/lif/dat/1999en_299A0710_01.html. [Note added by the editor.]

Canada Relations adopted on 22 November 1990 and to the Joint Political Declaration on Canada-EU Relations and its accompanying action plan adopted on December 17, 1996;

HAVE AGREED AS FOLLOWS:

I. Purpose and definitions

1.   The purpose of this Agreement is to promote cooperation and coordination between the competition authorities of the Parties and to lessen the possibility or impact of differences between the Parties in the application of their competition laws.

2.   In this Agreement,

"anti-competitive activities" shall mean any conduct or transaction that may be subject to penalties or other relief under the competition laws of a Party;

"competent authority of a Member State" shall mean that authority of a Member State set out in Annex A. Annex A may be added to or modified at any time by the European Communities. Canada will be notified in writing of such additions or modifications before any information is sent to a newly listed authority;

"competition authority" and "competition authorities" shall mean:

  (i)   for Canada, the Commissioner of Competition appointed under the Competition Act, and

  (ii)   for the European Communities, the Commission of the European Communities, as to its responsibilities pursuant to the competition laws of the European Communities;

"competition law or laws" shall mean:

  (i)   for Canada, the Competition Act and regulations thereunder, and

  (ii)   for the European Communities, Articles 85, 86, and 89 of the Treaty establishing the European Community, Council Regulation (EEC) No 4064/89 on the control of concentrations between undertakings, Articles 65 and 66 of the Treaty establishing the European Coal and Steel Community (ECSC), and their implementing Regulations pursuant to the said Treaties including High Authority Decision No 2454,

as well as any amendments thereto and such other laws or regulations as the parties may jointly agree in writing to be a "competition law" for the purposes of this Agreement,

and

"enforcement activity" shall mean any application of competition law by way of investigation or proceeding conducted by the competition authority of a Party.

3.   Any reference in this Agreement to a specific provision in either Party's competition law shall be interpreted as referring to that provision as amended from time to time and to any successive provisions.

II. Notification

1.   Each Party shall notify the other Party in the manner provided by this Article and Article IX with respect to its enforcement activities that may affect important interests of the other Party.

2.   Enforcement activities that may affect the important interests of the other Party and therefore ordinarily give rise to notifiable circumstances include those:

(i)   that are relevant to enforcement activities of the other Party;

(ii)   that involve anticompetitive activities, other than mergers or acquisitions, carried out wholly or in part in the territory of the other Party;

(iii)   that involve conduct believed to have been required, encouraged or approved by the other Party or one of its provinces or Member States;

(iv)   that involve a merger or acquisition in which:

- one or more of the parties to the transaction, or

- a company controlling one or more of the parties to the transaction,

is a company incorporated or organised under the laws of the other Party or one of its provinces or Member States;

(v)   that involve the imposition of, or application for, remedies by a competition authority that would require or prohibit conduct in the territory of the other Party, or

(vi)   that involve one of the Parties seeking information located in the territory of the other Party.

3.   Notification pursuant to this Article shall ordinarily be given as soon as a competition authority becomes aware that notifiable circumstances are present, and in any event, in accordance with paragraphs 4 through 7 of this Article.

4.   Where notifiable circumstances are present with respect to mergers or acquisitions, notification shall be given:

(a)   in the case of the European Communities, when a notice is published in the Official Journal, pursuant to Article 4(3) of Council Regulation (EEC) No 4064/89, or when notice of the transaction is received under Article 66 of the ECSC Treaty and a prior authorisation from the Commission is required under that provision, and

(b)   in the case of Canada, not later than when its competition authority issues a written request for information under oath or affirmation, or obtains an order under section 11 of the Competition Act, with respect to the transaction.

5.   (a)   When the competition authority of a Party requests that a person provide information, documents or other records located in the territory of the other Party, or requests oral testimony in a proceeding or participation in a personal interview by a person located in the territory of the other Party, notification shall be given at or before the time that the request is made.

(b)   Notification pursuant to subparagraph (a) of this paragraph is required notwithstanding that the enforcement activity in relation to which the said information is sought has previously been notified pursuant to Article II, paragraphs 1 to 3. However, separate notification is not required for each subsequent request for information from the same person made in the course of such enforcement activity unless the notified Party indicates otherwise or unless the Party seeking information becomes aware of new issues bearing upon the important interests of the notified Party.

6.   Where notifiable circumstances are present, notification shall also be given far enough in advance of each of the following events to enable the other Party's views to be considered:

(a)   in the case of the European Communities,

(i)   when its competition authority decides to initiate proceedings with respect to the concentration, pursuant to Article 6(1)(c) of Council Regulation (EEC) No 4064/89;

(ii)   in cases other than mergers and acquisitions, the issue of a statement of objections; or

(iii)   the adoption of a decision or settlement,

(b)   in the case of Canada,

(i)   the filing of an application with the Competition Tribunal,

(ii)   the initiation of criminal proceedings,

(iii)   the settlement of a matter by way of undertaking or consent order.

7.   (a)   Each Party shall also notify the other whenever its competition authority intervenes or otherwise participates in a regulatory or judicial proceeding, if the issues addressed in the intervention or participation may affect the other Party's important interests. Notification under this paragraph shall apply only to:

(i)   regulatory or judicial proceedings that are public, and

(ii)   intervention or participation that is public and pursuant to formal procedures.

(b)   Notification shall be made at the time of the intervention or participation or as soon thereafter as possible.

8.   Notifications shall be sufficiently detailed to enable the notified Party to make an initial evaluation of the effects of the enforcement activity on its own important interests. Notifications shall include the names and addresses of the natural and legal persons involved, the nature of the activities under investigation and the legal provisions concerned.

9.   Notifications made pursuant to this Article shall be communicated in accordance with Article IX.

III. Consultations

1.   Either Party may request consultations regarding any matter relating to this Agreement. The request for consultations shall indicate the reasons for the request and whether any procedural time limits or other constraints require that consultations be expedited. Each Party undertakes to consult promptly when so requested with the view to reaching a conclusion that is consistent with the principles set forth in this Agreement.

2.   During consultations under paragraph 1, the competition authority of each Party shall carefully consider the representations of the other Party in light of the principles set out in this Agreement and shall be prepared to explain to the other Party the specific results of its application of those principles to the matter under discussion.

IV. Coordination of enforcement activities

1.   The competition authority of each Party shall render assistance to the competition authority of the other Party in its enforcement activities to the extent compatible with the assisting Party's laws and important interests.

2.   In cases where both Parties' competition authorities have an interest in pursuing enforcement activities with regard to related situations, they may agree that it is in their mutual interest to coordinate their enforcement activities. In considering whether particular enforcement activities should be coordinated, either in whole or in part, each Party's competition authority shall take into account the following factors, among others:

(i)   the effect of such coordination on the ability of each Party's competition authority to achieve the objectives of its enforcement activities;

(ii)   the relative ability of each Party's competition authority to obtain information necessary to conduct the enforcement activities;

(iii)   the extent to which either Party's competition authority can secure effective preliminary or permanent relief against the anticompetitive activities involved;

(iv)   the opportunity to make more efficient use of resources, and

(v)   the possible reduction of cost to persons subject to enforcement activities.

3. (a) The Parties competition authorities may coordinate their enforcement activities by agreeing on the timing of those activities in a particular matter, while respecting fully their own laws and important interests. Such coordination may, as agreed by the Parties' competition authorities, result in enforcement action by one or both Parties' competition authorities, as is best suited to attain their objectives.

    (b) When carrying out coordinated enforcement activity, each Party's competition authority shall seek to maximise the likelihood that the other Party's enforcement objectives will also be achieved.

    (c) Either Party may at any time notify the other Party that it intends to limit or terminate the coordination and pursue its enforcement activities independently and subject to the other provisions of this Agreement.

V. Cooperation regarding anticompetitive activities in the territory of one Party that adversely affect the interests of the other Party

1. The Parties note that anticompetitive activities may occur within the territory of one Party that, in addition to violating that Party's competition laws, adversely affect important interests of the other Party. The Parties agree that it is in both their interests to address anticompetitive activities of this nature.

2. If a Party has reason to believe that anticompetitive activities carried out in the territory of the other Party are adversely affecting, or may adversely affect the first Party's important interests, the first Party may request that the other Party's competition authority initiate appropriate enforcement activities. The request shall be as specific as possible about the nature of the anticompetitive activities and their effects on the interests of the requesting Party, and shall include an offer of such further information and other cooperation as the requesting Party's competition authority is able to provide.

3. The requested Party shall consult with the requesting Party and the requested Party's competition authority shall accord full and sympathetic consideration to the request in deciding whether or not to initiate, or expand, enforcement activities with respect to the anticompetitive activities identified in the request. The requested Party's competition authority shall promptly inform the other Party of its decision and the reasons for that decision. If enforcement activities are initiated, the requested Party's competition authority shall advise the requesting Party of significant developments and the outcome of the enforcement activities.

4. Nothing in this Article limits the discretion of the requested Party's competition authority under its competition laws and enforcement policies as to whether or not to undertake enforcement activities with respect to the anticompetitive activities identified in the request, or precludes the requesting Party's competition authority from undertaking enforcement activities with respect to such anticompetitive activities.

VI. Avoidance of conflict

1. Within the framework of its own laws and to the extent compatible with its important interests, each Party shall, having regard to the purpose of this Agreement as set out in Article I, give careful consideration to the other Party's important interests throughout all phases of competition enforcement activities, including decisions regarding the initiation of an

investigation or proceeding, the scope of an investigation or proceeding and the nature of the remedies or penalties sought in each case.

2. Where it appears that one Party's enforcement activities may adversely affect the important interests of the other Party, each Party shall, consistent with the general principles set out above, use its best efforts to arrive at an appropriate accommodation of the Parties competing interests and in doing so each Party shall consider all relevant factors, including:

(i) the relative significance to the anticompetitive activities involved of conduct occurring within one Party's territory as compared to conduct occurring within that of the other;

(ii) the relative significance and foreseeability of the effects of the anticompetitive activities on one Party's important interests as compared to the effects on the other Party's important interests;

(iii) the presence or absence of a purpose on the part of those engaged in the anticompetitive activities to affect consumers, suppliers or competitors within the enforcing Party's territory;

(iv) the degree of conflict or consistency between the enforcement activities and the other Party's laws or articulated economic policies including those expressed in the application of, or decisions under, their respective competition laws;

(v) whether private persons, either natural or legal, will be placed under conflicting requirements by both Parties;

(vi) the existence or absence of reasonable expectations that would be furthered or defeated by the enforcement activities;

(vii) the location of relevant assets;

(viii) the degree to which a remedy, in order to be effective, must be carried out within the other Party's territory;

(ix) the need to minimise the negative effects on the other Party's important interests, in particular when implementing remedies to address anti-competitive effects within the Party's territory, and

(x) the extent to which enforcement activities of the other Party with respect to the same persons, including judgments or undertakings resulting from such activities, would be affected.

VII. Exchange of information

1. In furtherance of the principles set forth in this Agreement, the Parties agree that it is in their common interest to share information which will facilitate the effective application of their respective competition laws and promote better understanding of each others enforcement policies and activities.

2.	Each Party agrees to provide to the other Party on request such information within its possession as the requesting Party may describe that is relevant to an enforcement activity that is being contemplated or conducted by the requesting Party's competition authority.

3.	In the case of concurrent action by the competition authorities of both Parties with a view to the application of their competition law, the competition authority of each Party shall, on request by the competition authority of the other Party, ascertain whether the natural or legal persons concerned will consent to the sharing of confidential information related thereto between the Parties competition authorities.

4.	During consultations pursuant to Article III, each Party shall provide the other with as much information as it is able in order to facilitate the broadest possible discussion regarding the relevant aspects of a particular transaction.

VIII. Semiannual meetings

1.	In furtherance of their common interest in cooperation and coordination in relation to their enforcement activities, appropriate officials of the Parties' competition authorities shall meet twice a year, or otherwise as agreed between the competition authorities of the Parties, to: (a) exchange information on their current enforcement activities and priorities, (b) exchange information on economic sectors of common interest, (c) discuss policy changes which they are considering, and (d) discuss other matters of mutual interest relating to the application of competition laws.

2.	A report on these semiannual meetings shall be made available to the Joint Cooperation Committee under the Framework Agreement for Commercial and Economic Cooperation between the European Communities and Canada.

IX. Communications under this Agreement

Communications under this Agreement, including notifications under Article II and requests under Articles III and V, may be carried out by direct oral, telephonic or fax communication between the competition authorities of the Parties. Notifications under Article II and requests under Articles III and V, however, shall be confirmed promptly in writing through normal diplomatic channels.

X. Confidentiality and use of information

1.	Notwithstanding any other provision of this Agreement, neither Party is required to disclose information to the other Party where such disclosure is prohibited by the laws of the Party possessing the information or would be incompatible with that Party's important interests.

2.	Unless otherwise agreed by the Parties, each Party shall, to the fullest extent possible, maintain the confidentiality of any information communicated to it in confidence by the other Party under this Agreement. Each Party shall oppose, to the fullest extent possible, any application by a third party for disclosure of such information.

3.	(a)	The competition authority of the European Communities, after notice to the Canadian competition authority, will inform the competent authorities of the

Member State or Member States whose important interests are affected of the notifications sent to it by the Canadian competition authority.

(b)   The competition authority of the European Communities, after consultation with the Canadian competition authority, will inform the competent authorities of such Member State or Member States of any cooperation and coordination of enforcement activities. However, as regards such activities, the competition authority of the European Communities will respect the Canadian competition authority's request not to disclose the information which it provides when necessary to ensure confidentiality.

4.   Before taking any action which may result in a legal obligation to make available to a third party information provided in confidence under this Agreement, the Parties competition authorities shall consult one another and give due consideration to their respective important interests.

5.   Information received by a Party under this Agreement, apart from information received under Article II, shall only be used for the purpose of enforcing that Party's competition laws. Information received under Article II shall only be used for the purpose of this Agreement.

6.   A Party may require that information furnished pursuant to this Agreement be used subject to the terms and conditions it may specify. The receiving Party shall not use such information in a manner contrary to such terms and conditions without the prior consent of the other Party.

XI. Existing law

Nothing in this Agreement shall require a Party to take any action that is inconsistent with its existing laws, or require any change in the laws of the Parties or of their respective provinces or Member States.

XII. Entry into force and termination

1.   This Agreement shall enter into force on signature.

2.   This Agreement shall remain in force until 60 days after the date on which either Party notifies the other Party in writing that it wishes to terminate the Agreement.

3.   The Parties shall review the operation of this Agreement not more than 24 months from the date of its entry into force, with a view to assessing their cooperative activities, identifying additional areas in which they could usefully cooperate and identifying any other ways in which the Agreement could be improved. The Parties agree that this review will include, among other things, an analysis of actual or potential cases to determine whether their interests could be better served through closer cooperation. Attached to this Agreement are three letters exchanged between the Parties. These letters form an integral part of this Agreement.

IN WITNESS WHEREOF, the undersigned, being duly authorised, have signed this Agreement in duplicate, on the seventeenth day of June in the year one thousand nine hundred and ninety-nine, in the English, French, Danish, German, Greek, Spanish, Italian, Dutch, Portuguese, Finnish and Swedish languages, each text being equally authentic.

FOR THE EUROPEAN COMMUNITY

FOR THE GOVERNMENT OF CANADA

*   *   *

Selected UNCTAD publications on
transnational corporations and foreign direct investment

A. Individual studies

World Investment Report 1999: Foreign Direct Investment and the Challenge of Development. 578 p. Sales No. E.99.II.D.3. $45.

World Investment Report 1999: Foreign Direct Investment and the Challenge of Development. An Overview. 86 p. Free of charge.

Foreign Direct Invesment in Africa: Performance and Potential. 89 p. UNCTAD/ITE/IIT/Misc. 15.

The Financial Crisis in Asia and Foreign Direct Investment: An Assessment. 101 p. Sales No. GV.E.98.0.29. $20.

World Investment Report 1998: Trends and Determinants. 430 p. Sales No. E.98.II.D.5. $45.

World Investment Report 1998: Trends and Determinants. An Overview. 67 p. Free of charge.

Bilateral Investment Treaties in the mid-1990s. 314 p. Sales No. E.98.II.D.8. $46.

Handbook on Foreign Direct Investment by Small and Medium-sized Enterprises: Lessons from Asia. 200 p. Sales No. E.98.II.D.4. $48.

Handbook on Foreign Direct Investment by Small and Medium-sized Enterprises: Lessons from Asia. Executive Summary and Report on the Kunming Conference. 74 p. Free of charge.

International Investment towards the Year 2002. 166 p. Sales No. GV.E.98.0.15. $29. (Joint publication with Invest in France Mission and Arthur Andersen, in collaboration with DATAR.)

World Investment Report 1997: Transnational Corporations, Market Structure and Competition Policy. 420 p. Sales No. E.97.II.D.10. $45.

World Investment Report 1997: Transnational Corporations, Market Structure and Competition Policy. An Overview. 70 p. Free of charge.

International Investment towards the Year 2001. 81 p. Sales No. GV.E.97.0.5. $35. (Joint publication with Invest in France Mission and Arthur Andersen, in collaboration with DATAR.)

World Investment Directory. Vol. VI: West Asia 1996. 192 p. Sales No. E.97.II.A.2. $35.

World Investment Directory. Vol. V: Africa 1996. 508 p. Sales No. E.97.II.A.1. $75.

Sharing Asia's Dynamism: Asian Direct Investment in the European Union. 192 p. Sales No. E.97.II.D.1. $26.

Transnational Corporations and World Development. 656 p. ISBN 0-415-08560-8 (hardback), 0-415-08561-6 (paperback). £65 (hardback), £20.00 (paperback). (Published by International Thomson Business Press on behalf of UNCTAD.)

Companies without Borders: Transnational Corporations in the 1990s. 224 p. ISBN 0-415-12526-X. £47.50. (Published by International Thomson Business Press on behalf of UNCTAD.)

The New Globalism and Developing Countries. 336 p. ISBN 92-808-0944-X. $25. (Published by United Nations University Press.)

Investing in Asia's Dynamism: European Union Direct Investment in Asia. 124 p. ISBN 92-827-7675-1. ECU 14. (Joint publication with the European Commission.)

World Investment Report 1996: Investment, Trade and International Policy Arrangements. 332 p. Sales No. E.96.II.A.14. $45.

World Investment Report 1996: Investment, Trade and International Policy Arrangements. An Overview. 51 p. Free of charge.

International Investment Instruments: A Compendium. Vol. I. 371 p. Sales No. E.96.II.A.9; Vol. II. 577 p. Sales No. E.96.II.A.10; Vol. III. 389 p. Sales No. E.96.II.A.11; the 3-volume set, Sales No. E.96.II.A.12. $125.

World Investment Report 1995: Transnational Corporations and Competitiveness. 491 p. Sales No. E.95.II.A.9. $45.

World Investment Report 1995: Transnational Corporations and Competitiveness. An Overview. 51 p. Free of charge.

Accounting for Sustainable Forestry Management. A Case Study. 46 p. Sales No. E.94.II.A.17. $22.

Small and Medium-sized Transnational Corporations. Executive Summary and Report of the Osaka Conference. 60 p. Free of charge.

World Investment Report 1994: Transnational Corporations, Employment and the Workplace. 482 p. Sales No. E.94.II.A.14. $45.

World Investment Report 1994: Transnational Corporations, Employment and the Workplace. An Executive Summary. 34 p. Free of charge.

Liberalizing International Transactions in Services: A Handbook. 182 p. Sales No. E.94.II.A.11. $45. (Joint publication with the World Bank.)

World Investment Directory. Vol. IV: Latin America and the Caribbean. 478 p. Sales No. E.94.II.A.10. $65.

Conclusions on Accounting and Reporting by Transnational Corporations. 47 p. Sales No. E.94.II.A.9. $25.

Accounting, Valuation and Privatization. 190 p. Sales No. E.94.II.A.3. $25.

Environmental Management in Transnational Corporations: Report on the Benchmark Corporate Environment Survey. 278 p. Sales No. E.94.II.A.2. $29.95.

Management Consulting: A Survey of the Industry and Its Largest Firms. 100 p. Sales No. E.93.II.A.17. $25.

Transnational Corporations: A Selective Bibliography, 1991-1992. 736 p. Sales No. E.93.II.A.16. $75. (English/French.)

Small and Medium-sized Transnational Corporations: Role, Impact and Policy Implications. 242 p. Sales No. E.93.II.A.15. $35.

World Investment Report 1993: Transnational Corporations and Integrated International Production. 290 p. Sales No. E.93.II.A.14. $45.

World Investment Report 1993: Transnational Corporations and Integrated International Production. An Executive Summary. 31 p. ST/CTC/159. Free of charge.

Foreign Investment and Trade Linkages in Developing Countries. 108 p. Sales No. E.93.II.A.12. $18.

World Investment Directory 1992. Vol. III: Developed Countries. 532 p. Sales No. E.93.II.A.9. $75.

Transnational Corporations from Developing Countries: Impact on Their Home Countries. 116 p. Sales No. E.93.II.A.8. $15.

Debt-Equity Swaps and Development. 150 p. Sales No. E.93.II.A.7. $35.

From the Common Market to EC 92: Regional Economic Integration in the European Community and Transnational Corporations. 134 p. Sales No. E.93.II.A.2. $25.

World Investment Directory 1992. Vol. II: Central and Eastern Europe. 432 p. Sales No. E.93.II.A.1. $65. (Joint publication with the United Nations Economic Commission for Europe.)

The East-West Business Directory 1991/1992. 570p. Sales No. E.92.II.A.20. $65.

World Investment Report 1992: Transnational Corporations as Engines of Growth: An Executive Summary. 30p. Sales No.E.92.II.A.24. Free of charge.

World Investment Report 1992: Transnational Corporations as Engines of Growth. 356p. Sales No.E.92.II.A.19. $45.

World Investment Directory 1992. Vol. I: Asia and the Pacific. 356 p. Sales No. E.92.II.A.11. $65.

Climate Change and Transnational Corporations: Analysis and Trends. 110p. Sales No. E.92.II.A.7. $16.50.

Foreign Direct Investment and Transfer of Technology in India. 150 p. Sales No. E.92.II.A.3. $20.

The Determinants of Foreign Direct Investment: A Survey of the Evidence. 84p. Sales No. E.92.II.A.2. $12.50.

The Impact of Trade-Related Investment Measures on Trade and Development: Theory, Evidence and Policy Implications. 108 p. Sales No. E.91.II.A.19. $17.50. (Joint publication with the United Nations Centre on Transnational Corporations.)

Transnational Corporations and Industrial Hazards Disclosure. 98 p. Sales No. E.91.II.A.18. $17.50.

Transnational Business Information: A Manual of Needs and Sources. 216 p. Sales No. E.91.II.A.13. $45.

World Investment Report 1991: The Triad in Foreign Direct Investment. 108p. Sales No.E.91.II.A.12. $25.

B. IIA Issues Paper Series

Lessons from the MAI. UNCTAD Series on issues in international investment agreements. 56p. Sales No. E.99.II.D.26. $12.

National Treatment. UNCTAD Series on issues in international investment agreements. 104p. Sales No. E.99.II.D.16. $12.

Fair and Equitable Treatment. UNCTAD Series on issues in international investment agreements. 64p. Sales No. E.99.II.D.15. $12.

Investment-Related Trade Measures. UNCTAD Series on issues in international investment agreements. 64p. Sales No. E.99.II.D.12. $12.

Most-Favoured-Nation Treatment. UNCTAD Series on issues in international investment agreements. 72p. Sales No. E.99.II.D.11. $12.

Admission and Establishment. UNCTAD Series on issues in international investment agreements. 72p. Sales No. E.99.II.D.10. $12.

Scope and Definition. UNCTAD Series on issues in international investment agreements. 96p. Sales No. E.99.II.D.9. $12.

Transfer Pricing. UNCTAD Series on issues in international investment agreements. 72p. Sales No. E.99.II.D.8. $12.

Foreign Direct Investment and Development. UNCTAD Series on issues in international investment agreements. 88p. Sales No. E.98.II.D.15. $12.

C. Serial publications

Current Studies, Series A

No. 30. *Incentives and Foreign Direct Investment*. 98 p. Sales No. E.96.II.A.6. $30. (English/French.)

No. 29. *Foreign Direct Investment, Trade, Aid and Migration*. 100 p. Sales No. E.96.II.A.8. $25. (Joint publication with the International Organization for Migration.)

No. 28. *Foreign Direct Investment in Africa*. 119 p. Sales No. E.95.II.A.6. $20.

No. 27. *Tradability of Banking Services: Impact and Implications*. 195 p. Sales No. E.94.II.A.12. $50.

No. 26. *Explaining and Forecasting Regional Flows of Foreign Direct Investment*. 58 p. Sales No. E.94.II.A.5. $25.

No. 25. *International Tradability in Insurance Services*. 54 p. Sales No. E.93.II.A.11. $20.

No. 24. *Intellectual Property Rights and Foreign Direct Investment*. 108 p. Sales No. E.93.II.A.10. $20.

No. 23. *The Transnationalization of Service Industries: An Empirical Analysis of the Determinants of Foreign Direct Investment by Transnational Service Corporations*. 62 p. Sales No. E.93.II.A.3. $15.

No. 22. *Transnational Banks and the External Indebtedness of Developing Countries: Impact of Regulatory Changes*. 48 p. Sales No. E.92.II.A.10. $12.

No. 20. *Foreign Direct Investment, Debt and Home Country Policies*. 50 p. Sales No. E.90.II.A.16. $12.

No. 19. *New Issues in the Uruguay Round of Multilateral Trade Negotiations*. 52 p. Sales No. E.90.II.A.15. $12.50.

No. 18. *Foreign Direct Investment and Industrial Restructuring in Mexico*. 114 p. Sales No. E.92.II.A.9. $12.

No. 17. *Government Policies and Foreign Direct Investment*. 68 p. Sales No. E.91.II.A.20. $12.50.

The United Nations Library on Transnational Corporations
(Published by Routledge on behalf of the United Nations.)

Set A (Boxed set of 4 volumes. ISBN 0-415-08554-3. £350):
Volume One: *The Theory of Transnational Corporations*. 464 p.
Volume Two: *Transnational Corporations: A Historical Perspective*. 464 p.
Volume Three: *Transnational Corporations and Economic Development*. 448 p.
Volume Four: *Transnational Corporations and Business Strategy*. 416 p.

Set B (Boxed set of 4 volumes. ISBN 0-415-08555-1. £350):
Volume Five: *International Financial Management*. 400 p.
Volume Six: *Organization of Transnational Corporations*. 400 p.
Volume Seven: *Governments and Transnational Corporations*. 352 p.
Volume Eight: *Transnational Corporations and International Trade and Payments*. 320 p.

Set C (Boxed set of 4 volumes. ISBN 0-415-08556-X. £350):
Volume Nine: *Transnational Corporations and Regional Economic Integration*. 331 p.
Volume Ten: *Transnational Corporations and the Exploitation of Natural Resources*. 397 p.
Volume Eleven: *Transnational Corporations and Industrialization*. 425 p.
Volume Twelve: *Transnational Corporations in Services*. 437 p.

Set D (Boxed set of 4 volumes. ISBN 0-415-08557-8. £350):
Volume Thirteen: *Cooperative Forms of Transnational Corporation Activity*. 419 p.
Volume Fourteen: *Transnational Corporations: Transfer Pricing and Taxation*. 330 p.
Volume Fifteen: *Transnational Corporations: Market Structure and Industrial Performance*. 383 p.
Volume Sixteen: *Transnational Corporations and Human Resources*. 429 p.

Set E (Boxed set of 4 volumes. ISBN 0-415-08558-6. £350):
Volume Seventeen: *Transnational Corporations and Innovatory Activities*. 447 p.
Volume Eighteen: *Transnational Corporations and Technology Transfer to Developing Countries*. 486 p.
Volume Nineteen: *Transnational Corporations and National Law*. 322 p.
Volume Twenty: *Transnational Corporations: The International Legal Framework*. 545 p.

D. Journals

Transnational Corporations (formerly *The CTC Reporter*).

Published three times a year. Annual subscription price: $45; individual issues $20.

ProInvest, a quarterly newsletter, available free of charge.

United Nations publications may be obtained from bookstores and distributors throughout the world. Please consult your bookstore or write to:

United Nations Publications

Sales Section	OR	Sales Section
Room DC2-0853		United Nations Office at Geneva
United Nations Secretariat		Palais des Nations
New York, NY 10017		CH-1211 Geneva 10
U.S.A.		Switzerland
Tel: (1-212) 963-8302 or (800) 253-9646		Tel: (41-22) 917-1234
Fax: (1-212) 963-3489		Fax: (41-22) 917-0123
E-mail: publications@un.org		E-mail: unpubli@unorg.ch

All prices are quoted in United States dollars.

For further information on the work of the Division on Investment, Technology and Enterprise Development, UNCTAD, please address inquiries to:

United Nations Conference on Trade and Development
Division on Investment, Technology and Enterprise Development
Palais des Nations, Room E-9123
CH-1211 Geneva 10
Switzerland
Telephone: (41-22) 907-5707
Telefax: (41-22) 907-0194
E-mail: medarde.almario@unctad.org

QUESTIONNAIRE

International Investment Instruments: A Compendium

Sales No. E.20.II.D.

In order to improve the quality and relevance of the work of the UNCTAD Division on Investment, Technology and Enterprise Development, it would be useful to receive the views of readers on this publication. It would therefore be greatly appreciated if you could complete the following questionnaire and return it to:

Readership Survey
UNCTAD Division on Investment, Technology and Enterprise Development
United Nations Office in Geneva
Palais des Nations
Room E-9123
CH-1211 Geneva 10
Switzerland
Fax: 41-22-907-0194

1. Name and address of respondent (optional):

_____

_____

2. Which of the following best describes your area of work?

Government	○	Public enterprise	○
Private enterprise	○	Academic or research institution	○
International organization	○	Media	○
Not-for-profit organization	○	Other (specify) _____	

3. In which country do you work? _____

4. What is your assessment of the contents of this publication?

Excellent	○	Adequate	○
Good	○	Poor	○

5. How useful is this publication to your work?

Very useful ○   Of some use ○   Irrelevant ○

6. Please indicate the three things you liked best about this publication:

_____

_____

_____

7. Please indicate the three things you liked least about this publication:

_____

_____

_____

8. Are you a regular recipient of ***Transnational Corporations*** (formerly ***The CTC Reporter***), UNCTAD-DITE's tri-annual refereed journal?

Yes   ○   No   ○

If not, please check here if you would like to receive
a sample copy sent to the name and address you have
given above   ○